LISTENING

to the

UNKNOWN

Second Edition

James Alan Conlan

Ryehill Publications Ireland

Ryehill Publications
O'Brien's Bridge
Co. Clare
Republic of Ireland.

Second publication Mid-summer, 1999
First published in Ireland
by Ryehill Publications January 1999
987654321

Second Edition
ISBN 1-902136-03-9

Printed and bound in Ireland

Cover painting:
Midsummer Eve
by Denise Ryan
Reproduced by permission of the artist

To My Beloved

'I' am the wind my love
The gentle breeze that touch your hair
'I' am the sky
The moon
The countless stars
Every sound
In all things 'I' am found
My love
My sweet and gentle love
In this heart
Your heart
Greater than the sky
The laughter, tears of joy am 'I'
This 'I'
Your 'I'
Just 'I'

*

Works by James Alan Conlan

Dance of the Goblins, **(October 1997)** the first of a trilogy subtitled, *The Human Condition,* is a part autobiography of the author's traumatic experiences as he re-awakened to the truth of life. It is a journey of innocence to light up the truth of your heart.

Listening to the Unknown **(First edition)** **(Jan. 1999)** illustrates the distinction between one's true nature and one's acquired nature with the intention of opening the door to the unknown for those who are ready and willing to listen. Through this door the mysteries of the entire creation await your discovery.

'In Celebration to life **(May, 1999)** offers the way of release from the feared loneliness that is the controlling factor of the personal self. This book may appear as a challenge to the psychological pillars of society and the assumed authenticity of the scientific mind holding many bound to a false reality. Nonetheless, it comes as an open gift to you, to help you realise freedom, so you can celebrate being the love and truth you really are in every aspect of your life.

Listening to the Unknown **(Second edition)** **(Mid-summer, 1999)** comes with a re-edited index giving easier access to areas of particular interest, as requested. There are some minor changes to parts of the original text to facilitate clearer understanding. The additional chapter dealing with questions arising from the previous publication is a book in its own right and may prove additionally beneficial to those who have already tasted the inner experience from reading the first edition.

Chaos The Omnivorous Beast **(Oct. 1999)** questions the impoverishment being inflicted upon the self by one's false veneration to mind-perceived gods. It examines beliefs and how they directly support this false veneration. This may be extremely disturbing for those who seek uneasy shelter under the erroneous ideologies of a religious nature. We can only be the truth when we face the truth of the situation. Five thousand odd years of denial, is it enough?

CONTENTS

***

Introduction

What is love? What is life without love? We think we know. But really! Do we? Do you know? As one of the masses you are born, you live and you die. But do you really know your true nature? Do you really know the truth of love? If you do, then you are one of the few and you will enjoy the challenges you will easily recognise in this book.

The truth of love? What is truth? According to the wise, truth is not in the telling of truth, it is in *being* the truth. This is so simple, yet so profound that we all seem to miss it. I have come to realise through my own transgressions in this make-believe world that there is nothing of truth in the way we normally live. We desperately try to fit in and please in accordance with the values of our acquired nature. Nonetheless, it is seldom more that appeasement. This acquired nature is what seems to be superimposed on each and every one of us by the disenchanted masses seemingly lost to perpetual darkness. The darkness is sustained by humanity's blind veneration to the gods of this anguishing world, even the make-believe gods of organised religions. These are just some of the issues we are about to explore.

It is obvious to many that humankind is presently undergoing an enormous shift in consciousness. All of our societal structures are not only being threatened by this but they are slowly disintegrating in front of our eyes. These are, indeed, extraordinary times and we seem to be on the threshold of a phenomenal awakening. This is what humanity is actually facing. Or is it? Well, everything we know that forms our security, everything that is fixed, is based on the past and these psychological foundations are being seriously challenged by scientific revelation. Past is dissolving, but at a much faster pace than ever before.

Chronologically, these changes are all very recent in our existentialist world exposing the projected implant of humankind's insecurity, even the insecurity that man feels in the presence of woman. Man of the past could not tolerate, man could not look into himself. Fear of the truth drove him away, so woman had to be subordinated, then nature and everything else that reflected his own insecurity. The stream of religious dogmas obliged as the mental yoke while brute force obliged as the physical and the ego-man projected this anguishing world as it is from himself. This world is his mask that he strives to preserve and this has become his all-consuming anxiety.

This is man's problem. But the answer to every problem is within the problem itself. Galileo shattered man's self-importance with the revelation that Earth is not the centre of the universe as had been previously accepted and man was then obliged to acknowledge that his presence as an earthling is merely mediocre. Man had considered himself as being in the image of God, then Darwin threw in his evolutionary theories stating that man has descended from the monkey. Marx propounded that the soul is a myth and that consciousness is merely a by-product of matter. Mankind was dethroned. Then Freud submitted that reason does not exist, that man is an irrational mess and merely a victim of the unconscious. Now modern science is shattering the few remaining strings of self nobility as man is being faced with the new possibility of seeing himself cloned. According to Delgado we are all but machines to be used and manipulated at will and this seems to be the current trend, the current direction en-masse.

Nonetheless, all these discoveries are part of humanity's projected consciousness and I propose that there is something much deeper afoot. The ones among us failing to understand what is happening are being driven into indescribable hopelessness. What is occurring is going to bring even greater tribulation for those still clinging onto their existentialist props, be they scientific or religious, and refusing to let go of the past. Many are going to be shocked and dismayed even though it is all being predicted. While for others there is going to be great joy and great celebration, especially for those unfettered by attachments, open and free in their hearts to embrace the unknown.

The current shift in consciousness is unprecedented and many who are aligned to its speed through stillness are discovering the seed of infinity within. This is not as a replacing belief-structure but as an actual fact. Humanity is on the threshold of understanding in a way that has never been possible before. All of this is happening right now in the speed of this time, hence the many unexplainable occurrences being experienced in the daily lives of the ones who are sufficiently awakened to notice.

Should you, the reader, be prepared to journey with me, then I entreat you to listen as we gently explore the challenges about to be made. I am merely a voice in the darkness, in the wilderness of humankind's lunacy, calling to you to wake up. I am not speaking to the masses for the masses are doomed, this is an universal fact and it has been so since time as we know it began. I am speaking directly to you, you alone, where life is happening right now in your beautiful body. This is all that matters, for everything outside of this is but a passing occurrence.

Who am I to be making such statements? The discursive mind will want to know what are my qualifications, for such is the nature of the mind. Well, life in itself is one's greatest qualification. Life is my ink. We are here to experience what must be experienced. It is allowing oneself to be born into a maze and then setting out to discover one's own way back to the source. For each and everyone born into a personal life this is the immediate quest, is it not? Why else are you here if not to experience the truth of yourself?

What is my worldly experience? On the educational front, if you can call it education, I have a primary degree in social research and a post graduate diploma in philosophy that has something to do with conflict resolution. In the business world I have swallowed the bait, lived in the fast lane and danced every illusion I encountered to its own bitter, sweet end. Being possessed by the spirit of the entrepreneur I worked for many years as a financial broker with my functions varying from negotiating specialist, investment instruments to peddling life-assurance policies for a variety of life-assurance companies. Part of this work involved being mediator and counsellor to partnerships commencing and to others going drastically wrong while drawing from the experiences of my own relative successes and failures.

There seems to be so many ideas and so much to do with each set of doings giving rise to its own set of problems. Even the solving of problems merely give rise to others where the only consistency seems to be in the continuous flow. Yet, the diversity of people and the commonality of problems are all encapsulated within the one big, melting pot. Indeed, we are all in it together as the oneness of humanity whether we personally like it or not.

When I was a steel-fixing contractor in the latter part of the sixties I had occasion to participate in the construction of towering apartments in the East End of London. This was the new world then, the great move forward from the rows and rows of terraced houses unnecessarily occupying what was commercially assumed as valuable space. Then, less than twenty years later I found myself back as a student immersed in the sociological study relating to these same apartments and the devastating effects they were having on the local community. No one had thought of this in advance for these were effects beyond the consciousness of that particular period.

It is seldom one sees beyond one's immediate interests. This is the human condition where past can be seen but rarely the present as though we are walking backwards through time. We are here to enjoy according to our measure while the all-consuming importance of some yesterday foregone is the raw turgidity of the human consciousness possessing today.

We seek through personal desire, for desire is our driving force. There was a period when I built houses in my efforts to quench the insatiable thirst when each new achievement was envisaged as the one to bring the ultimate fulfilment. Nonetheless, these houses came and went as part of my worldly expression and they passed on to others expressing similar thirst to expand, acknowledge or demolish. Previous to that, I worked as a labourer on the railways and dug out tunnels by hand and machine in the bowels of the earth beneath the city of London to help pay for my upkeep during my first attempts at saving some money for college. This was the personal plan when no problems were initially foreseen. But the money seemed to disappear as fast as it came keeping up with the pace of the immediate expression. It was all very consuming at the time, even in the affairs of the heart where I can say that I have been both passionately loved and aggressively abused by woman. But there are no mistakes. We are here to be awakened through experience, are we not?

This book is not merely concerning our personal relationships. That I leave to the overburdened psychiatrists struggling with methodologies still dependant on the past. Nor is it about the pros and cons of finance, I leave that to the utter confusion that it is in itself.

There are mountains of experts out there aggressively seeking the edge on each other, all having the immediate answer, the immediate formula, as the entire business-machine of finance blindly cascades along to the edge of the next abyss. But so be it, for it is all in the play of this living experience. I have spent nine years of my life in that business and I challenge any expert at any level of its expression to face me, or to be more precise, to face herself or himself as to what they are really doing with their lives.

However, this is a challenge to all who are living to the whims of the personal, for no matter who we are or what we are doing we are being incarcerated in some form or other by the money-machine. We are all being subtly conditioned to venerate this 'money-god' from the moment we leave the womb until the undertaker's bill is finally paid.

We are not setting out to judge what is right and wrong, for all judgement is within the limitations of our conditioning that is our confinement, rather this search is a challenge to see with a clearer vision into the truth of the world which we are being programmed to serve.

Should Delgado be correct in his assumptions then we are all but machines, predictable en-masse. This we need to impartially examine if only to realise what we are not.

You need to see and understand your conditioning that is your acquired nature, you need to see and understand this through an non-judgemental silence before your deeper reality can be realised.

Your life should always be a joy, whatever the circumstances. You are not a machine, you are blissful, eternal presence. This is your true nature, the love that you really are, as the radiant blossom truly liberated from a world full of thorns and thistles.

You do not have to live with the strife, the confusion, the mental anguish, no matter how serious, how all-consuming your problems might seem, you never need suffer again for you do not have to suffer once the truth of your true nature is fully realised. This is our journey together.

There is but one 'I'
You are it

CHAPTER 1

Who Is This 'I' Whom You Call Yourself?

The leaf falls. The breeze blows it along the ground. This is its first and last journey away from its root of attachment. It is now in a world of its own. Its colours ripen according to its nature, be it a golden brown or a bright and pertinacious red and it dances in temporary freedom, loosened from its temporary abode, as it sings its new found freedom to itself.

There is a continuous movement as the leaf flutters and tumbles along, propelled by the breeze into a merry-go-round tune of song. And then, alas, it gets caught in a nook or a crevasse, or perhaps in a mound of countless others the same. There it remains in fading personal distinction as the all-patient mother earth gently absorbs it back into her bosom through the dust of itself. In this time all of its personal nutrition, momentarily enriched by this flash of its own omniscience, again carries on in its time-honoured journey back in through the roots of nature, back into the source from whence it has come. It will never again re-appear in its personal distinction as the one that it was in its moment of personal dance.

So let our hearts be awakened to the imperishable truth, that you and I are but this leaf on the ground. All of yesterday's year is but the fading vibration of this moment of *now* where life endlessly breathes as the perennial key to the timeless. But we seem to have become absorbed with the personal import of how we appeared a moment ago or what a tomorrow might bring. It is as if we are forever outside of ourselves as we endlessly struggle to grip onto this fleeting body of blood in its momentary flash of sensory wonder.

Like the leaf falling away from the sap of the tree we are thus blown along by the winds of ourselves as we become lost through our minds. We see the world about us as something apart and then we set out to arrange it in accord with our personal desires, each of us at difference and immediately conflict arises. We become totally irresponsible when we lose sight of our true nature as we become tossed by the turbulence of the acquired. But do not believe me. Ask yourself if this is not so, if this is not the way the world of our personal creation appears when we break from the sap of our true essence?

This acquired nature is the fleeting commotion which we fervently take to be the one and only reality. It is the worldly illusion we create by captivating ourselves with the belief that this apparent world of our own personal making is what we must battle and struggle against in order to fulfil our personal desires. Then we wonder in dismay at all the destruction about us. Our social structures are designed to sustain and improve this world while ignoring the fact that no matter how perfect we make it, yet it remains a world of fear and anguish, of pleasure alternating with pain. We fail to understand that the world is as we are. It is our immediate reflection. When one truly sees that one *is* the world then one can be free of one's desires and fears and one can be totally responsible for the senseless sorrow being inflicted on humanity by this acquired nature of the cumulative of personal selves.

Still this is the ongoing story of each of us individually born into a particular mould of a society that is our immediate reflection. We become part of the continuing saga, a number as such among numerous others. But what does this mean? Why is it important? Why do I write about it? It is nigh impossible for us to personally see how we become trapped in the mould, having lost sight of our true nature, our true essence in being, as we set about defending and upholding the societal prison we solemnly take to be real.

We become lost through our notions, through the beliefs we endeavour to cling onto, braving the pain of denial while, more often than not, our hearts are totally in bits. What is pleasing to us might give us temporary release, but it is only a matter of time before all of it goes. There is no real release from the trauma, not even through the inevitable death we perceive from within these limitations that we rigidly support through our fears.

We live through these fears, imprisoned as such while failing to openly address them. Denial is our only perceivable avenue of escape. Even our beliefs of another existence, of some heaven hereafter, can be challenged as being nothing more than escapism as we vainly endeavour to extend our denials beyond this deepest and furthest fear of unescapable, personal death.

Still, we stick by our conditioning with our heads in the sand. When our rigid, societal convictions are questioned by reason we delusively search for some other appropriate appeasement rather than facing the actual truth. We refuse to listen, for the truth is too painful to accept. This seems to be the unrelenting, human condition for the past few thousand odd years of recorded happenings. The objects being used by man and woman may have changed considerably over this time but the personal self and all pertaining to it has hardly improved. The strife, wants, pride, jealousy, hates and fears continue their unchanging dance beneath the personal mask.

Whenever our conditioning is flooded by the light of trans-parency coming from a Krishna, a Buddha, a Socrates, a Christ or indeed anyone awakened among us, we tremor in fear of the inevitable death of this acquired nature of the self in the light of such wisdom. This death we will not allow so we react to the light-bearers by defacing them, religionizing them, poisoning them, crucifying them or declaring them mad. The light has to be ignored as long as we are unable to face into this greatest fear, that is the unavoidable death of this personal self, while failing to acknowledge that the personal self is but a temporary occurrence.

The frenzy of the existentialist side of the self keeps us trapped in the transient world endlessly dodging the truth. We are hijacked by our acquired nature through our discursive minds. When we openly look at ourselves the evidence is plain to be seen. Our story through chronological time clearly illustrates how the human mind repetitively binds itself in all sorts of meticulous beliefs. Nonetheless, all beliefs are the psychological base for all of our conflicts. This is an undisputable fact. Every war that has ever been waged has been waged in defence of some particular doctrine or other, even the doctrine of peace.

Then the questions arise; Is it possible for the human mind to ever overcome its own limitations? Is there a way of release avail-able to us other than the limited known? Is there a way of know-ing the truth of oneself? I suggest there is and it can be achieved by tapping into an universal intelligence that surpasses rational thought by looking through an open awareness from a point where the mind transcends its restrictive limitations. This is awakening consciousness.

These are some of the questions we are about to explore and this is the proposition being posed as we challenge our under-standing of love, reincarnation, even Ufos, but a few of our impercipient convictions in this attempt to discover how we can really look and listen when we are not merely looking and listening through our usual conditioning. This looking is impossible to those who are lost to the conditioned mind, so one must be willing to let go and be willingly naked in oneself in order to explore the unknown.

The secrets of the entire creation are available to us once we discover the key. Nonetheless, it is not going to be an easy task. We will have to transcend our philosophical minds before we can touch the philosopher's stone and this calls for real effort. We philosophically tease ourselves with our notions that an answer to the truth of existence can be deductively found through scientific discovery. But scientific research is pertinent mostly to matter. Great discoveries have been made, still every scientist to date has had to meet with the similar fate of shrivelling and dying to all that has been discovered.

There are but the few who have come to realise a much deeper understanding of the intrinsic nature of life and death. It is this new understanding that we are endeavouring to unfold and before we can commence we must first unload our current programme. We must be prepared to let go, to be empty and free. This is the first prerequisite.

The truth can only be heard when the ear has opened to hear what is new, that is when it ceases to listen through its conditioning of past. Our conditioned selves can only pick up the intonations of truth through the rigid structures of mind as our established ways of seeing and hearing and thinking that appear as a comfort to us. When we are unwilling to let go of these transitory comforts we dis-allow ourselves the opportunity of great realisations awaiting to blossom. We enter this life, live through our personal fears and waste it in limbo. Whether here present or hereafter this is the soulless situation of our acquired nature.

Through our fears we shrink back into our second childishness without making the effort to discover the meaning of life. It seems that a long and arduous journey of preparation is necessary before we can transcend our known limitations. This we oblige on ourselves. New discoveries are continuously being made, but we seem to dissect them to impotence through the mind being transfixed to the relative known rather than opening ourselves to receive these discoveries in the light of the new and this is our ongoing restriction. This is the tenacious security we use as a shield for the inner insecurity of the personal self. The world about us is the immediate reflection of this brought about through our accumulative fears. So the question arises;

How does one gain freedom from the known?

Books pertaining to wisdom tell us that one needs to unconditionally look at oneself. In order to do this one needs to focus one's awareness on the consciousness of *being* life in the sensation arising through the sensory body. Were one to earnestly examine this sensation of *being* life as it enters through the human brain, then perhaps, one may discover that life, perennial life, is formless is essence. At this stage this is merely a suggestion. But one can understand how formless life passes through each cyclical leaf from the moment it appears as a bud on the branch of the tree until it eventually falls to the ground. The tree itself is a form of life, as is the cat, the bird and myriad others that are each individually supported by the eternal presence of formless life.

Nonetheless, the only place in existence where you, the individual, can know formless life in the sensation of *being* life is in your body right now. This is a fundamental truth when we examine together this truth that we are. So it can be accepted that one's body is a form of life while one's *being* is formless in essence.

Being is the formless presence, the perpetual radiance shining into existence through one's immediate form. Let us not pass this point in haste without first realising the deep significance of what is being said. This is a primal key to our journey of discovery. If we miss it then we oblige ourselves to remain in the darkness.

Then the question arises as to who is this 'I' who is *being* life in the body?

We can instantly acknowledge there is but one 'I', the 'I' that each of us address as ourselves. This is the 'I' within you that is now being addressed, not my particular I, or your particular I, but the universal oneness in each and everyone. This universal oneness cannot be known through the mind, for the mind is the personal I, the personal self, and the architect of the transient that is not even a shadow of the universal. The mind cannot surpass itself. But the universal 'I' that is one's radiant presence totally dissolves the mind wherever it shines, unhindered by the personal, into the mind's existence.

How does this 'I' tie in to formless life? How does it link? What is the connection?

This enquiry immediately leads to the deeper question, "Who or what am 'I'?"

We can understand how the molecules of the body change in shape and form over a period of time. We know the body must eventually die. It is not a whole lot different from the fallen leaf dancing itself back to dust. Inevitably the body ends up as food for the worms, then being the worms themselves, an unacceptable fact but true, nonetheless. There must be something unseen to our mental vision, something more that is permeating through all this dancing and changing. Yet, there is only 'I' to perceive it in this body as life that is known to you and me right now through the *being* of life as it is.

The body is merely the portal to the mind, that is the porch to existence. The mind is the modem through which 'I' connect to immediate life as I touch, taste, hear, see and smell all that I am on the face of this earth. 'I' am alone, totally alone. This, I propose, but you must not believe it, for believing is not knowing. It can only be known when it is realised in one's own experience.

This 'I' whom you are is sensational and actual life. This must be true, for everyone and everything else outside of life in your immediate body can be nothing more than forms of life being perceived by this 'I' in the body perceiving, where actual life, in the sensation and *being* of life, can only be known directly. You do not need to do any research to verify this for the verification is immediately within you and being experienced through the sensation in the *being* of life in each moment of *now*.

When this sensation of life is permanently established in the actual *knowing* of life, then you will find that you are in a new place consciously. This is the 'I', the witness, the bodyless and mindless observer whom you are, as you enter existence through the body at this moment of *now*. I consider that we can agree upon this.

As we return to this point of the 'I' in this book I wish to emphasize that I am never referring directly to myself. I am merely speaking from the one universality that is equally within us all. In order to truly hear what is being said it must be heard as the 'I' within you, the individual looking out at existence through your immediate body. Individual means indivisible. This 'I' that is herewith addressed is the 'I' that you speak of when addressing yourself. Should you objectify it by placing it on me now writing these words then you are missing what is being said.

There is only one 'I' in or out of existence as one knows it and you are that. Putting first what is first this is an universal fact. So let us take cognisance as we perceive through universal intelligence the universality of 'I', of the 'I' that you really are, the 'I' that I am, eternally am. This much we can establish through reason so we can safely drive an anchoring peg on the face of this exploratory cliff that we have started to climb together.

Universally speaking, 'I' am here in existence only in this moment of *now*. 'I' am never yesterday, nor tomorrow, 'I' am always *now*. Life is formless before it hits the brain. This is what 'I' am when I am looking into 'Me'. The very first form 'I' take in formless life is the form that 'I' am in this body. Then all other forms of life appear. This first form creates all other forms. When the individual man or woman that I am in this immediate body goes to sleep then all other forms disappear. When I wake up again I play with the many forms of life through my most immediate creation which is this formal body.

Please check it out in your own experience. Can it be challenged? Where else right now are you in the *being* of life apart from life in your body? There is no where else. There is no other life known in your experience as in the sensation and *being* of life but in your body, wherever you are, whoever you are. The masses are but forms of life as a shadow outside of the one individual, indivisible self where the sensation and *being* of life is being actually experienced right *now*.

This is what you are, you the individual, indivisible self where all life has its beginning and ending. You are the point, the central point of the vortex spinning out into existence. The mind cannot get a hold on this for the mind is chronological time, it psychologically consists of past and future whereas 'I' am timelessness. Putting first things first this is where it all begins. If we fail to grasp the significance of this then everything else about to be explored is going to be missed.

Let us examine it closer by focusing the attention on the essence of *being*. When you first awaken in the morning after a restful sleep you are for just an initial moment in this state of *being* life. Most of us have experienced this, although we may not have given it the attention it deserves. Then the first thought enters the mind and it is always the 'I' thought. After the 'I' thought the world re-appears. One needs to be sharp to detect it. Then the mind-weed of one's acquired nature floods back into the clear space and one's living condition of turbulence, relative peace or whatever one's state recommences all over again.

What if one could permanently be in that space directly before the 'I' thought enters the brain? Could this be the self-realisation that the many are seeking? Could this be the invisible door to the unknown? Perhaps, it is through this door that the secrets of the entire creation are waiting to unfold to you who are earnestly seeking to truly understand. This we are about to explore as we break through the frontiers of human consciousness.

These frontiers are the state of the human condition en-masse that keeps one locked outside of one's true nature. Do we not endeavour to please and impress? Should we look at this closely we can see that the masses are but a collection of colliding personalities with each one bound up in his own or her own self-consideration. Perchance, this self-consideration is the illusion we serve. When we take this external trauma of the masses to be our all-consuming interest believing it to be of the greatest importance we unknowingly deny ourselves nature's endless demonstration of the absolute reality.

We allow ourselves to be bound in service to an external existence that is but the steam from the kettle, vapour returning to water then returning to steam again. We give ourselves religions, we give ourselves souls and we search through the vapour of ourselves for saviours to save us. Yet, as nothing comes out of nothing there can be nothing to be saved.

Still, the restless mind in its own acquired ignorance seems to be re-cycled again and again through each of us born to serve it. This ignorance is the illusion we cling onto when we become attached to the personal self through our own self-considerations while refusing to accept that the personal self is but a fleeting quiver in time. Even time is part of the illusion when seen through the light of the greater reality. But the acquired nature of the personal self has neither the inclination nor the access for such understanding.

The truth of it all seems too awesome to comprehend. Indeed, it can never be understood from where we gather en-masse convincing ourselves that the external, restless world of the mind's creation is the one and only reality. This is the mind-weed that floods us each morning at the moment of waking and in this we are being blindly driven through our efforts to serve ourselves, even to the point of personal vanity in our assumptions that we may be of service to others.

The personal self hankers for excitement and so the world of ourselves tries to fulfil through the force that is our economic system. Then we feed this excitement into our children thus turning them outwards and away from the light of their being that is their natural, radiant presence. The dis-ease becomes rooted. More and more is desired. Still there is no permanent satisfaction as we stitch ourselves up in our emotional worlds of psychological anguish, happy one day then unhappy the next. We try and we try for temporary reprieve, always searching for something outside of oneself, yet all our remedies are seldom more than patching our worn-out clothing, endless solutions re-creating endless problems.

What can one do? Where can one find the inspiration to transcend this self-perpetuating mess? Inspiration? The answer is in the word, is it not? These mental tendencies of humankind are 'spirally' twisting outwards. Such is our intellectuality and through this we become further enslaved. The more intellectual we become the deeper we entrench ourselves. The world is aghast through its searching for external answers. The word inspiration means to go 'in', to go in through the 'spiral' and to re-enter one's core. Here lies the source to all 'in-spiration' where everything external can be seen and understood exactly as it is and not through the conditional tense that only finds place in the mind.

The source is the inner flow, silently humming its perpetual song. When one re-aligns to this then one can openly partake in the external world without being swallowed by the illusions. This is being truly responsible. One can at any time, at any place, in any situation feel the inner presence and *be* it. While objects of excitement come and go as fodder for one's acquired nature, one's 'inspirational' source is the constant, unchanging presence within. One only needs to be awakened to this, but such awakening calls for inner silence.

One needs to look to the inner realm, in through the universal 'I', the only 'I' whom one is in existence. The discursive mind can logically assimilate that the 'I' must be the direct way back to the source. But one cannot enter the source through logic as logic is dependent on mind. This is the dilemma. The source is in the spontaneity of life itself. It is love in existence. This is the door to infinitesimal spacelessness and the way of true discovery, even for the scientist obsessed with the stars and an expanding universe of matter.

The mind cannot know the source. It becomes involved by dissecting it, analysing it and creating philosophical meaning to it. One can never enter, can never *be* it through the mind. The universality of all is the 'I' that you are, the 'I' that I am. Once one comes to know this, to fully know this, in the actual *being* of it, then all of one's psychological world and all of one's personalisation is instantly dissolved.

I propose that the inner, behind the 'I' thought, is our true essence, it is the only permanence. The outer is the psychological. Even the astronomer looking through the telescope can never, as such, reach beyond the matter of himself or herself. Seeking the source of 'I' is the long and laborious journey back home. Here the persevering few pass through the inner 'big bang'. This 'big bang' is the point where one actually transcends the consciousness of perceivable matter. The passing through is sudden and immediate. It can only occur when the long and laborious struggle of letting go of the accessible known finally explodes within the seeker and the seeker instantly dissolves. This is the awesome moment of realisation when one's acquired nature comes to its end.

This is the death of the personal self that can only occur after one has taken the courage to step out of the conditioned masses, to step out of the comforts of the old, the commonly accepted, for it can only be then that one can enter the vastness of the unknown. This is the re-entry into the light that is the universal intelligence. Then it is truly seen that the outer, expanding universe is but the reflection of the inner, a fact that can never be understood by the discursive mind.

The mind is in favour of the old for here it has established its hold, here it clings onto the relative comforts of fixed opinions, fixed beliefs, all producing fixed societal norms as the stagnant waters of the living dead. The mind is fearful of the new because it only knows how to deal with it by either rejecting or re-interpreting it in accord that is consistent with the old, established order. Therefore the unknown is always disturbing because the new is always a challenge to existing beliefs, thus creating stress and expending enormous energy as a result in trying to hold onto the old, in trying to preserve the expired.

Hence the mind re-creates its own form of intelligence from the recurring past, the form of intelligence that gives birth to the universities and the laboriously long corridors of philosophical and religious thought as the mass support for its own denial. When the light of the unknown suddenly appears it is either ignored or destroyed, for the mind by its discursive nature refuses to acknowledge its own impotence.

This limited mind could not tolerate Socrates. Ignoring him was not sufficient. The truth of his presence would not go away, it was too penetrating, too threatening to the societal limitations, so he had to be killed. Then Christ, the greatest illumination of all in this time, came among us and through our self-inflicted limitations we did it all over again, as we are still doing to the essence of Christ today through our own interpretations of convenience, this being the wilfulness of our acquired nature. Whether these interpretations are personalised or institutionalised, these are, nonetheless, interpretations of convenience through which the masses hide from the light.

This is how it actually is where the mind is always in conflict with the new, even the scientific mind only seeing through the fixed ideas of past as it struggles to hold onto the relative conveniences of the old. This is the force, the wilfulness of the worldly side of ourselves, refusing to let go of the ignorance. As such we are the living dead, merely walking and talking corpses denying ourselves the reality of life.

Life is spontaneous, always new, always in the *now*, while the mind of our acquired nature is always equating to the old, always living through the past and this is the reason why life and the mind can never meet. When one is bound up with the mental tendencies then one cannot *be* life, no matter how intellectual, how clever one might seem, one is living in darkness with all one's energies spilling into a bottomless pit of appeasement.

When one pays close attention to the cycle of nature as it unfolds around us and in us that much can be realised. It can be seen that the example of the falling leaf reflects the nature of our minds and bodies. They are transient, impermanent. Even the souls of these bodies as perceived by our minds are all but a part of the outer illusion. But this is not for believing as believing is also part of our acquired nature, the demon of anguish we serve. One must seek out the source of 'I' through the inner eye of one's being where the *being* of life is experienced and discover the universal intelligence for oneself. Guidance is needed for this and the guide appears only to the level of one's perceptibility.

The stories recalled in this book are the reflections of my own discoveries as this acquired nature battled in vain to sustain itself when it was suddenly caught in the penetrating presence of one who had realised the inner radiance. This battle waged through the endless illusions rising before me, through the passions, intrigues, misplaced love and betrayals of my life as I tried to live out the endless deceptions created by my wilful and restless mind. So it continued until I, the false I which I had become, finally surrendered and died.

Should one have the awareness to face into oneself then one can begin to realise the inner and universal 'I' from the depth of one's being. Should one not have this awareness then so must one remain a slave to one's undiscerning mind, one must remain in one's hell. Nonetheless, this too is part of the creation and there is nothing wrong with being in hell once one knows it, for when one knows it then one naturally stops perpetuating it. Such is awareness finding its way.

However, when we are ignorant of this fact, when we are ignorant of our acquired nature then we imagine that hell is somewhere else, somewhere outside of ourselves, somewhere beyond our immediate state, and we fail to see that hell is right here in this moment of *now*.

We fail to understand that hell is the acquired nature of the human condition, as my condition, your condition, this mass hypnosis as countless personae personally incurred in varying degrees of inner conflict.

Should you be fortunate enough to come to the end of the personal self, should you be totally in bits, crying for release and begging for freedom as your personal world is exploding, then you are privileged indeed, believe it or not. This freedom is the freedom from your conditioning that is driving you so far away from your source, so far away from the truth of 'I', the one universal 'I' that I am, that you truly are, this being your essence, your perpetual radiance, your immortality.

When person, personality or mask is no longer sucking you dry, then the 'presence' of all whom you are shines forth unhindered by frontal disguise. This is freedom from self. It can only be truly understood when one is at one with the 'presence' through *being* it each moment of one's life.

The 'presence' is the source while the person is the denial. One needs to be astutely attentive to understand the implication of this for it is beyond worldly understanding. The intellectuality of the masses can philosophise about it for ever but it cannot be realised as such, it can only be hypothesized, theorised and categorised into conflicting religious patterns that is this self-perpetuating hell.

There can never be truth in the masses, for the masses are merely the externalised projection of 'I'. This you are aware of in yourself, bur seldom acknowledge as you endeavour to live in accord with the projection, being ruled as such by your mind. You are duped to serve the illusion with all of your energy, until your energy is spent. But, everyone living are obliged to face the reality at the moment of death. Then it is suddenly clear, a life having been wasted caught up with the crowds when it could have been lived in the light of one's presence.

In your heart it is known there can never be hope or salvation in the masses, for the masses are forever doomed while the 'presence' forever is. Such is the play of existence.

Be it, know it and enjoy.

Listen to the silence

CHAPTER 2

Love? What Is Love?

L ove is the medium of life, the unending flow of the creation. It is the grace we perceive as being God, the communion of all in one, the vibrant between the subtle and coarser elements. It is the air and the water, the fire at the centre surrounded by the outer crust of the earth. It is the harmony between the nucleus and its orbiting electrons, the unending dance spiralling outwards through the Milky Way, it is you and I, our true nature, our very essence in being. Love is *being* in existence.

But we, the multitudes, cast ourselves out of this understanding that is the perennial garden of life. We cast ourselves out of our true nature, the truth that we are, through our own emotional disturbance of personal issue. We vacate the 'I' and lose sight of *love*, so to speak, by imposing our wilfulness on the natural order, when the giving hand becomes the claw ruthlessly grasping for self-satisfaction. We set about objectifying love while suffering the pain of the loss, seldom knowing what is lost, each of us to our own personal desires for a particular lover and even a particular god to satisfy the hunger of this acquired nature of the ungodly self that takes up abode within us.

This acquired nature of humankind is the ongoing affliction. When the infant is born it is immediately exposed to decay as the conditioned masses exerting the will of the personifying demon, even through the natural wonder and natural love of the mother. It is the societal pulse, the societal speed, as the outer reflection of the retarded, human consciousness perpetuating its ignorance upon the vacant abode of the innocent born again and again into this loveless bondage. This is the world of our own creation, the loveless place of the personal self.

Man seeks out woman and woman seeks out man in the name of love to satisfy the agony within and one goes with the pleasure of personal satisfaction until it runs dry, until no more can be squeezed to ease the personal pain of one's inner aloneness. Then one blames the 'other', but rarely the self, for one cannot bear to look inward, one cannot bear the naked reality of seeing the self personally possessed by the demon. So the wretched denial continues as one listens to the songs of so-called love, the music of the mad world while one hopes in vain that the next lover might fill the gaping hole in one's aching heart.

You need to be appreciated, you need to be loved, but the world is uncaring for it is there only to exploit and to take whatever can be taken. You might call out in blind despair, "Why is the world so cruel?" while failing to see that we as ourselves are this uncaring world. This is the acquired nature of humankind as the collective wilfulness of personal selves at varying levels of conflict. All one needs to do to verify this is to look at oneself.

One's personification is a consolidated block of resistance within the magnetic pull of the larger societal expression. Within this field of resistance the human mind which is a limited containment of data and memory comes into the play. Through this limitation the collective resistance of grouped personification sets out on missions of scientific research in its efforts to re-discover its own identity. It is so that the educational systems have come to venerate the scientific god. But the western evolution of thought, that is the mind, is now being obliged to acknowledge the inner neglect where all this scientific research is still failing to bring one to a clearer understanding of love. This remains your immediate hell as you can only repeat your previous anguish while you are being sucked into the outward spiral of the societal, magnetic field.

Then you try to measure love and grasp it according to your particular needs as seen through the limited mind while constantly in defiance of nature gently speaking, gently reminding you to let go. This is part of your resistance. But you do not listen as you fight for your personal wants, brother against brother for some particular woman, sister against sister for some particular man, mother for her particular child, child for his or her particular toy, impassioned human for one particular cause and so your hell continues.

Then when natural death takes the loved one away, the person is suddenly engulfed with the terrible pain, the terrible emptiness, the terrible vacuum that nothing can fill. You may even retaliate against your god for the terrible loss and rightly so, for this god is seldom more than the convenient god of your acquired nature. This god can give you no lasting relief, no permanent retrieve from your recurring anguish.

Life and death are intrinsic. We may refuse to listen to life but all of us are obliged to listen to death. Nonetheless, we pretend it is not there. We ignore the fact that death is inevitable. It is always someone else who dies. As a person I am obliged to logically accept that the body must die, but never this self, so I look upon it as having a soul. Consequently, I follow the collective lie convincing this self that a heaven hereafter awaits where this body and soul might again re-unite, or failing that, then I, as this personal self, will reincarnate in another place with another body.

35

Thus the loveless demon continues being served.

You can only discover through your own experience and the harder life speaks to you then the more fortunate you are, even though this is seldom acknowledged. You tend to become absorbed in your pain, in your own sad story as though it is the only one in existence, and so you fail to hear the message of life. In this relative world it is a gradual process where time is needed for something to happen in time. Still we fail to acknowledge death and we are always traumatised when a loved one suddenly leaves us. This would not be so if we were to truly understand death for it would then be a celebration rather than being such a trauma. So I will speak of love through my own most immediate experience of losing a loved one when the reality of life exploded my turbulent world and brought me back in through my senses obliging me to listen, silently listen.

It had been an unusual Sunday. I lay in my bed in the deafening silence, my mind battling against the inner unfolding of nature's secret. I did not wish to listen for the reality was too painful to accept. The time was well past midnight, somewhere into the early hours of the last day in May. I was mentally succumbed, yet nursing an utter refusal to accept nature's inevitable. My world of permanence was threatened. The reality of life was not conforming to my own unrelenting attachment to what I still wished to believe.

I was then living in a bungalow as a single parent with my two young daughters some five miles from my own parent's home. My mother and father were always together in mostly everything they did and everywhere they went. They expressed their love in serving the love that they shared. Rarely would I see one without the other. Their visits to us had been a regular occurrence until some weeks previously when my mother decided to spend some time with her twin sister who was living at the other side of the country. I only learned of this when my father visited us one evening alone and, seeing the question on my face, told me that my mother had gone.

That moment was the first flash I got. Seeing my facial reaction he proceeded to say that my mother had only gone to stay with her sister for a month but that was not the message registering within me. I had been struck like a thunderbolt by the cold, hard reality that a moment where she would forever be gone was recorded within me and that this utterly, unacceptable moment was gently edging upon us. I can only describe it as a sensation that vibrated through every particle of my body. Nonetheless, my mind refused to acknowledge this untapped intelligence coming to the fore within. It was unacceptable, painful to consider and I forcefully dismissed it like we usually tend to do when suddenly faced with the unpleasant.

This seems to be the way of things when one only believes what one wants to believe. It is the denial that keeps one locked up in ignorance, ignoring the deeper intelligence within, the deep reality of life. This denial comes about through our fears, being afraid to face what we see and being afraid to let go of our attachments. Our own superficial reality superimposes itself to the extent that we fail to acknowledge the truth, for the truth is always too painful for our acquired nature to accept. Our greatest fear, the fear of death, results from this condition and I do not just mean the death of the personal self but the death of one's nearest and dearest.

That Sunday had been an eventful day. Some days previous my mother had admitted herself to the Mater Hospital in Dublin whilst on her way back home after spending three weeks with her twin sister in Navan. She had felt a pain in her chest as they

37

walked together on the busy Dublin streets and she requested a nearby policeman to call an ambulance. She phoned my father after being medically examined and assured him that she was all right but would be staying in the hospital for a few days under observation. She insisted that she did not need us to visit, that it would be only a matter of time until she would be home. No one felt unduly concerned. The pains had come before and we had all lived with her heart condition pushed to the back of our minds since the first heart-attack some nine years previous. My mother was a survivor and with a wonderful zest for life. She overlooked my denials as to the seriousness of her condition, she overlooked my personal discomfort in facing the truth of the situation.

When Sunday arrived a feeling arose within me that I should drive to Dublin to see her, regardless of her plan to come home on the following day. She always used to tell me that in spite of my rambling I somehow seemed to be in the right place at the right time. For my part I took this intuitive side of my nature for granted without questioning why. My father and two friends decided to accompany me and we set off on the journey across Ireland together. The hospital had strict visiting hours and visiting time was just about over when we arrived. I told the others not to look lost or ask for directions lest we may be denied access but to follow me as though we knew exactly where we were going. I relied on my instincts to show me the way and I walked through the corridors eventually coming to a room where she stood alone by her bed.

The others arrived moments later and just in time to be told by the orderly matron that we all had to leave. My mother came out with us to a corridor by the hospital entrance and we all sat on a bench-seat together. She tried to tell me as gently as she could what the heart-specialist had told her. She would come home on the following day but we must accept the fact that most of her heart was deceased. But I dismissed this as nonsense and tried to assure her that she would be perfectly all right, while refusing to see that I was merely trying to reassure myself. I insisted that I would drive back to Dublin on the following day to collect her once she was officially discharged.

My mother sighed and silently touched me. Our lives together had been exuberant. She had been more of a close friend than a mother as I travelled through childhood, adolescence and into my manhood. We had our moments of great passion and great aspiration and those special moments in the silence where nothing needed to be said. She was always spontaneous and free, always open to the next discovery that life might unfold. She danced my dance and shared my delights. She was there in my moments of greatest sadness, silently sharing my pain and she looked on in wonder at the adventurous side of myself.

She knew, she understood, for she was fully aware as a young and beautiful woman when I first entered her consciousness as a voice in her inner ear and she instantly responded with the love of her heart. I came into existence through her loving consent. But the world of myself grew up around this knowing, like the weeds smothering the corn, and I was absorbed by the weeds of this world. My mother never forgot. She was aware of the fuller story from the moment I came into life from the seed of her womb, then through the pain of birth followed by the psychological pain of seeing her son being slowly absorbed by the mercenary world.

Our story had been intimate and honest. But I was not being honest with her now when she needed my honesty the most. She was facing death in isolation for I was unable to be honest in myself and accept it. I had become absorbed with my personal self, with my own personal desire of refusing to let go of her physical presence. Through my selfishness I refused to acknowledge the imminent and because of my own refusal to embrace the truth of the situation she was obliged to take this last step alone.

I had come into being through her conscious awareness. Then in my lack of right discernment I had become psychologically attached to my personal world of which she was seen as a permanent part in her role as mother. But this could not be so forever. Clearly I knew this, but I did not wish to know for the reality was too painful to face.

We left her alone with my father for some time. When we returned to say our goodbyes she looked into my eyes and within her all-knowing gaze I saw a deep anguish speaking in silence to me. She wept to herself as we all walked away. I wanted to believe through this existentialist side of myself that I was returning on the following day to bring her back home, but try as I would the reality of this happening would not come to life within me. As I drove the long journey back to Clare I was vividly aware of the surroundings, trying my hardest to bring the following day's journey into existence according to my own desires. But there was no inward assurance arising. My intuitive nature was silently speaking. Nevertheless, I refused to acknowledge what I was being instinctively told. I would not accept, I would not listen.

It had been a long Sunday. My refusal to acknowledge the disturbance within caused an anxiety that increased in momentum from the early morning right through to the midnight hour. My daughters, also, had gone through an active day staying with their cousins and they were now fast asleep in their rooms next to mine. I lay silently awake looking into the darkness about me on that warm summer's night. My mind would not settle as I battled with myself that everything was going to be all right, that tomorrow was going to happen according to my own particular desire.

It must have been three in the morning before tiredness gradually took over my body. It was a fretful tiredness as my mind remained active, still semi-conscious trying to work out what could not be worked out. Eventually it cleared as sleep overcame me. The following morning exploded when I was awakened by my father and younger sister tapping on the bedroom window. In my nakedness of body and emptiness of mind I jumped out of bed and opened the window to greet them. It was so how I received the terrible news that my mother, had died. Death, the cold reality of death shivered through my body. It was a numbing sensation.

The trauma of a funeral is something most of us experience at some time in our lives. Often it takes such a trauma to shake one out of one's groove. We tend to become so absorbed in living and keeping up to the terrible speed of our wants that we scarcely give ourselves time to pause and to ponder the meaning of life. Where does the one dearest to you go when taken from you through death? It is such a cold finality. Personally, I could not accept what had happened. My mother was dead but within me I could still feel her presence.

The first six weeks were the most traumatic. She had gone from us forever. It was the harsh reality but to me she was not gone. She had changed, she was unseen, as she changed her appearance so many times before, but she was not gone. Some of my friends tried to point out that I was in a state of denial but I knew this was not the case. My mother's body was gone, forever gone, but all that she was remained fully alive within me. It was then that I first knew I seriously needed to listen, to silently listen. The secrets of the creation were less than a moment away. Somehow through the unknown, through the great emptiness of the void within, my mother was still part of my life.

At first I found it difficult to comprehend, for up to that time I had been totally consumed in the physical body of matter. The fire energy of life absorbed me in my late teens as I went into an outward spin, consciously discarding the wealth of insight that was flowering through me in the light of her presence. Although I seemed to know this at that time, still I also knew that I had to enter into the maze of this living confusion. The mystery of life can only be known through the actual experiencing of it. Life is here to be lived. There is no other way.

Adolescence is a personification. The battles commenced between my personal desires and the natural rhythm, between what I personally wished to experience and what life issued forth to me. My mother never once impeded my urgent aspirations as she patiently listened, reflecting all the exuberance that was happening within me. Whether my projects blossomed or dismally failed she was there in unchanging appreciation.

Each time I entered the inauspicious forests of the living my mother patiently sat at the other side waiting for me to re-appear. Sooner or later I would come to the end of chasing the shadow of my personal notions, of this she seemed always cognisant by allowing me the space without hindrance to achieve or to fail. Whenever I became lost to the worldly illusions she was not unduly concerned, she knew me much deeper than that, she knew me behind my personal masks and she trusted the wisdom of silence. This was her speed of consciousness, even though she lived as an ordinary mother with her doubts and fears whenever she lost herself to her feelings.

In her clarity, however, she showed me the meaning of love. She showed me that in the knowing of love I am love. This is not the falling in love and the falling out of love as tends to happen with lovers. Such is the immaturity that is part of our acquired nature and it is usually driven by a personal want as one seeks what is pleasing to oneself. Falling in love can never be permanent. If one falls 'in' love then it is possible to fall 'out' of love. Such interpretation of love is relative to someone or something and is always temporary whereas *love* in itself is eternally present.

As I matured a little, wising up to my emotional fixations and moving away from my natural innocence, my mother noticed my heart growing colder. Again she was there to remind me that, although I am not above the emotions or feelings of love, they are beneath my true nature for love is neither emotion nor feeling. While feelings and emotions come and go still love always remains as the perennial flow of life. I did not fully understand the meaning of this until I was overcome by my feelings and emotions when she suddenly died. It was then I realised that the love was still there, even more than before, as the personal had been totally severed. Relatively, everything had changed, yet nothing had really changed.

I discovered that death does not separate, it changes as everything in existence keeps changing, but it does not separate love. Long after my mother's death I discovered she was still there to help me to realise love. The outer has changed but the inner remains exactly the same. What she had shown by example still speaks to me through the silence. Her presence is love and her person has died back into the love that is forever the love within me. This is my heart-centre, this is my being, forever as one in the blessed eternity.

Stillness is the way, the only way to this realisation. Stillness transcends the personal and the personal self is the problem with its particular fears, particular wants and particular emotions. We mistake the personal to be our true essence and we waste our energy trying to uphold it against the weight of the world opposing.

Even the word 'personal' tells us this, should we examine. Personal comes from the word 'persona' which means 'to mask' and behind this mask we suffer our pain, our personal anguish, while we endeavour to smile to the uncaring world. But one is not this mask, one is not even touched by it. You are aware of this as you look out at the world through your particular mask. The mask is around you but not in you. You are not this and you clearly know it.

You are forever still at the core of your being, it is the pure, unchanging presence. Stillness is the way to the centre, to the 'I', through the 'I', while the mind-weed is the hurricane spinning about you and holding you captive. You know the stillness within yourself, yet you seldom realise it by actually *being* it. There is always something or other being desired that keeps you outside of your centre.

I knew I had a long way to go as I battled through my personal desires in the slow and tedious journey of fulfilling them and the more I fulfilled them the more I realised they had to be fulfilled. It is, indeed, an addiction. But something had changed within me. I began to see this addiction for what it really is and I was no longer fulfilling my desires to please myself but rather to come to the end of them. I was beginning to realise the futility of it all and I could sense the freedom even though I was still not free from the personal self.

The desires I speak of are not those relating to the necessities of life, these are one's needs. I am referring to those cumbersome desires which are driven by the forces of marketing, self driving self, desires such as feasting, alcohol and sex being one of the strongest. There is nothing permanent, no lasting fulfilment whatsoever to be found through any of these desires, this I was obliged to acknowledge. When I began to realise the transient nature of my world I was driven to search for a deeper understanding. Towards this my mother had encouraged me as I matured through the floods of my personal wants. All my years with her were more than enriching and now she was gone, no more to be seen, no more to be heard, no more to feel the warmth of her touch or her gentle fragrance about me.

The book she was reading before she left was still on the table beside her bed where she had placed it. My father, having a deep respect for her privacy, had not disturbed it while she was away visiting her sister before she died. The book was on transcendental meditation and it lay untouched until I noticed it some weeks after her death. I picked it up from where it rested face down and open and read what it said,

"According to Maharishi, the ideal of education is, 'To create a fully developed man who is knowledgeable, resourceful, responsible, successful, fulfilled and of maximum use to himself and to others. Thus, an educated man is not one who merely has knowledge, but one who is able to use that knowledge effectively'."

It was a poignant message highlighting my inner neglect. I had become a man of the world, absorbed in action and driven by the reactionary world cascading about me from one dilemma to the next. There was no time for pause between my business activities and my obligations as a single parent of two young daughters. At that time I was working as a contractor in cargo distribution. It was speed followed by crisis followed by speed again. I am sure it all sounds familiar.

During that hectic period of my life my mother spent her last nine years expecting death to occur at any moment. She had been forewarned and her only concern was the trouble she was putting upon us. I had been un-awake to her presence as she walked alone in her own inner journey during those final years. Then she was quite suddenly gone through the wall of physical death and out of physical reach, no more to be seen by my earthly eyes.

Nonetheless, I could still feel her love within me. It was as though she had passed into the love, had absorbed and enriched it. Through the love that she was I could now see beyond the relative reality of the changing world about me. It seemed as though I was consciously in a new place where there was less doubt and fear, less confusion within.

Two months after her death I happened to be driving my lorry of freight past the local university and quite unexpectantly felt her presence burning right through me. It was as if she was telling me to wake up to life, to stop my madness and call into this college.

"But I do not have time," I silently argued, "I have a load to deliver and many calls have to be made".

"If you were dead you would have more time than the world is made of," the voice said in my head.

I drove into the college grounds, parked my lorry and sought out the reception. I had no idea what I wished to study and asked the lady at the desk what courses were available. She told me that all places were already allocated but then helped me by checking the register for cancellations and discovered a vacancy in the mature students slot for European Studies. I had the necessary educational requirements and she entered my name on the list and reminded me how lucky I was seeing that it was the last day for late registrations.

Although I was still unaware of it at the time, the circumstances of my life had considerably changed. I had felt that it would have been too traumatic for my father to live on his own after my mother's death and I had moved back home with my daughters as a temporary measure. But my father immediately took up the role of parent and councillor to the three of us. This gave me unanticipated space in my life to seriously consider the sudden opportunity of returning to college to continue with my own educational path.

I engaged an extra driver to handle my deliveries so I could avail of the placement being offered. From a monetary viewpoint it was not a practical decision as there was no guarantee that it would work out in the measure of financial reward. Nonetheless, I made the conscious decision to explore the deeper realms by placing my trust in the unknown. This is how the journey began, although there is no actual beginning. I needed to partially break free from the world of business and I accepted that I could only progress one step at a time once I opened to what was unfolding. I knew that I would have to relinquish my impressions and acquired opinions before I could receive the fresh and the new. This is how it actually occurred but it took me five years instead of four to graduate as I struggled through my financial shortfalls. Although all is immediate, but in our relative state it is a gradual process. When the day of graduation finally arrived it was a day of dedication to the love which my mother had so elegantly served in bringing all of it to life within me.

What is this love, one might ask?

It is not what we normally take to be love. The love that is known by the world usually has its root in some particular want. When love for another is generally expressed it is based on some desire to possess or to use. This is the ground that is part and parcel of our acquired nature. It is the legalised abuse to the meaning of love. We all crowd and clamour to serve ourselves. Even the zealously religious usually indulge some sentiment or some personal want for a heaven or a life more appealing hereafter. This is not love no matter how much our priestly nature convinces. This emotional expression of love is based on selfishness, such as the clinging to a parent, a child, a lover. In fact anything of the mind cannot be love for the mind is always seeking some end.

Love cannot be cultivated through cultured expression or produced under artificial terms as seems to be the notion of the worldly wise. This does not work, as we all know from our own experience in the turbulent world about us if we look at it honestly. We may study a course on the philosophy of life but philosophy is not love, nor is theology, nor any other course of study.

Then what is love?

In my own experience love is the medium of life. It is *being* rather than 'becoming' something or other. *Being* love can only be known in the *now*. One must live love to know love. It is *giving* in absolute freedom. There is no claw, no want, no condition. The air that the body freely receives is love. The air expects nothing in return. It is freely there for all, regardless of social, moral, religious or indeed any other mental conviction. Nature is natural love. Human nature is superimposed through the mind and it is in the mind where the purity of love is contaminated. This mental contamination even affects the air that we breathe.

We may try to find love through religion or society, but these only serve our acquired nature. It is always speculation through thinking about love, through self-consideration, but not in *being* love. The personal self comes and goes, as the passionate lover, the priest, the philosopher, the sage, while love is the omnipresence of all that is.

Love cannot be practiced, not even through emotional sentimentality for all emotions and sentiments are part of the conditional mind. Love has to be lived every moment of one's life in order to be known. This I discovered through all my experiences of what love is not. It is awareness that makes experience possible. As light is the colourless presence in the rainbow so also is awareness in every experience. Pure awareness is impartial reality where one seeks not only what pleases but sees what is true. This is not philosophising. Indeed, anything mental is part of the human condition, part of humankind's self-perpetuating anguish. The nature of the mind cannot be love for the mind is always conditional, always temporal, whereas, love is all. One must *be* love to know love.

There is always some want in the love as it is commonly expressed. We must first relinquish this personal force to want, to possess, if we are to *be* love. We must first return to the original state of stillness within, with nothing arising, before we can re-enter the harmonious *being* of love. This is not an easy task when we are tied and bound to our worldly desires. But the truth of the matter remains. One can never know love until one *is* love. That is when one is not being driven by the shell of oneself. To *be* love, then there cannot be want.

In the stillness of this desireless state love is the medium through which creation comes into being, where life and death are one and the same. It is through this medium that past, present and future are all in each moment of *now*. It is the medium through which my mother speaks from where she always was and always is. Love is. This I was initially shown by her example and then saw through my own experience after coming to understand that life and death are intrinsically the one expression. When the body dies it dies into love. It is the unpersonalised state of perpetual love. When you truly love, there is neither subject nor object, there is only love. This is our immortal state.

In our blindness we objectify love, then we expect to receive it from some other. When one *is* love then one is not this objective world, one understands the state of the world and one can see how the world objects to love. Such a world has no real substance. It is merely a projection of consciousness that is only recognised by the mind and perceived through the senses. It has no permanence, no immortality. In the light of one's true nature it is not even a momentary occurrence. When this is known through the source then one can blissfully enjoy the creation where one is not desiring the world through one's personified feelings and one is freed from the emotional demon of illusion, the gaping hole in one's heart.

When I travelled to Australia in search of the truth some twelve years after my mother's death I was still partly immersed in the feeling of love, still subconsciously searching for love to express itself in an external form to fill the vacuum within. I was in transition, ascending from the feeling of love to the knowing of love. It was a traumatic transformation and most disturbing emotionally. Although my personal and emotional self at that time was mortally wounded yet it was lingering as part of the hunger for a personal love.

But my life had dramatically changed. The superficial world in which I had allowed myself to plunge no longer sustained any lure. My worldly desires could no longer entice me into giving them chase. The consummation and ending of each desire was flashing through me simultaneous to its initial arousal. The beginning and ending all seemed to be in the same moment.

I had discovered a stillness within and in this place of stillness I was experiencing a speed of consciousness that was phenomenal in relation to anything I had previously known. This was new, totally new. I could feel as though I was psychically bristling and even in silence I could feel this bristling within me being a silent disturbance to others. People would look without knowing what they were seeing and then move along on their way. But the few who could see would smile through the sadness of what they were seeing and this was my comfort.

I felt as though I was being swallowed by an aching emptiness, an utter aloneness that was driving me to seek the company of the wise and the holy. This is how I came to spent three weeks in Australia in the presence of one who addresses himself as a spiritual master. This man's ego appeared to be massive and it needed to be to make such a claim. But it was not a worldly, acclaimed ego he appeared to display. This ego was driving him out to meet me from another source, a source that seemed to be placing him just one step ahead of the speed of consciousness within me at that particular time. Each moment I arrived at the spot where he appeared to be in his own understanding then he seemed to move just one step deeper and so it continued at phenomenal speed until suddenly all was transparent, like everything at once dissolving to light.

This occurred in the beautiful rainforests of Australia as the afternoon sun was casting its rays through the towering trees over the large marquee where I was sitting in his presence with about three hundred others from different parts of the world. Stillness was shimmering through us as we listened to his words and entered his silence. In the stillness of mind one is the great silence, before, during and after the word. So it was at that moment. We were gathered in service to love, each of us according to our lights.

There it suddenly happened. My inner vision became pristine clear and I was overwhelmed with inexpressible joy. I suddenly knew that 'I' am love in the here and now. I suddenly knew the truth of love in *being* as one with all.

This was my mother's parting message as this world of all of us faded from her. We faded as the dream, her special dream as she dissolved back into the void, back into the great beauty, the great emptiness that is the love in our hearts. It took twelve full years of searching through shadows for this realisation to implode. It took all of this time for the seed to crack open within me. And this is not even a ripple of the mystical experience that cannot be relayed through the spoken or written word. It can only be known in oneself when one is uncompromisingly empty, openly innocent, and truly trusting the unknown.

I walked deep into the rainforest and sat under a tree with all nature as one about and within. It was the most wondrous, inexplicable experience, beyond word, beyond description. It cannot be explained, it cannot be described, for the mind by its very nature can never understand the statelessness of no-mind. When I eventually returned to the gathering I knew it was done. I knew it was over for good. My personified world of 'becoming' had come to its end. I had passed through the death of my personal self. And *She* was there to embrace me through the arms of a beautiful woman, for I am man in existence and *She* is woman, not a particular man, not a particular woman, just man and woman as it was in the beginning is now and forever must be. So it is in the creation where 'I' am this life, this heart, your heart, the heart of all as the one heart.

If it has happened within you then you know exactly what is being said. One never needs to re-experience what one has been shown. Once it is seen it is seen and once it is known it is known.

Realisation is in itself not an experience, it is the discovery of the timeless factor in every experience. There can be nothing to follow but gratitude for this greatest of gifts, this greatest privilege to behold the realisation of one's true nature. It is from this place I speak as I speak about love. Speak I must, for such a divine privilege by its very nature must be shared and I am just an ordinary man having entered the immortality of my being through the medium of love that is here for one and all.

Earnestness is the only requirement once stillness is allowed to calm the restless mind bound up in its worldly concerns. It is only through absolute stillness that such knowing can enter one's understanding, such knowing that scorches the personified ego to death, such knowing that clearly shows this objective and transitory world as merely a projection of consciousness, as is, indeed, the subjective self.

The spiritual master gave me the key when he said there is but one 'I' and one 'Me'. I trusted him, I allowed these words to work on my heart until their awesome truth suddenly and unexpectedly exploded within. I had been listening to his words as he spoke them over and over again. Then I found myself listening to the silence behind the words. My mind seemed to split open. I could hear him with my ears and understanding as he spoke out through the ego of himself, out through his own personal issues, out through the 'I', out into my world. Then, directly behind the 'I' in myself I was suddenly hearing and understanding through the universal language of silence.

This perpetual silence is filled with all abundance, so much so that the spoken word is but an interruption. What I experienced cannot be explained for the word can only come after the thought, the first thought, the 'I' thought. But I can say this, there can be no going back. When one enters through the 'I' one discovers immortality. This one 'I' that I am is the 'I' in your heart whom you address as yourself. As we journey together, you and I, we journey into this light, into the inner being of all that you truly are, all that you eternally are. This is perpetual love, perpetual meditation, perpetual life.

I had finally cleared the way to allow it through when I had given up all my beliefs, all my notions, opinions and prejudices, when I had allowed all my garbage to be burned. I had to be willing and open to completely empty myself before I could *be* the great silence of no-mind. This is the inner stillness that is the way, the only way where it is possible for one to discover the truth of love. The closest to this in the relative world is the ecstatic state experienced when two lovers in the making of love totally melt into each other. This is the awesome wonder of life that is one's true nature in the *being* of love in existence.

This is not the relationship between minds. The dependence between two minds is what the world mistakes for love and this is what keeps us confined. This is always conditional, there is always a personal agenda whereas the *being* of love is boundless.

Religions are of the mind, philosophy is of the mind, reason is of the mind, but when the transformation to the state of no-mind occurs then one comes to know God as the highest quality of love. This is the ecstatic God-madness, like the God-madness of Buddha when he, forsaking his worldly treasures, chose to be a beggar, or like the God-madness of Jesus riding on a donkey into Jerusalem knowing full well that he was about to be crucified but ready and eager to give himself up in totality to love.

This is the great celebration, the great ecstasy of life in each moment of *now* in the timelessness of *being*. Here 'I', the one universal 'I', am always with you, always as one heart pulsing through the nucleus of the atom and spinning out through the Milky Way, forever as one, forever *now*. And here am I as formless life in this body, forever with my dear mother, where in truth there is neither mother nor son, just love, perpetual love pulsing throughout existence. This, I have discovered to be the greatest freedom, the greatest realisation. It is your true essence and the awesomeness of all that you are.

When man and woman come together in the making of love

they enter into the ecstatic being of oneness. This is the greatest beauty, the touching of the cosmic pulse of all that is before, after, within and without the creation. It is the humming of the bee, the perpetual rhythm of life where all of the world, indeed all of existence, is spinning about this one cosmic centre. It is the truth of all that you are in each pulse of your body that is happening right now where you are this formless life at one with every facet of love-making throughout all of existence.

When this great truth suddenly exploded within me I realised the meaning in the words, "I am in the world but not of the world". Then the world claimed me back as my karmic wheel continued spinning from its own momentum. I had reached the pinnacle of my worldly expression in the world of finance and that world was still weaving its fury about me in the form of a particular woman obsessed through the force of her wealth. One does not step out, one does not abandon, the play must be allowed to reach its own conclusion for this is the nature of the world and the world is as I am.

My business and brief encounter with man-made wealth is gone, all my worldly accumulations are gone. I rest here with nothing. That feverish urgency to succeed in a personal world of conflict filled with confusion is over. It is done. Many wonder at how I seem to keep going. The very few who know, the very few who have passed through the eye of the needle, they smile in the silence for in silence it is known. In silence nothing needs to be said. It is as it is. This is the acceptance. Knowing is the greatest privilege on the face of this earth. Then one must let go of the known for whatever is new.

Life is the unknown, forever new, while the known is forever old. Letting go of the known is allowing the pulse of life to be each moment freshly experienced. Love is always new. It

becomes old when one tries to take, when one becomes a clutching claw, this being the way of the psychic entity, the acquired
nature of the personal self. Then it is not love, it is greed masquerading as love, merely out to possess, out to plunder, using all
types of masks even those of the worldly gurus blinded by their
own sexual desires. This is a blasphemy to the preciousness of
love that is the most sacred of sacred between woman and man.
But the sword of truth is always here to cut through the self-made
gurus of this relative world who use the light to plunder the sacred
essence. Life is the perennial flow of the unknown spilling into
the known, slowly but surely unfolding the cloaks of deception
where all ultimately dissolves back into the oneness.

The deception is given ground when one is afraid of the aloneness, when one feels one needs a particular partner in life before
one can be love in oneself. Is this not how most people feel?
Indeed, many become totally lost to this, even to the point of per-
juring themselves in denial. The truth cannot be faced. Then the
ways of the world are given importance, cloaking the lie. Even
religious institutions are used and self-centred prayers pleading to
an external god, all to fulfil some personal desire. But no matter
how much the mind seeks some outer remedy to fill the raw, nauseating vacuum within, nonetheless, there can be no such escape
from this inner aloneness. The aloneness has to be eventually
faced, it has to be ultimately accepted.

Even the green-eyed monster of jealousy that is capable of driving the one possessed to murder only exasperates the inner dis-
ease. There is no escape outside of oneself. There is no place for
the inner demon to hide when one has the courage to face the
impostor self masquerading as love. This is facing into one's
aloneness by honestly facing the truth.

My mother tried to show me her aloneness on that fateful day before the morning she died. She had reached that moment of acceptance. It was finished for her. It seemed as though she was looking at the world from a different place and she could see through the illusion, she could see through the artificial nature of our love. She could see through the shallowness of it all for now she was obliged to see having fully accepted death. She had crossed over the divide from the superficial reality and she was alone.

Still, her heart was filled with the overwhelming love she held for us all. Her silent disturbance was in having to leave us in our blindness and having to leave me still trapped in my own foolish dreams, for I was not ready to awaken. I could see the stillness and the knowing in her eyes, even her silent acceptance of my refusal to acknowledge. But nothing happens before its time, as the spiritual master reminded me many years later, and that particular time, when my mother was about to depart this world, was not my time for awakening.

I could not understand then what I understand now and even with this understanding I realise how little I know in the face of all that is to be known. When my mother's final moment was upon me, still no matter how much I had tried or had wished I could not be with her, not even in the oneness that we had previously shared when wrapped in the beauty of nature about us in those early years of my youth.

That eve of her death was a much deeper state, a much finer consciousness than the coarseness of my own worldly expression. She wept, but it was the silence in her heart that deeply penetrated me, that deep immortal silence that swallowed me into its stillness. She withdrew from me, she withdrew form my world, in her aloneness, total aloneness, she died.

There was so much more I had wished to say. I was not prepared, I was lost to my personal world and I was out of tune with the sweetness of life.

This is how it was as it is with most, the foolishness arising from personification. But when one dies to the personal self, when one passes through, then there is no need to say goodbye, for each moment is lived in fullness. One is right up there in every aspect of one's life where there is nothing to be fixed, nothing to be put right, for all is right with oneself when there is no personal agenda dictating. Then every moment is the moment of goodbye as every moment is the moment of hello and there is nothing to be grieved.

Should you have something to put right with anyone then you are imprisoned by that. See it as it is, say it as it is, then you are free, you are right up there in the moment, every moment, accepting death as it occurs. This is the great understanding of perennial life in the great aloneness where there is no separation in the one 'I' directly behind the personal. This is love in existence.

As one steps into the unknown one is this aloneness, this absolute aloneness. This is how it must be, this is the trust, this is love, forever one's love, forever I serve 'It' and may it forever be so.

CHAPTER 3

Courtship? Who Are We Fooling?

First, let us examine the difference between love and courtship. When one is a servant to love then one is the master of the self, whereas, courtship is courting one's personal desires. Love gives unconditionally, it liberates, only love knows how to give, while desiring is the opposite, it implores, it begs, it exploits, it takes for itself.

Slaves are those who only know love as that expressed through desire. These are the masses doomed to recurring anguish. Their spouses and lovers are seen by them as their possessions, like everything they believe they possess, while the reality is that their possessions actually possess them. They are imprisoned by their desires and they live in slavery. The love they possess is lust. It is displayed all over the plastered morality of their societal faces, even to the extreme of lusting after a mind-weed god.

In the light of this knowing let us explore the play of the sexes. You are familiar with yours, so I will continue by relating to you some of mine. You will find similarities and, perhaps, see through the restrictive circles that we allow on ourselves.

When I had barely entered my teenage years I fell madly in love with a girl called Ann. She was wild, beautiful and free. It was not only her beauty with her tossed hair and dancing eyes that I found most attractive, it was her free spirit, her naturalness, that totally intrigued me. I was captivated by her radiance and each time she entered my space I experienced that strange but familiar burning sensation in my solar plexus.

Ann was a challenge to everyone. She did not live by the norm and the prudish were in constant fear of her unpredictable spontaneity. She had no reservations whatsoever on what she might say or what she might do. Other girls feared her, hence she was mostly alone. She was even too challenging for the boys, for not only could she outsmart them but she could out-box them as well. At the local dances Ann was the best at jiving. She taught me how to dance the rock-an-roll and we both took delight in the speed as we jived and twirled in our youthful exuberance together.

The night of my grandmother's funeral she allowed me to kiss her full on the lips after we went down by the river while all my family and most of the neighbourhood were praying in the chapel for the repose of my grandmother's soul.

This was a awesome happening, as well can be imagined, when the first kiss is experienced. That moment seemed to go on forever and it is still enriching me now.

Passion, sweet, sweet passion, it is the greatest wonder of life. There is nothing to compare to such rare moments and to the innocence of love before the worldly wise take hold of our senses.

The late evening shadows had descended upon us as Ann and I passionately caressed by the still waters of the Shannon. It was an awesome occurrence that moved me to write her this love poem,

Love it is the greatest thing
Since time itself began
It has survived through waging wars
Down through the ages ran.

Adam loved his lady Eve
Then love was meant for man
But now it seems just meant for us
You and I my dearest Ann.

She was exhilarated, so much so that she showed the poem to everyone on the school-bus, much to my mortification. Although I enjoyed her spontaneity, yet I was courting the alternative macho expression in my efforts to be accepted as leader of the boys. Now they were jeering the words and reducing the heart of the poem to my love-struck stupidity by falling under the spell of a girl. I was losing my place in the gang and the force of their jeering threw me into an awkward silence to the point of ignoring the presence of love.

This is how it seems to be in our youth as we so quickly get ourselves caught up in the societal expression. We start out as boys by ignoring love in order to appear to our peers as being cool and we foolishly take this to be manly. This was Ann's early experience in seeing the unnecessary pain being caused by man's stupidity in his inability to be true to life, to love and to the awesome fire of passion. The openness and spontaneity of her untarnished true nature could not be freely appreciated by the acquired nature that was slowly but surely enveloping myself. I speak on how it occurred through my own experience, realising of course that Ann's experience may not have been similar. However, I regained my place in the gang at the price of losing my love.

Ann was there for the remaining time of my youth but we only came together in the dance. The school-years swiftly passed. Then the night of the last dance arrived and again we embraced before the impatient world swallowed us into our separate destinies. That was our last farewell.

I was swift and foolish in disassociating myself from the passionate enrichment that life had freely offered. The shallow personality of my personal self was by then absorbing most of my available energy. One needs to be alert to the moment as the waters of life all too swiftly flow by. You know how it is in youe own experience.

"Man chooses the woman who chooses the man". I think it was Oscar Wilde who first made this statement. Well somebody did, for it has been said and I consider it a judicious observation.

I seem to have lived a dozen lives since love first showed me its purity through the childhood innocent of Ann's loving heart. Then I gave myself up to the world believing it to be the true reality. I courted this realm trying to impress it through many professions and still love occasionally appeared as a gentle reminder.

Whenever it appeared through the heart of a loving woman it enabled me to momentarily see the madness I was relentlessly creating in this world of myself. It seemed that the madness was my recurring expression. Still, each time love came close to my heart through the presence of a woman of love the worldly illusion of mental impressions grew bigger and bigger to pull me further away. The karmic recurrence of my first abandonment of love in its purity continued to spin.

This is our world. This is the pain and confusion we seem to be serving. Each of us have our own personal experience, our own traumatic occurrence, and while they all may appear to be different, nonetheless, they are all much the same. The old and the wise can tell us that this becomes more and more obvious as one is nearing the end of life's journey. Should we examine one personal trauma then we can come to a clearer understanding of all, for it is the same old story on this well-worn stage of existence in one form or other recurring again and again.

Your situation can be understood through mine, as my situation can be understood through yours. We are all but mirrors of each other, even though we spend most of our lives striving to be different. There can be no one excluded. No matter who or what one thinks of oneself still one is not different. On the surface one may appear to be different, but directly beneath neither gender, creed, class nor colour can truly differentiate. It is the one big melting pot of pure consciousness blazing through consolidated consciousness reflecting as matter.

I had forsaken love for worldly impressions, until eventually I called to life to show me the way. When I had suffered enough I pleaded with God for release while still foolishly trying to hold onto the reins. Inevitably woman in the form of hell's fury had to arrive. The scene was being set in this make-believe world that I had set out to serve when I was unexpectantly chosen by a particular woman to be her particular man. This woman had given herself up to a similar world and I refused to acknowledge her so. In retrospect it is easy to see that she was uncomfortably too close to my own acquired nature. It was certainly not what I had wished to find in woman as I had more than enough to suffer at the time by facing into this acquired nature in myself.

Although I did not fully recognise it at the time, it was the world of my own creation at the edge of the ultimate abyss. I had been courting this world of my acquired nature for most of my adolescent life, as most of us do, and had finally arrived at that point where I was now expected to take the ultimate step in dealing my heart to the devil. But love is always present, even if not seen through one's own foolishness when one is lost to the worldly glamour. We build our own bonfires and the greater the ego then the greater is the burning.

Whatever one's problem in life, by whatever hand one may

seem to be suffering, at the end of all the appropriation of blame, it is oneself who is calling it up. It is oneself who choses to remain. All one has to do is to walk away but one does not realise this until one has been burned enough. We call up our fires to burn out our demons within. Strange as it seems, this is exactly how it is. We are all interconnected. As one burns out one's own demons then the demons of others immediately about one are instantly exposed. No matter how secure one feels in one's personal beliefs of convenience, yet one will discover this fact should one come into the physical presence of one who has passed through the fire of the personal self. This is the fire that is ignited by the cosmic fusion arising through the courtship dance between woman and man.

Looking back at the situations of our lives we understand how our reasoning is that of our acquired nature. It is easier to see in retrospect. When I was ensnared through my own desires by a particular woman using the power of her worldly wealth it became a battle of personal wills. I failed to see how she was loading me with all of her world as she played on my strings using every conceivable method to make me feel guilty. Should I have had the clarity of seeing things clearly I would have realised that I had nothing to be guilty about except the one fact of refusing to be her lover, for this was an obligatory part of our relationship as far as she was concerned. No matter what I did or how successful I was in our business arrangements together I was forever guilty in her eyes for denying her this sexual intimacy. For this denial she willed me to fail. The problem reached a critical mass when a lover briefly entered my life. The obvious avenue open to the woman then flooded with rage was to create total destruction in all my worldly affairs and this she successfully achieved. It had to be so. To every action there is an equal and opposite reaction according to science. The destruction of my world is the extent of her own personal grief. More than meets the eye needs to be seen and understood. We are all the victims of our own creation in one way or another when we look beneath the surface.

It took the presence of a spiritual master to awaken me from the nightmare. Through this I realised how terrible it would be if I should exit this life while still in compromise to the 'money-god' of this mad world which was the immediate reflection of my own acquired nature at that particular time. This is the most horrifying trepidation imaginable when one suddenly realises the awesomeness of love that one has been trading to the devil as one's acquired nature. The contrast between love and such courtship is unimaginable.

Words cannot explain it, but I can relate that I had the privilege of witnessing hell and this is one of the rarest privileges on the face of this earth. Having seen what I have seen I know that I can never again be apart from my true nature.

This is not a terror of losing my personal self, for all self has to be relinquished. What I really experienced was the multi-dimensional presence of *being* all that I am, which I had never before realised, as I precariously balanced on the edge of the terrible abyss. This is what I was abandoning through the wilfulness of my own personification.

From this I can say with absolute certainty that the soul you may think you have does not exist even as the minutest particle of all that you really are. This I was about to molest, about to hand over to oblivion, for this is hell and in hell there is no return, that I speak from my own experience. When you know this, I mean really, really knows this, then you would not, even for a moment, be of service to your acquired nature. The fact of the matter remains that whatever you serve in life so you die serving. There are no exceptions, as one plants so one reaps. This is the universal law and I am not making the rules.

What a terrible calamity it would be should I die for anything other than dying in service to love. This I realised was my greatest anguish when I had become fatally ensnared in the worldly web of deception. I suddenly knew then that I had to break free when my condition had reached a critical mass and awareness told me that we are born into this life only to serve love. I can speak with absolute certainty that this is the only purpose to life. There is no other reason, no other purpose, believe it or not. It is only you, the individual, who knows through your heart who or what you are really serving.

The devil takes unto itself all of those serving their acquired nature. This is the universal play. We are all devil bound as we are and so shall we die whether we get a religious burial or not. But, one does not have to wait for physical death before one enters the pits of hell, for we are the portal of hell in this mini-dimensional existence. It is all in the unfolding in each moment of *now*, forever *now*, and the greatest gift that can ever be given is the gift of sight to those who are blind as the play of life and death forever continues.

The gift of sight is not easily attained on the coarser levels of existence and it can be further blinded on the subtler levels by the seductive play of the occult presenting itself as a new fascination. Access to these forces is immediate to one when fully opened to truth. But, should one become dependent on such it is like walking backwards with one's back to the light where oneself is playing into the darkness of one's own shadows. It is still the play of the acquired nature of self that is seeking further personal advantage.

This does not only apply to devil worshippers but also to theologians, philosophers and, indeed, to all facets of the mind-weed through which the acquired nature of the self tries to interpret. We must not allow ourselves to be fooled. There is no mystery in the occult.

Society en-masse denies man's potentiality as societal ignorance forms a block of resistance. This block is like damming the river of life and a huge reservoir builds up. This is the reservoir that sustains the occult and if one is part of the damming force then it is one's own energy that it feeds upon. It is as simple as that. All one has to do is to see it exactly as it is. Then it has no power, whatsoever, and should one realise one's true nature in the *being* of it then anyone in one's presence depending on the occult will be instantly rendered impotent. There is no power that can have superiority on one who is self-realised.

"Man chooses the woman who chooses the man". In my own experience it is certainly true. There was a time in my earlier years when I foolishly thought that I, as a young man, was fully in command of my own destiny as far as women were concerned. Nonetheless, in hindsight I can now understand that the few times I won a woman's heart only occurred when the woman actually allowed it to occur. It may be the man who seems to do the asking but it is always the woman who decides while all of her men are precariously balancing on the edge of her whim.

One lives by probability alone. The woman allows herself to be propositioned by the man of her particular choosing and her regular annoyance is in refusing the men who are not. The woman's frustration of course is when the man of her dreams is besotted by the sight of another woman who may or may not have her sights set on him, or when the foolish man is too preoccupied trying to impress his peers. This seems to be the way of things in the noisy clattering of living out our fantasies, frustrations and elusive desires in the manner in which we seem to display the mating tendencies of our acquired nature. It is the devil singing and dancing through all of us. The devil is our acquired nature and we foolishly give it a character with a horny image that we wish to see as other than personal self.

Experience teaches us to acknowledge this play of existence pertaining to the mating inclinations of man and woman. In order to examine it together, to see if it is really true, we need to impartially look at the sexual games in which we engage.

When we are grasping for temporary appeasement for sexual desires or relief from inner loneliness we usually mis-align ourselves due to our lack of awareness relating to the rules of the game. If woman chooses not the man then all the mating manoeuvres of the man are in vain. She may choose to play with him for a little self-amusement while she fills in the time until the man of her choosing arrives. Then, should he arrive, that is the end of that or the start of the real commotion!

The play of never-ending characters so continues in this relative world while each of us take it as a very personal affair with the emotionally burdened psychiatrists trying to unravel the ravelling!

A particular man befriended me with his personal problems. It is a good example of how we behave. He was more than twenty years married and his wife had grown tired of being used as a convenient release for his sexual needs. The older he was getting the more demanding he was becoming and their relationship had come to the stage where she could no longer find any loving feelings in her heart for him. She had more than enough. But he needed his fix. He pleaded with her through his mounting frustration, even masturbating himself in her presence one night while kneeling by the bed that he still forcefully shared with her as a matter of contractual right. Needless to say, she was not impressed.

He was asking me if he had grounds for divorce, particularly when she turned her back on him and went to sleep after telling him that he was pathetically disgusting. I tried to remind him that I was a financial consultant. That is what I had been told when I was groomed by the life-assurance business to be a life-assurance salesman. I had no extended qualification from the appointed financial genies relating to his specific field of enquiry. My purpose was merely to sell him an investment bond so I could enjoy the commission.

Then one morning I called to his house to discuss the opportunities relating to a particular financial instrument some eager fund-managers were putting together. But he was unable to receive me as he happened to be on his way out to church. He invited me to join him in prayer if I wished. In the course of the curious profession as financial consultant, in which I had at that time been engaged, this would have been just one of many such peculiar occurrences. We both ended up on our knees in front of a candle-lit altar quietly listening to the words of a priest. This religious man reminded the small congregation of mostly elderly people that Christ is not dead but is fully alive in each of our hearts.

We only need to wake up to realise it," was the message he hammered home to the few scattered souls awaiting their final departure.

"This is the real tabernacle of Christ, your very own body, as are the bodies of everyone," he repeated again and again through the course of the service.

Later, after leaving the church, we sat down in a cafe, re-investing in our worldly concerns, while the truth in the words of the priest was conveniently buried. We talked over coffee, me about my investment bond and he about his sexual plight, with neither of us listening to the other.

I placed the colourful bar charts on the table before him that I had carefully pre-arranged as part of my own presentation. I showed him copies of the positive predictions put together by the investment genies without caring to even consider anything pertaining to the opposite. I reminded him of the prevailing advantages relating to currency exchange and all the other benefits pertaining to the pending transaction. The sale had to be closed and this was my only concern.

"We should move on it now", I tried to encourage.

I silently felt that I had already more than earned the commissions to be made on the deal. The charts were more than impressive, I thought, as I covered the table before him. This man was spurred by the same greed as myself for the quickest possible returns. This new investment bond was the latest instrument I had been given and I talked through all the opportunities immediately at hand. But he was not responding. He was not even listening as he spoke of his wife being his problem. This was his immediate torment as he started thinking aloud about his loneliness and isolation in the uncontrolable sexual surges charging through his body like the hot flushes of a horny teenager.

"Damn it! 'Tis a woman's duty", he said in a sudden outburst that filled the cafe. I was taken completely by surprise.

"Woman must surely know the sexual frustration in man," he continued at the top of his voice.

"Man has to fuck! This is his nature. When I took her to be my wife, for Christ's sake she said at the altar that she would love, honour and obey. Now she turns her arse on me and I am forced to masturbate this sexual tension out of my body! This is not doing her duty! What does she expect me to do? Look for sexual release on the streets? Or join with the balding middle-aged men in the nightclubs and seedy sex joints? Is this what she is driving me to do? Is this what she wants? For Christ's sake! Forgive me Jesus. Oh! forgive me for using your name! But for Christ's sake you made me! What do you expect? I am a sexual man, you know how much I need to fuck! This woman you inflicted upon me is failing to do her duty".

The cafe was suddenly filled with an uneasy silence broken only by the sound of a few rattling cups and saucers being washed in the kitchen. We were instantly the centre of attention and a life-assurance salesman is particularly sensitive at the point of a sale for rarely he truly believes in what he is selling. I stared into my empty cup without even seeing where I was looking, for I was totally taken off guard and not knowing where to direct my attention, or where to hide my face.

"This bloody well entitles me to a divorce", the outraged man emotively continued, banging his fist on the table.

Perhaps he was watching too much television for this was the only place where divorce was at that time happening in Ireland! Murder was the only direct method available to a beleaguered spouse wishing for absolute release and I am aware of at least a few situations where it was professionally administered. But the law is reluctant to interfere with family matters for this is deemed as the field of the Church. Anyway it is rarely that a woman is driven to murder more than one husband in a lifetime so one engaging in such action is not usually seen as a societal menace. Stealing a purse is far more serious. What an unusual society we support!

We had become the focus of attention in the cafe. Then I began to feel why should I allow myself to be intimidated by the people about me. Even if I were a toothbrush salesman I was merely in this situation peddling my goods. Business is business and I suddenly realised that before I could make any progress or, indeed, make any commission from the sales presentation I would first have to address his immediate problem. His self-centred attitude was in conflict with mine and even more so when he started raving about the great sacrifices he had personally made by becoming a reformed alcoholic and placing the blame of all his demise on his wife's refusal to have sex with him.

He was far too dominant in his behaviour for my own self-centred desire to get the sale of the bond concluded, this being my only interest which was not even getting a partial airing. It must have been a comedy of errors to our audience. He was more than persistent in his efforts to gain my support. But he succeeded in bringing me to the end of my tether when I found myself drawing from the words of the priest relating to the theme of his sermon that Christ is not dead but alive in each of our hearts. His outrage had to be challenged.

"Perhaps it was Jesus speaking to you through the heart of your wife when she spoke to you that way telling you how pathetic you had become when tossing yourself off in her presence like you did," I boldly suggested.

He was taken aback and he straightened himself in his seat with a question-mark of amazement all over his face. I knew that I had caught him off guard and it gave me the courage to continue.

"Perhaps if you should see Jesus in her, for she is the heart most immediate to you where the priest was telling you to look, then you would not be so anxious to fuck her!"

His mouth fell open in the deafening silence descending upon us. The lady who was serving the tables smiled to herself as she closely passed by while making a conscious effort to catch my eye. This served me the necessary energy to continue the assault while he was stunned into silence.

"What is the point in praying to the heart of Jesus on your knees in front of an altar and then going home to your bedroom to fuck the same heart of Jesus in your wife? Surely your attitude does not make religious sense".

I could feel myself on a roll and riding on the crest of the wave of his personal problem. But no more could be said. An uneasy hush descended upon us. Our coffee cups were empty, had gone unnoticed, and I allowed the silence to prevail while I waited for his response. Whether or not I had blown the sale of the bond I was obliged to hold onto my ground. There could be no going back for what had been said was said.

Eventually he spoke, but almost unheard.

"You are right", he sullenly muttered.

Nothing more on the subject was mentioned. The space was cleared for my investment presentation to proceed. This was my vested interest. We can see how cruel we are. The colourful charts filled the vacuum as more coffees were ordered and drank.

But he was not quite ready to proceed. He needed his wife's approval. He needed authorisation from her before he could decide. I discovered I was presenting my jargon to the wrong partner as it had now become obvious that she was the boss. So I did the logical thing that a salesman would do and made an appointment to meet them together.

It was over a week later when I called to their house on the appointed evening, but he had made it his business not to be there for the meeting as planned. Nonetheless, his wife was present to greet me and at first she apologised for his absence as she amusingly remarked,

"He must have totally forgotten. Or maybe he really doesn't want to meet you," she continued with a smile.

"He's not quite himself since you spoke with him last week after you both went to church together. You know, I cannot figure him out, he has suddenly gone so quiet in himself. I thought I knew him but now he's acting so strange. He even jumped out of bed a couple of nights ago and got down on his knees and started praying to me, calling me Jesus Christ and begging me to forgive him! There is something unusual going on. You know, whatever you have been telling my husband I think you are getting him seriously confused".

The woman was right of course. A life-assurance salesman is not necessarily a good marriage guidance councillor, or sex therapist for that matter. And her husband was not far off the mark in describing the common difficulty in men and how they spill their frustrations into the bars, nightclubs and seedy sex parlours. He felt he was morally right in keeping his sexual frustrations restricted to his marriage bedroom. His wife seemed to be coping with this until I arrived on the scene and added fuel to the fire of the issue with my over-direct suggestions.

"I can cope with his unreasonable behaviour", she said, then she jokingly added, "But I cannot cope with this role of being Jesus to him that you seem to have put into his head".

It all may seem to be very amusing. Nonetheless, when we look at the plight of someone other than ourselves, we can see how ridiculous it is. Yet, these are the types of games we seem to play under our misguided interpretation of love. These are our courtship procedures that serve not love but serve only our acquired nature, our own personal wants.

We have to acknowledge that there seems to be something amiss in the lines of communication between the genders, but the law relating to courtship remains unmoved.

"The man chooses the woman who chooses the man".

In my own experience, as man inclined towards woman for my deeper desires to be met, I can only discover the truth of it all by looking into myself. Should I be man in sexual need then I am but one of the multitudes. I am as the more foolish of men in dire expectation fluttering about the sexually alluring, like wasps furiously buzzing around an open jam-jar.

But the woman is still in command of the play. Even in this situation it is still the woman who inevitably decides whom she will take to her bosom while the rest engage in incessant competition with one another, if not to win the woman's attention then to win the attention of the world as a paltry substitute. So we seem to continue the play while failing to address the hidden cause of all such actions. This is the man-made world of sexual projection.

When we look at it closely we can see how this world is endlessly re-created as contemporary men in assumed importance prance like peacocks with cellular phones and hot sales agendas. Men seem to be always searching for something to do or something to show that might create a temporary advantage for captivating a pleasing female to use as a dump for their sexual desires. This might not be the apparent intention in the subtlety of the dance but it is usually the force behind the engagement. Although modern man may seem to have cultivated himself more than this, nevertheless, he has merely cultivated his denial of the truth. It is hard to accept that one is being used by the devil dancing its way through the human psyche as man's intention precariously hanging off the end of his penis. It takes an awakened woman to see it.

We set out to compete. It is this acquired nature that seems to consume us from the moment we wear our first shoes. Why must it be so? Why must we waste our energies in pursuit? In the kingdom of cats I have noticed a characteristic of the mature male driving him to kill the newly born, male kittens. Apparently, he is instinctively driven to do this so he can maintain the exclusiveness of his own domain. This is an animal instinct that seems to be not too unfamiliar among humans. While the play may be more discerning yet the intent is much the same.

Men compete with men for the sexual rights over a particular woman and women compete with women for the sexual rights over a particular man. In order to outshine all one's fellow competitors the exploiting manoeuvres continue. Then one becomes totally absorbed in the manoeuvres, this being the world one endlessly creates. Even when a conquest is made one soon becomes restless as one hankers again for the buzz of this mating performance. Again one is out in the field subconsciously searching to reassure the self of its own egotistical agility. It may not necessarily be for another liaison, unless it arises, but it surely is for adding additional plumes to the deflating, egotistical tail.

Is this the root of our problems? Is man abdicating his true essence to performance as such?

The woman, misguided by the lure, allows her decision to be made according to this surface reflection of temporal sheen and yields to the acquired nature of man. When this acquired nature reaches the peak of its frustrations by masturbating itself in her presence then the ingrained intent is unmasked and she suddenly looks upon it all in utter dismay. Now she shows her disgust for now she is obliged to acknowledge what she failed to acknowledge in the beginning.

She allows herself to be absorbed by the dazzle that is usually the mask for such deeper intent, even in the depths of herself. This is our world dressed up through consumerism where all the wizardly, financial manoeuvres from Wall Street to Tokyo, London and back are merely its outer expression. It has gone beyond immediate recognition. This dazzle has layered itself upon layers of itself. Wanton frustrations expand in this outer projection where humanity seems to have dismally lost contact with its true nature.

Indeed, one can hardly hope to understand what is one's true nature from where one usually perceives. The transient sheen has become much deeper than the temporal show performed as the mating dance by the clones re-birthing to serve it. The mass ignorance super-imposes itself through the masses upon the masses and the individual is duped into ignoring the natural law.

The terrible plunders on the sanctity of woman, the terrible inflictions imposed upon her through men's instruments of religion, economics, social political systems, men who set themselves up as demi-gods and women hypnotically following, these terrible systems of violation have evolved through our self-acquired nature overshadowing our true essence. This is the nature of the world we create and endeavour to serve with each man and woman pushing and shoving for his own or her own personified interests. This is our conflict where all our applied methods of conflict resolution are little more than temporary appeasement for the psychic monster invading the human realm.

Should we question ourselves by impartially examining the force that is relentlessly pushing us along we might come to realise the reality of this perpetual mess, how we spend our energies in rigorous pursuit of gratification for withering flesh. This is the modern world, the world of 'becoming', where the woman instead of choosing the man has herself become lost to the glitter. This is not to place the fault on the woman for we are all as the one humankind and it is the strutting of the business-like male now lost to the courtship ritual that seems to be currently perpetuating this abominable situation.

This courtship ritual has evolved from ancient tribal customs to be the performance, not only of monarches and closeted bishops but now appearing as the modern world of money and business we serve.

It is the world of men made by men that is serviced by men and women as men in furious momentum. There can be no service to love when it is all in service to self-satisfaction. The frustration it causes has brought sexual man to his knees masturbating his terrible anguish in front of the conceptual image of sexually perplexed and sexually disenchanted woman.

Where is the love in all of this dancing and prancing of plumes? Where is man and where is woman in service to love? The world of inevitable death seems to have been triggered by the wilful restlessness of our acquired nature seeking its own continuity. This is the man-made world that is eating into the crust of the great mother earth, the fuel of the fire burning through the hearts of men and women as anger and greed. One only has to look at the hourly news bulletins to verify this. It is mostly the same old story with different actors and different events but all expressing the same putridity of man's inhumanity to man.

Then on the rare occasion woman appears in her true essence in service to love and she opens the heart of man to receive her. This is the heart of the goddess that is surely the innermost nature of every woman. Woman realises this in herself when she melts back in through the sensation of *being* love that is her true nature within. This is not the objective love of being in love with another that always, sooner or later, leads to inevitable doom. It is the love that she is when she is fully at one with the inner light that is her real illumination.

It is only the embrace of her true nature that purges man from the restless side of himself. Woman's true nature is in her *being* as the goddess, in *being* love. Man can only be his true nature when he is in service to love. He can expect nothing but added frustration from a woman who is not a woman of love for a woman as such is but a reflection of his own sexual torment within. But when man serves the goddess in woman then he is *being* his true nature. Should he consider his true nature as other than this then he must surely be spiritually dead.

When we look at the world around us we see it is teeming with walking and talking corpses direfully in need to fuck one another. These are the multitudes of men and women wilfully abandoning the truth that they are. We seldom realise who or what we are really serving while we are all being driven by the force of the sexual demon let loose. Man can experience nothing but inevitable anguish from women of sexual hunger. Here he is being externally confronted with the immediate reflection of his own macho demon from whom he is unconsciously endeavouring to escape.

As part of the masses one can only become demented while displaying oneself as a dancer of worldly desire. Tasting the bitter-sweet fruits leaves one even more bitter within when the taste-buds run dry

This seems to be how it is in our immediate world that has become a world of litigation, with crowded courtrooms endeavouring to unravel each mess by additional ravelling. It is a delicate compromise when trying to appease appeasement as the goblins of innate indulgence continue to dance through the human psyche.

But the times are changing as time always has done for this is the nature of time. Having danced the dance we seem to be now approaching the end of this epochal term. Women have served the

sexual demon to the point of total excess and the heart of wom-
ankind is now screaming, "Enough! enough of this madness".
The true nature of love can never be that of this worldly expression. It is inevitable that the female principle has to respond if
there is truth in the saying that to every action there is an equal and
opposite reaction.

We are entering the era of *She* rising through the veins of
woman. This is the goddess, woman's true nature taking up the
sword of freedom in the awakening heart. In *her* presence the
demon has no place to hide for all its masks are transparent. Its
medium is being vanished from existence and its multitudes of living dead are being frizzled back into oblivion. It is happening
right now and all one needs is a good pair of nostrils to smell it!

Man can only escape from his self-made captivity through *her*
embrace. Before he can truly receive this immortality he must
first be ready to let go of his acquired nature that is deep-rooted
through the genetic code and the innate psyche of the human
expression. He must see the reality of his loveless situation. Man
can only discover this through the experience of love in the *being*
of love in his heart. Before he can enter here he has to first get it
right with woman, for *She* is his immediate God. Whether he
accepts it or not, there is no heaven here-now or hereafter for man
who cannot get it right with woman and this getting it right is
much deeper than sexual association. The world is saturated with
sex-ridden men as the eunuches of women's frustrations, while
man of love and woman of love are the rarest phenomenon on the
face of this earth.

Love cannot be had through the love-seeking, self-gratification
of worldly desires being gorged and gobbled. This is what the
world has mistaken for love and this mistake is the perpetual pain.
It is the confusion. We consume ourselves with our buzzing com-

puters and scientific applications of assumed importance. We have become the seekers of self-pacification for this acquired nature that we have become impoverished to serve, having severed our true understanding of love.

The water-diviner seeks out the source of the waters beneath the surface of the earth. This is the skill of water-divining. It is not easily achieved. It is indeed a delicate task and if one is not sure then much unnecessary digging has to be done. One is obliged to try and try again until the water is found. So also we need to divine the self to re-discover the divine love that is our true nature.

We can never see or hope to understand this divine love through the eyes of our acquired nature that is the smothering self endlessly seeking the pleasant. This worldly self is the delusion that justifies its existence through convenient beliefs such as where we blindly continue our plundering under the notion that an exterior god in the image of man is here to redeem us whenever we feel ready in ourselves to be redeemed. Let us not be so deluded by these gods of salvation whom we are conditioned to believe in by the worldly side of the personal self.

Men, let us be honest, there is no exterior god to save us. Woman of love is the saviour of man. Should I, as man, appear unlovable to the heart of a woman of love then this is my place for correction in this moment right now. There is no place else, no matter how much one wishes. It takes a real man to go down on his knees to a woman of love to ask her forgiveness. And it takes a real woman of love to reach out to the heart of the man through the shivering, unlovable beast that he has become in his loveless world of 'becoming'.

For better or worse as far as man is concerned, it is woman who decides. When I was a man driven by the fire of worldly passion

I was naively unaware of this fact. Like most men I insisted where women resisted and I resisted where women insisted. I had thus become swallowed by the worldly expression of self. Then a woman of the 'money-god' plundered my space, for it was ripe for plundering, and I allowed my integrity to be compromised as I danced the devil's dance with my energy spilling into the worldly illusion in service to money. This is the piper's tune and the piper always demands to be paid.

Many get swallowed in this living hell where there seems to be no way out of the mess, of one sort or other, that seems to escalate out of nothing in particular. One may please and appease but it only gets worse while one fails to face the truth of the situation, for one's immediate situation is always the truth challenging one's acquired nature. This is exactly how it is. Whatever the circumstances, whatever the suffering in one's life, the bottom line remains that these circumstances are one's immediate task, one's immediate God, for it is only in the circumstances of one's life where the truth is directly speaking.

One might set out to fool oneself by going on religious pilgrimages or chasing enlightened masters or becoming 'holier than thou', but the fact of the matter remains that one's real purpose for being in existence is always directly present, even though at times it may seem impossible to see.

While one twists and turns for a better kind of living, always in search of something or other, one fails to address the immediate. Fear of facing the truth of the situation is the unacknowledged bogey that keeps on driving one the other way.

I gave nine years of my life as a broker in the world of finance where considerable wealth accumulated but only again to be lost. Then out of the blue a woman of love appeared. I was suddenly re-awakened to a depth forgotten through the blindness of my own acquired nature. In the midst of my greatest turbulence I was brought to a stillness within. The noise in my ears was silenced to all but the song of her love. The fragrance of every flower was her fragrance, every smile was her smile, every touch was her touch, every taste was that pleasing to her. My searching was over for ever it seemed, even though I had not been aware that I was still searching. In the time of our wondrous embrace we were two together as one, hand in hand with the natural law both serving the wonder of love. I was thus consumed with the rapture of love's fragrance being reflected to me through her presence.

This is what is termed as falling in love. But even such love is not *being* love, for there is still a personal want, a personal need and falling in love is rarely more than a temporary occurrence. I am sure we can agree upon this. How many times have you fallen in love? Still one must not close off from the world. One must not hide behind one's previous pain for such prohibits the spontaneity of all that is new.

I challenge this acquired nature we serve and how we blindly search for pleasures to blot out our hidden anguish. The mind cannot for a moment be still for stillness shows up the truth of one's pitiful state. This world of 'becoming' is our reactionary race away from the truth. The millions of bodies in this financial equation are merely its pawns to be consumed and excreted at will. Our world of exploitation is on automatic pilot with no one in particular accountable for the loveless situation. This I speak from my own experience having been the lord of the dance, the dance of the living dead. I have entered and tasted and placed its crown on my head and now I am being dragged through the mortuary chamber of its final expression.

In this dance of the worldly we all wear the masks of glitter as outer assertion courting outer assertion. Fresh blood, new arrival, here I discovered myself masquerading as king with the sultry queen of the dance courting our way into hell.

Nonetheless, everything is as it is and when a godly man threw me a line I had thankfully realised that the embodiment of my acquired nature was not to be rescued. This self has to be burned and it must go on burning and burning until it burns itself out. There are the few who return from the fire. The few who do have a story to tell and each is obliged to tell it.

Times are changing, they say, whoever 'they' are, in this brief, two thousand, odd years of courting the devil. Let us continue together on this journey of discovery through our living quandary in a world we take to be real as we court this infinite time, but limited nonetheless, to each of us courting. We must divine the truth of this self and the source of the being, as the diviner divines the source of the waters if we are to re-cognise the devil we are courting within.

The secret of knowing may be the realisation that I, as myself, can know absolutely nothing. From this nothingness one may come to realise the blessed eternity in this moment of *now*.

Here lies the courtship in the court of the timeless. But, before you can see it, before you can know it as man or woman, you must first acknowledge the ridiculous nature of the transient self.

The realisation occurs in the depths of the fire. Let fear not be a barrier to this greatest experience of all. Your acquired nature has kidnapped your innocence. It has stolen you from your first love, your first kiss by the waters of life. But you are enriched by the wondrous passion that burns through the solar plexus. You can forever *be* this state, *be* this enrichment. Your acquired nature is here to be burned. All you need do is face up to this fact.

Go on, ask the devil to dance!

CHAPTER 4

Reincarnation? What Is There To Reincarnate?

There is a new religious concept flourishing in the West that is fast becoming a fervent belief. It seems to be spreading like wildfire. Mostly everyone on a spiritual path are fully aware of it. It is the myth of reincarnation and I am going to explode this myth for the ones who have the courage to listen. The devout Christian might initially be pleased, for the myth of reincarnation creates a disturbance to the coveted belief in a Christian heaven as the place for a life hereafter. But I hereby declare that such a notion is equally untrue. Both these beliefs are part and parcel of one's acquired nature. All of it is nothing more than mind-weed being cosseted by those who live in the fear of facing their own unreality.

What is reincarnation? The mind understands the concept and many believe it as such but let us not indulge ourselves in concepts. Conceptualization serves only one's acquired nature and through this one can never reach a clear understanding, for one is still obliging oneself to hide behind one's fears. Then how can one know? How can one transcend the restriction of the mental realm?

Many may say, why bother. That is okay. For every seed that germinates there are countless others that rot on the ground. It is all in the perennial flow of life. But for the one who is earnestly interested, for the one who is really ready to awaken, who is ready to move out of the circling ignorance of self, then such a one is obliged to enquire.

While ignorance prevails as the mass-hypnosis of the common mind, this being the tinsel, communal security, the discerning few see through its shallow imprint. These are the courageous ones who are ready to challenge the norm. You, who are reading these words, are one of the discerning few. Whether you agree or disagree with what is being said, this does not count, for all that really matters is the fact that you are engaged in enquiry.

An enquiring mind is not the common mind. How is this so? Well, first we need to look at ourselves, not analytically but impartially. This is difficult for we are all conditioned in some manner or other and through our conditioning there will arise our value judgements. Nonetheless, we can still look, being consciously impartial while seeing these value judgements arising from within the bounds of their own limitations but not engaging in them.

Western humanity is in a spiritual dilemma. I can speak of this for I am western man. Here in the West we have scientifically evolved by applying our reason to matter while leaving the understanding of our spiritual nature in a relatively infantile state.

But one may argue to the contrary. The West is predominantly Christian, is it not? This may be so but I propose that the religious manner of Christianity as practiced by the West seems to elude a spiritual essence. This is aptly demonstrated in my native country of Ireland and I use it as the microcosm for the purpose of illustrating the western situation.

We are all natives of somewhere or other in this relative world and should one truly wish to understand society then one must first understand one's own. However, before one can truly understand anything about any society one must first understand one-self. This is putting first things first. It is only when one truly understands oneself that one can clearly see the societal expression for what it really supports. Then one can see beyond the relative impositions induced through the collective ignorance of one's immediate surrounds.

Ireland is predominantly Christian and, like mostly everywhere, it has its own peculiarities. We hardly need to be reminded of the Irish situation of conflicting Christian expressions where one brand of Christians, proclaiming to be godly, are blasting the brains of the other. But this is the nature of Christianity, promoting and encouraging division. History is an abounding illustration of this. It cannot be argued, it cannot be denied, the nature of Christianity is conflict and everything expresses itself by its nature.

The Irish are still suffering the effects of a divided opinion that is centuries old. They have made themselves the victims of cause and effect, like the circular ripples expanding outwards on the still waters as the effectual disturbance after a pebble being carelessly thrown. But it is more like a boulder that enters the waters of Christianity. As a relative calm eventually returns to the centre yet the rippling effect going out to the periphery takes much longer to recede.

It can be observed that the violence emanating from the central point of conflict between the church bodies may seem to have evolved to a smoother level thus giving the impression that tolerance now abides between the factions of Christianity. Nonetheless, the root of violence remains. It is only more finely disguised as the nature of the conflict becomes more subtle and the clergy distance themselves from the atrocities being caused by Catholics and Protestants killing each other. The church leaders eagerly denounce violence but yet they fail to face their own dishonesty by disallowing the light of truth to penetrate their own denials. They condemn the effect while remaining themselves within the same bounds of cause and effect. Anyone holding the office of pope is obliged to serve the dishonesty. It must be infallibly so when the institution that is its body can only survive through upholding division. "We are all children of God", words spoken by most of the leaders, but only children of God as according to one's particular opinions. The religiosity of the western world is an indulgence of factions greedy for power. This is the sad reality.

The Irish dilemma is the ripples of time, past ignorance regurgitating the present. Then a relative peace is sought through some form of compromise. The hatchet is buried for now while the real issue of the conflicting, acquired nature remains unaddressed. It is seldom one wishes to look at one's ignorance. It is easier to look and appropriate the blame on the other, then to seek out some relative compromise through some partial retraction while failing to address the underlying issue. One needs to be astutely attentive to hear what is being said for we are now addressing the turgidity of human consciousness being expressed through the conflicting veins of Christianity.

Christianity? Let us look at it more closely. In my experience as a child I could not help but rebel. Although I innocently believed in a god, yet I could not believe in the ways of the church, nor in my immediate teacher at school who could only communicate her religious convictions through the excessive use of violence. This was her mental anguish and the only outlet she had for relieving her pain arising from the violence against woman that she was obliged to endure under the psychological yoke of religiosity. It was the only way open to her through which she could react and her pain was inflicted on the innocent children.

The analytical mind might immediately jump on the notion that I may be carrying a chip on my shoulders resulting from this, for such is the nature of the analytical mind, but let us put that notion to rest. I went on to be an altar-boy and was devoutly Christian even to the point of seriously considering the priesthood. But when I reached seventeen and the time was upon me to go into a religious college I began to seriously look at the church in an effort to harmonise my understanding of God with that being institutionally expressed. One very honest priest advised me not to be too concerned if my spiritual aspirations were not being fulfilled but, "In practical terms", as he put it, "Look on the priesthood as a good career where one has a free house, usually the best in the parish, one has a good car, a commanding position and money as well, all guaranteed for life".

It was a good proposition, indeed, I had not approached it that way before, but it failed to induce the final decision. Instead, it caused me to question the authenticity of the clergy, particularly the ones commanding the higher positions. These questions only began to arise after I partially overcame my inner guilt arising from my zealous attraction to the opposite gender as not being the only cause of my unwillingness to face into a celibate life. The double standards between the religiosity of the clergy and their personal attitudes in their day to day living were causing considerable conflict within me when I first entered Galway University to study commerce instead of theology.

In university I naively expected to receive some clearer understanding but there was no enlightenment to greet me there, only professors who were unbelievably insular in themselves and commanding a pomposity in the local society like the lords of the past. They had nothing of wisdom to teach. Indeed, I learned more

about life in one of these professor's four-poster beds while courting his beautiful housemaid than I learned in all of my time on the
university campus. That lovely colleen from the Arran Islands
knew more about the natural rhythm of life than all the mouldy
professors could possibly know even if all their intellectuality was
lumped together.

The cold harshness of further religious entrenchment dominat-
ed the scene at that time under the authoritarian influence of a
puritan, Catholic bishop who had a terrible hang-up about sex.
Some of the local gardai who were policing the streets under this
man's instructions spent their nights harassing courting couples
parked by the seaside enjoying the natural delights. It seemed this
bishop was trying to extend his dogmatic tyranny against the natural order of the creation in his efforts to make it criminal as well.
Such was the cold, outer expression of a religiosity feasting off
guilt.

But that was the ignorance of those times and what has ignorance to do with the topic of reincarnation one might ask? Well,
one first needs to understand oneself if one is to understand who
or what reincarnates. One must look at one's conditioning in
whatever form it takes or in whatever expression it makes. One
needs to understand the insular nature of mass conditioning, even
in an open, secular society as some may seem to be now enjoying.
On the surface much may seem to have changed but little has really changed when the skin of it all is peeled back. The only real
difference is in the degree of insularity. As it was in the past so it
is in the present. Anyone thinking otherwise is still living in darkness and this is the nature of the common mind.

I speak of this ignorance as part of the past for the mind can
accept it as past. In this manner one can approach one's mind
without meeting resistance and when one goes deep enough into

the nature of one's conditioning then it is possible for the mind to see the ignorance as present. This is the intention to lure the mind into trapping itself. I am making no bones about this for we are travelling light, carrying no baggage and taking no prisoners. We are not entertaining opinions when we are dealing with facts so we know where we are before we continue.

In the Irish expression of spirituality something seems to be seriously amiss. While the message coming from the scriptures seems to be promoting love, yet the message coming from the Catholic church has promoted hate and division. Fear was the tool being used with a revengeful god, as the clergy's beacon, stoking the fires of hell. Every Sunday the multitudes piled into churches all over the land to receive their weekly dose at the altar. All other religious expressions other than Catholicism were viewed with deep suspicion. Indeed, all Protestants were perceived as dissenters by the body of the Catholic church. Catholics, were barred from entering the Protestant chapels, or from partaking in any of their religious services. This barring was not imposed by the Protestants, but by the Catholic bishops themselves, who had made the dogmatic declaration that those partaking even in a part of Protestant services were committing a grievous sin. This sin was deemed as being so serious that the ordinary priest did not have the power to grant absolution. The offenders were obliged to go to the bishop to be absolved, otherwise they could not escape from the bishop's revengeful god and the eternal flames of hell. People believed it, for they had no other choice when they were unable to see for themselves.

This was the mental subjugation being used as the power of a clergy seemingly oblivious to the fact that they were allowing themselves to be the instrumental anti-Christ masquerading as God's representatives on Earth. This is not to place blame on the

clergy for they were but part of humanity's expression of the ignorance of that particular time. Ignorance is the anti-Christ and
ignorance is one's acquired nature. The clergy had allowed themselves to become the seed scatterers of the revengeful hate which
ferments through ignorance. This hate became deeply embedded
in the human psyche and was later to be openly expressed in the
violent eruptions on the streets of Belfast and throughout the
province of Northern Ireland. This was not intentional, of course.
Few had the time or inclination to examine it deeply and many
genuinely felt that they were serving the good.

Behind the scenes it was a struggle for power and an institutionalised church does most of its thinking in centuries. The fall-
out from such thinking must inevitably spill into the centuries
ahead.

It became clear to me through my own experience that love
was not being expressed through the body of the Catholic church.
Nonetheless, love was the only message that I could interpret as
being the message of God. The fear-filling, revengeful god of the
priests was nothing more than a brainwashing sham. I began to
wonder why these church authorities were so willing to discard
love in their power struggle against one another and how people
could be so foolish by allowing the clergy such psychological control over their minds.

This is how it was in this insular society of Christian Ireland
with a religiosity unique to itself. The people were trapped
through their fears as many still are today.

It seemed obvious to me as a questioning teenager that we were
all fooling ourselves and in the course of such foolishness there
were the misguided nationalists creating further havoc. While the
few remaining Protestants in the Irish Republic kept a low profile
and got on with their business, the Protestants in Northern Ireland,

through their fears of being outnumbered by the growing Catholic population coupled with their inherent bigotry, continued in their scheming to subjugate the Northern Catholics.

These Protestants were deeply entrenched in their own form of ignorance that was being expressed through their self-justifications for the terrible wrongs they were doing and the lengths they were prepared to go to hide from their ignorance rather than facing the truth. They saw what was happening to the people of the South, how these people were being driven by a sectarian Church, how they were being controlled through their minds and this the Protestants were prepared to challenge while failing to challenge the defilement in themselves. Northern Catholics were shunned and excluded from every avenue of social advancement as a result of the reactionary mentality of the hard-line Protestants. Indeed, both Christian divides were chronically diseased psychologically, as the one's holding on to their sectarian beliefs still are to this day.

The Protestant clergy in the North had plenty of ammunition for their heated sermons, that some of them articulated in passionate fervour. But they refused to look at their own acquired nature and they failed to see their bull-nosed ignorance as being the root cause of the explosive situation on their own doorsteps. Fear and suspicion were the order of the time and this is the spirituality being expressed by both divides that feeding the doctrines of hate and mistrust cloaked in holy disguise.

It took the emotive wave of Civil Rights sweeping in from the West to break open the deadlock. This was followed by thirty odd years of atrocity inflicted on the innocence by the collective hand of cowards, the bomb being used as their convenient weapon. There is no integrity in the warfare being waged for there is no integrity in the imprint of the type of Christianity that has rooted itself in the psyche of the western world. Ireland, like most of the West, is spiritually impoverished. This is the unacceptable reality beneath the oppressive cloaks of piety.

There were plenty of religious dogmas to support the ecclesiastical supremacy over the masses, be they Catholic or Protestant, but there was little or no true spirituality. It was a loveless situation. The seeds of division were deeply planted to serve the poisoned fruit to future generations.

The people may consider that they have fully awakened to their misfortunate plight. People have, indeed, become more worldly wise and the Churches may seem to have temporarily lost their hold, but the psychic imprint in the mentality of the masses cannot be easily erased. It continues to simmer in the darker regions of the mind. Even though one may seem to have transcended this ignorance, yet the headless demon keeps turning the wheel of the misguided masses thus perpetuating the mental dis-ease. Whenever one of its outlets is blocked it concentrates on some other.

Christianity, as such, is the unspoken part of our acquired nature. Western humanity has made it the religion of crucifixion but not of love, for humanity's acquired nature can never be love. Times may seem to have changed but this is our past that is still our past in the present. Compromise is all that is sought as the solution for some relative peace, for compromise is the limitation of the conditioned mind. But there can be no real love, no real understanding, while we continue compromising to our own denials. This is the spiritual poverty of the western world that is so richly expressed in the Irish situation.

When one earnestly seeks to understand the meaning of life, of love, of truth, of death, of God, then one is obliged to look elsewhere. One is obliged to look beyond this ignorance being expressed through western religions.

In Hinduism this ignorance is categorized as *maya*. This Sanskrit word denotes the play of events that creates, preserves and dissolves the universe.

One particular night as I travelled by train I happened to be seated with a fellow traveller who was an assiduous student on such matters. Feeling the peace emanating from his presence and the serenity surrounding his face I could, indeed, vouch that he was a living example of the natural peace he had come to realise in himself. It was an easy conversation. We discussed our own interpretations of our personal discoveries with the intention of discovering our personal limitations rather than proving any particular point. Such is the course of the enquiring mind.

Eastern philosophies tell us through questionable translation that there is a lower and higher self. I use the word 'questionable' because one tends to translate through the mental build-up of one's own conditioning. The problem arising is that we usually translate into that which we set out to find. There is a subtle presupposition where we set out to prove what we already believe rather than unconditionally listening to whatever is present in the immediate unknown. So we close the door before we even begin and this is our problem.

Our ignorance is our ignoring. While we are bound by a notional duality then *maya* may be interpreted as the play of *Prakrti*, the lower self, while the higher is seen as *Purusa*, the *Absolute* within. *Purusa* is the realisation of the self being as one with God, or the realisation of the oneness of all. This is all very well. Nonetheless, these are the teachings from another culture relating to one's true nature that one may foolishly claim to understand while failing to first understand from one's own.

This begs to be challenged. We in the West have no direct

experience of such teachings and we can hardly expect to fully understand when even so few in the East have a clear understanding of this.

Other than the theoretical mind, western humanity has no experience of *Prakrti* or *Purusa* and one can hardly discover the truth of oneself through theories. But one does have experience of one's acquired nature. Born in the West as one with the West this is what one has become. This, one must first realise. The collective, acquired nature is what one is groomed by the West to serve, regardless of one's religious denomination where the occasional eruptions of conflicting opinion are but the occasional gasses belching to the surface of a putrid swamp, such as Christianity at variance in Ireland and, indeed, many other places as well.

Our minds are that of duality, good versus evil, right versus wrong. This is the ground of conflict where all others are perceived as other than oneself. There can be no escape for western humanity where one is conditioned to view oneself as other from everyone else, even as other from God. This is one's birth. It is one's living experience and this I can speak, for the language I use is that of the acquired nature of western man spinning to the tune of the western dance. The cunning, western mind may seem to fool the eastern masters but the 'I' within you cannot be fooled, even when seated on this shanty throne of the West.

The rational, western mind correlates through its acquired nature as it mentally seeks to understand the new. Objectively, it sees itself as apart from thought and it sets out to theoretically dominate through its business-like intellectuality. This strengthens the acquired nature through correlating further experience within its confines, so there can be no real escape from ignorance, there can be no fundamental change.

The creative comes only when the thinker is the thought, when there is no gap in between. Any articulation of the theoretical mind, any contrivance, any form of mental activity only gives strength to the egotistical, personal self, the little 'me' that dominates western thought. It is this ignorance speaking through the western mind as the self that now claims to be the higher self through its own philosophical interpretation. I propose that all of it is utter mind-weed for there is only self in the experience of the western mind and all self is ignorance.

Such notional concepts of the philosophers and the theosophists relating to a lower and higher self can only lead one into further confusion. Eastern masters speak of the same inner truth but such cross-correlation can hardly be understood by the acquired nature of the western mind that utterly fails to understand itself. This inner truth cannot be understood by the West, nor by anyone for that matter, for surely it can only be known through *being* it. At best the eastern philosophies can only remind the West, but one can only fully understand through the realisation of one's own true nature.

People live in an evanescent world and they refuse to fully acknowledge its transient character. The religious structures of convenience are failing to give one solace as a new and deeper reality dawns through the scientific revelations of the West. It is becoming more and more difficult for one to ignore the truth of one's situation. The West is in a spiritual plight as it searches for alternative means to justify its plundering world. This makes the people easy prey for alternative philosophies. One only needs to look at the number of worldly gurus frequently rising like lingering fireballs from the ashes of the smouldering past, while the substance of what is received from any of them is rarely more that past recurrence.

This is our spiritual dilemma. In the act of being shaken out of our beliefs of convenience we, in the West, are finding it more and more difficult to fool ourselves. Our external world is gathering incredible speed, more so than the train shooting along its track through the darkness of night. We are beginning to realise there is more to life than is mentally and religiously endorsed and we are being obliged to face up to our spiritual poverty. Our religious predicament increases as we are coming to see our plight more clearly for the pawns that we are, caught up in the web of ourselves. Apart from our religious institutions harassing to hold onto their power we are being further absorbed by the blight of consumer wantonness.

Although one might zealously serve one's wants through one's personified self-consideration, still a deep discomfort remains within. This discomfort is becoming more acute through scientific revelations as one begins to realise that one's basket of assumptions are not all what they seem.

Wants fulfilled is the breeding ground for further wants arising. The more one consumes the more one needs to consume. Still, no matter how much one consumes one remains empty inside. This raw emptiness remains and it grows more astute as the body gets older. The body is limited and one's conditioned mind is even more limited. The realisation of this becomes one's most immediate disturbance when one begins to awaken from one's immediate conditioning.

We, in the West, are conditioned towards eternal living and that is greatly different to eternal life. Eternal living is the self-perpetuating anguish of never being able to find a complete satisfaction not alone in physical comforts but even in spiritual needs. One is driven to seek through alternative religions and one may become emotionally involved in Buddhism, Hinduism or some other, but involvement as such usually only lasts as long as the emotion.

This is like the seeds of the corn taking root in shallow, or rocky ground. The depth is not there and soon the new growth withers and dies. Or one may become intellectually involved and such involvement has more longevity but the mind-weed grows around it and chokes it again as happens to the seeds that fall among thorns.

In the western world we have become saturated with creature comforts, with computers to do our thinking and automobiles to 'talk' us to our destinations. Even the poor beggar-man who could hardly find a blanket to keep himself warm is now likely to find two or more as he sifts through our accumulating waste. It is all so explosively sudden in chronological time with each of us feasting according to our personal cravings as the illusive dream is being served. We bind ourselves with our desires and finding new ways of satisfying these has been the ongoing obsession driving through our incessant thinking.

But the modern, technological world is outpacing our external, physical needs. There is more than enough. Sooner or later the outer poverty is going to disappear when scientific discovery causes humankind to transcend the current concepts relating to wealth.

This is part of the enormous shift in consciousness that is edging upon us. We are being obliged to pause, but when we pause we cannot avoid looking at ourselves. It is then we truly discover that behind our material wealth we are spiritually starved.

One is starved for love and this is the greater poverty that cannot be relieved through scientific discovery. Nor can it be relieved through the type of love one seeks from another for this also is an external need. It can only be relieved from within when one comes to the end of the line, when all else has been tried, when one is eventually obliged to give up chasing the illusion. It is only then that one can truly realise that the heart is love, as it was in the beginning, is now and ever shall be. This is the inner journey, the inner search for one's true nature that is about to explode in the West when the cup of sensuality has been surpassed.

But this only occurs when one is ready, for nothing happens before its time. Western humanity has obliged itself to travel to the end of its own materialism, this being its acquired nature. Its destination is the end of the line and so it must be, for it has abdicated to its desires. Eastern philosophies can help the weaker desires to be dissolved through introspection but the deep-rooted ones can only be up-rooted by recognising them for what they are through experience. The burning of self must not be denied. It is only through the burning of self that one's true nature can truly be known. This is the unfolding in the western journey. The burning makes way for the fertile ground.

Self-imposed, moral denial of deep-rooted desires has shown to be nothing more than postponement. Examining it closely, this seems to be the situation. One only needs to look at Christian morality in society, how it covers the ugliness with the skin of self-righteousness while the innocent are silently abused. Suppressing desires is ignoring the reality. When humankind finally discovers the emptiness after excessively tasting the sweet, or bitter fruits of the deep-rooted desires that possess it then surely it must break free from their seductive grip. What is there left to experience when the bubble has burst? What is there to taste when the taste-buds run dry? Still the multitudes continue serving the madness. The mass hypnosis remains.

Buddha sat under a tree refusing to move until enlightenment would dawn. That is his way as he sits in the heart to be found, while the western excursion seems to be the way of existentialist man and woman. It is the spiritual journey where the inner eye opens through one's experience. Western humanity obliges itself to serve the mirage to the end of the rainbow before the object of seeking finally turns inwards for the lonely journey back home.

It is noticeable how it is usually not until one has experienced the bitter-sweet fruits of living before one really starts looking introspectively. Whatever one knows at this stage one knows through one's own direct understanding. At least this is primary knowledge, but, like the fate of the seeds among thorns, many cast it aside. When death becomes imminent they seem to religiously fall back into some institutionalised groove that has no real spiritual significance beyond the appeasement of one's own acquired nature. The churches have nothing to offer apart from their shallow rhetoric. Thus one obliges oneself to finish out one's living as one dies back into ignorance.

It seems like an unrelenting circle of events as the time of living the illusion continues. One may have come to understand how the pursuit and seizure of sensory pleasures quickly dissolves as the receptive body gets bored and hankers for change, nonetheless, experience can follow experience without awakening the experiencer. The western expression struggles through psychological time accumulating wealth to satisfy the sensory wants of the ageing body running out of tempo. Such is one's dilemma when one fails to grasp that the eventuality of freedom can only occur in the desireless state.

When one is in want then one is bound to that want and one cannot know freedom. It is so how one keeps oneself locked outside of one's own true nature. But one cannot know this until such time as one comes to the end of chasing one's illusive rainbows and then earnestly seeks out the source.

Then it is time when one has drunk one's fill from the chalice of sensuality, when that moment inevitably arrives when one's senses can hardly distinguish the subtle varieties of taste. It is indeed noticeable how one's worldly vigour fades when there is nothing external left to please one's flooding drunkenness of mind.

From the sharp malt liqueurs of the North, like the coarseness of the rough sandpaper being used on the raw wood for refining, to the smooth and fruity wines of the South slipping over the raising taste-buds of eager desire, so one's succulent meeting of moments continue. The sensual magnet must be served as one is conditioned by one's world to do. It is the captivity one obliges oneself to follow before one can come back in through one's senses to eventually seek a relative freedom as the first step back home to one's true essence. The false must first be realised.

This is the situation in the western world with endless wants cascading over this fountain of life savagely swallowing the vision of one's true nature. All one's notions of what happiness should be are forever rising over the next horizon just out of one's reach. This is the imaginary juice, the elasticity of one's external thrust and the utter confusion of the multitudes spinning in circles. It is the bitter, cold reflection of the insatiable hunger that seems to be permanently locked in one's world-weary eyes. One needs to pause and observe.

This is the world of western humanity spinning into boundless space where one's energy is endlessly spilling towards the gratification of one's sensory wants. Here one is lost in one's trying to find solace through tasting with tongue something to equal the divine taste of love momentarily discarded while chasing the illusive juice of its shadow. One can know this through one's own experience of being a Westerner swallowed in the solemn belief that one's world of scientific invention will give one the ultimate joy.

You hasten to fill your house of desire with all that you can acquire. The energy of your body and mind feeds into the reckless chase and continuous find from your daily dose in the material markets of plenty. This becomes your obsession in life.

As a humanoid vacuum you are being programmed to suck up the objects of continuously changing matter from these emporiums of technological wonder that are incessantly flooding from the outer side of yourself. Each week, each day, indeed each moment of your life is constantly spilling away on this trip from nowhere to nowhere. The speed raises a storm of dust and you become blinded by this dust of your personal self.

Where must this journey lead you, pray tell? For this is a journey away from the truth of your being, is it not? You wade through your endless desires. You reach to a world outside for a perpetual happiness that seems more elusive to the restless mind than a crocodile sprouting wings. You seek and seek, yet failing to find, like lovers confused and tripping over themselves. It is an endless creation of dilemmas while failing to see that the answer to your dilemma is always within yourself.

The West is being awakened by the conquests of science in the exploration of matter. However, the train is of matter and thus the speed of the train is limited. Indeed, the speed of all perceivable matter in linear movement is not even likely to reach the lazy velocity of visible light. In this outward search you are legions away from the actual realisation of your own immeasurable speed of consciousness. When you bind yourself to the turgidity of matter you can never hope to see that pure consciousness is instant where the journey's end is already consumed before its beginning actually occurs, even as a flickering thought.

But this may be all too much for human intelligence still wallowing in the consumer corridors of chronological time. The western mind seems stuck in the belief that the body in which it positions itself as landlord and tenant is the one and only reality. It measures everything from within these confines in this realm of existence. Religions of convenience have evolved to sustain the illusion. Many naively believe that the body members of flesh, bones, sinews, blood and guts for processing excrement will magically re-member on a notional, last day to take up position again! This may or may not be so, as according to one's own creative desires, but who, pray tell, will look after the sewers? One needs to look more closely at what one is being conditioned to accept. Let us challenge it further.

Where is life, actual life, that one knows in one's own experience? Where is timeless life in the *being* of life? Surely it is in the body one takes to be oneself that finds its place in existence somewhere between the food that it eats and the excrement it passes each day. But one becomes attached to this bodily instrument manifesting between the food and the excrement and one takes it to be one's true reality. One measures and assimilates accordingly. Then one pulls down the sensory blinds and rigidly holds onto one's own emotional position. Just a movement either way and one is likely to find oneself either in the soup or the shit! How vain one becomes with one's facial make-up and more foolish still when one buries one's heads in the sand by accepting the rhetoric of the masses.

The train speeds along on its track. There is no other way it can go. It is caught in the motional grip between linear and circular steel scarcely outpacing the speed of the rust coming up on its tail. This is the West being awakened through the agent of western mind. But awakened to what, one may ask?

When this mind is challenged through reason as agent of intellect by philosophical light from some other dimension it still seems to deny the reality of its ephemeral domain. It astutely sets out to sustain its fearful continuance by converting to its own worldly wisdom the enlightenment it perceives through the cloud of its own misconceptions. As such it equates through the measure of its correlative memory, that is its accumulative past, and so the ignorance continues.

It is so that the past keeps re-birthing itself through the pawns that we are in our service to it. This is how the unenlightened mind blocks the perennial flow of light from entering one's opening awareness.

Western humanity considers itself to have attained scientific magnificence in the fields of energy and matter. The scientific mind has partially unlocked the secrets of the atom in its journey of research back in through this smallest particle in a perceivable element that can take part in a chemical reaction. The world of the mind is this reactionary world. The nucleus of the atom and its one or more orbiting electrons has long been discovered. In haste to split it in two humankind has come to realise its creative potentiality in the field of energy and its enormous destructiveness in the field of matter.

But here the journey of discovery abruptly stops for the scientist has not yet discovered himself or herself. Darkness abounds. The western realm of existence is still its accumulative past. Human intelligence is still being measured on past recurrence. These are the iron wheels of our intellectual carriage rolling along the man-made track. They call it *karma* in eastern philosophies, as I am reminded by the man on the train.

When the superficial, western mind is challenged with a deeper wisdom, it tends to rationalise the deeper reality it perceives through its own surface understanding. This is rational logic as the only functional logic understood by the West. To rationalise is to think in fixed proportions. This is the acquired nature of the western mind. Instead of acknowledging its limitations, the western mind continues to rationalise the truth in appeasement to its own limited world that is still turgidly evolving through the exploitation of resources and human endeavour.

This is the contemporary expression of the West seeking a commonality of religious acceptance to augment the central power structures that is the accumulative of democratic selves where the only acknowledged measure of quality is the measure of material comfort. The reaction to this is the escalating discontentment expressed through violence of one form or other where inner resentment seeks alternative outlets through drugs, or whatever means becoming available. Although more subtle than the raw, religious expression of the dark ages, nonetheless, the exploitation of energy continues being justified by the religiosity of the acquired nature pertaining to the western idiom.

However, it is now the subtle exploitation of ideas which is more destructive. The peculiar, western ethic endorsed through religious formulas is the deification of the self-dependence and individual autonomy of the western self. It is so how the repetitive image living from each individual energy-sweep gets its ongoing support. We serve a congenital society in static mass as we collectively become absorbed in static beliefs that sustain the continuity of material accumulation and economic despotism. This is the cold, outer face of the western world. When we observe it in a purer awareness, unaffected by denials, desires or fears, then surely this can be seen as an actual fact.

Western humanity's unprecedented, spiritual dilemma is now in the field of ideation. The importance of humankind has become secondary to the re-appraisal of legal structures justifying the intricate systems of exploitation in a world that is becoming more and more transparent in the light of its own discoveries. This is endorsed by the flimsy values we now place upon human life.

Warfare in service to greed is the unspoken societal norm as seen from the daily dosage of newsreels circumventing the globe. It is the collective expression of our personal activities. Western authorities play little more than verbal rhetoric to the utter, un-natural state of our collective, acquired nature as they, like the personal, serve their own vested interests. It is a melting pot of mutual appeasement.

Having lost contact with our true nature, we have become centre-less. We have no foundation to re-structure our faltering position. Our social evaluations are being focused upon the personal collective. This is like shadows trying to maintain their existence from shadows. Resulting from this peculiarity we are now witnessing that the justifications of our activities are becoming more and more difficult to uphold in the mounting complexities of warring ideas. These ideological challenges being faced by the western world are the basis of its spiritual crisis as the system endeavours to morally sustain its continuity through the changing, outer face of the western mask.

Western humanity is losing the search for consistency and continuity in its narrow, material world. In truth, the only consistency in the entire creation is continuous change. But our rational behaviour driven by the aspirations of our acquired nature is contrary to this. Each of us endlessly seek the perfect lover, the perfect job, the perfect house, the perfect religion, the perfect something or other as though to last for ever and ever. This is our outward thrust through our sensate values in search of some sort of permanent satisfaction.

The personal self desperately needs to be part of the collective of similar persons in order to sustain the illusion. Should the perfect situation arrive it is gone again in a flash of time, a day, a week, a month, a score of years. But this is ignored by the fearful mind. This is our systematic prison. It continues as such as long as I, the personal self, fail to face the truth of the situation.

Finding new definitions will not necessarily assist in seeing ourselves more clearly. Indeed, it is amazing how the illusion of the world we perceive continuously fools us. There seems to be always something or other one must desire. We create a morality of right and wrong to define the acceptable rules of the game as the forceful thrust of society tries to give every desire a moral code. In practice we notice that our desires are morally right or morally wrong only according to the prevailing circumstances. It all depends on how society perceives them. Thus, we have irregular consensus in our modes of legislation. The loudest voice rising from conflicting persons seems to give validity to moral distinction. This is the way we have become in our self-made world of 'becoming'.

Western humanity is the accumulative world of persons jostling for personal desires to be each fulfilled, thus creating a basis for conflict between the personal self and the rest of the world. This is the contradictory mendacity of western society sapping away at our energies. We are forever at war with each other. The only peace we can hope to secure is in our mutual acceptance as to the level of warfare we seem to engage.

Our relationships are built upon this anomaly and most sadly of all, the relationship between man and woman. There can be no real love in this when the hidden objective is for personal satisfaction. This self-consideration is evident between us where each one is out for his own or her own personal agenda. We personally suffer from these constraints inflicted by the personal hand of the collective self. This is our heedless torment and we need to seriously examine our tenacious condition.

Should one honestly look at one's individual situation one can see that one's energy reservoirs to fulfil one's personal desires are limited. One seems to be endlessly struggling against this limitation when one sets out to seek gratification for one's personal, sensual hunger. But in this self-seeking quest one inevitably clashes with other persons pushing and pulling for similar, personal fulfilment. It is a world based on conflict where most of our religious adaptations are based on the mutual, moral code defining the perimeters of action.

This seems to have evolved as the religious expression of our western world that lives on personified matter. This is our western Christianity, the spawn from the priest-ridden past. It is what we, as the personal collective, have become as we load our aspirations in our service to the 'money-god'. There can be nothing spiritual in this for it is in itself an utter denial to love, to life, to truth, to death, to all that is naturally Godly.

When we look at it honestly we can see how western religion has matured in line with economic growth as the convenient, moral justification for this heedless side of our acquired nature. We have even given ourselves conceptual souls and deny ourselves the message of Christ by appointing him as our convenient saviour for a swift passage through our inevitable doom to eventually arrive at some conceptual, heavenly abode. We conveniently ignore inevitable death. We can only accept this death as happening in some distant tomorrow as we cower in our fears from the unacceptable thought. Where can there be truth in this? Surely, this is the mass exodus of the ignorant foolishly accepting the false security of numbers.

We are personally bound in our personalities. There is no escape for the one who perceives from within these confines. My energy as a person is limited, as is my intellectual perception when I am driven by my personal desires. But should my desire be that of all humanity, or even all life, then the energy to fulfil such desire must surely be boundless. This cannot be fully understood while one is still bound up in one's own personal predicament as one of the many in mutual appeasement.

One needs to see through convenient, belief structures embedded in the psyche. One needs to examine the acquired nature of the collective, western self that spawns the societal limitations on personal man and woman. This needs to be clearly understood in order to come to the realisation as to the hopelessness of the western condition as long as western humanity fails to understand itself.

Through my own experience as western man I have come to acknowledge this fact. There can be no salvation for one's acquired nature, not even through adopting the eastern, philosophical concept of attaining to self-realisation as being the realisation of one's higher self. There can be no higher self in the acquired nature of western humanity. There can only be higher ignorance. This higher ignorance is what I am as theosophical or philosophical, western man. This is the fact of the matter. Equating to a higher self is the crystallisation of this ignorance for the western mind and not the dissolution of it.

What is understood as self-realisation in eastern philosophy becomes lost through the subtle interpretation misappropriated by the acquired nature of the West. Western man and woman are bound by the mind through the mind. The personal self, no matter how much it tries, can never transcend its personal predicament. It can only be dissolved by allowing itself to dissolve. Then what remains is the transcendence. This is the boundless state and the doorway to freedom. But it takes a courage that is even beyond the imagination of the western mind to allow the personal self to be burned out to this.

The illusion of the West is sustained by the personal self trying to assimilate and ratify each new idea in accordance with its acquired nature. It thus perceives an evolving consciousness through the limitations of what it already knows. Cognition is the act of knowing and the difference between one life form and another is the degree of cognition.

Western humanity is enslaved through the wants of the emotional, mindful self, be one a business-person, a queen or a bishop, the degree of cognition is buried in sluggishness in accordance to one's personification. Thus one clouds one's awareness enshrouding it in ignorance as one ratifies each new tenet of knowledge by conforming it to one's own unperceived limitations.

This is the self-perpetuating past, the shadowy vapour that one perceives as reality. It is the emotive world that is presently bursting at the seams with useless information, like the current web of information technology circumventing the globe as illusion mirroring illusion down a narrow corridor of infinite mirrors. It is how one continues to bamboozle oneself when making spiritual assertions from within the confines of one's own self-imposed configurations.

The known is the limitation that man and woman place on themselves. This is the discursive mind bound-up in its past assumptions stuffing itself silly with mountains of useless information as cushioning for its assumed reality. This, surely, must be the subtle expression of ignorance where one's cup is overflowing with useless data. What can one hope to receive when one's cup is already full? Surely one needs to empty this cup, to break free from the known, before one can meet with the new.

But one cannot break free when all one's energies are absorbed on the surface play of matter as one dances on the outer periphery. Wasted as such, one's spirituality is still in an infantile state. Now the time is upon western man and woman where they can no longer sustain this outer shell of the self. Its own hard crust of convenient, static beliefs is no longer able to cloak the spiritual vacuum. Strange as it appears, this crust is now splitting at the seams under the glare of the mind-exploding, western scientific. The West seems to be approaching a new realisation through this existential side of itself. The more one discovers the more one realises how little one really knows relative to what is unknown. This is the new frontier of western humanity, the current buzz, the current consuming excitement.

However, it is also the current neurosis for the western mind. Its pillars of past are collapsing at a phenomenal pace. The mind is always in fear of the new. It is comfortable with the old for it knows its ground, with the old it builds its security, but with the new it is always impotent. Life is always new while the mind is always old, always expressing through its knowledge of past, so the mind is always in conflict with the new. When one fully understands this, not just intellectually, but actually, then one can understand that life and the mind can never meet. This, one needs to acknowledge instead of allowing the conditional mind to continue finding ways of avoiding this fact.

Reason can bring one this far, it can bring one to the realisation that there is something more than mind, that there is something much deeper to one's being than what is mentally endorsed. This something must be explored if one is to move out of the sensual darkness created by human consciousness spinning through matter. One needs to impartially look, impartial meaning being free of all mental connotations, being totally empty, before one can possibly move even one step beyond one's own limitations.

One's awareness is the refinement. Consciousness is a subtle attribute of matter. It spontaneously appears in all organisms, subtle or dense, this being their energetic field. What commences as pure consciousness gradually congeals into grosser modes such as that being experienced through the senses of the human body. In human consciousness there is a character who is conscious, while awareness is undivided and characterless. One can be aware of being conscious but one cannot be conscious of being aware. Awareness is the changeless reality. The world appears and disappears through consciousness, while awareness remains unchanged.

When one dies one does not leave the world as the mind would surmise. It is the other way round where the world actually recedes from the one who is actually aware. The world gets smaller and smaller. Gradually friends and relations disappear, then one's nearest and dearest, until eventually nothing is left except the consciousness of oneself. This too recedes back in through the imprint of one's final all-consuming thought. Memory as the totality of the known disappears, as does everything pertaining to mind. Then nothing is present apart from pure awareness.

Consciousness arises in pure awareness where the world appears and disappears. In consciousness the person appears through the senses spontaneously perceiving the totality of the known according to its lights. Time and space is gradually perceived through the mind where a past and a future formulates. So it occurs that human consciousness creates a chronological order. The mindful person sets out to improve the organism of consciousness that it perceives as itself, but inevitably the organism of matter must wither and die. The awareness recedes through infinitely finer states of consciousness back in through the point of nothingness.

This point of nothingness in existence is *now* where every breath of life is also every breath of death in the timelessness of pure awareness. One needs to focus on the source of awareness. One needs to enquire as to who or what is being aware. This is going in behind the 'I' thought. One needs to connect with that, whatever it is or is not.

When one enters the stillness of no-mind there is no body of conscious matter, there is only awareness. Then it can be understood that matter and consciousness are merely aspects of awareness. But when perceived through the existentialist mind, that is the byproduct of space and time, then human consciousness becomes intensely dense. The personal self sees itself as being in the world and fails to realise that the world is in the self, the self that is referred to in eastern religions as the higher self. But the mind cannot know this for it can only be so in the placenessness of no-mind.

The transcendence from mind to no-mind is the slow procedure of the human mass gradually moving through the dimensions of consciousness. This is the western journey in the scientific exploration through matter. As each shift of consciousness occurs it causes major upheaval in the societal structures, for the mind builds its security on past and as consciousness shifts then major chunks of past are instantly dissolved. This can be clearly understood when one looks back upon the historic journey of human consciousness over mind-recorded time. It can be seen that its evolution is gaining incredible speed when compared to what is recorded through memory. This, of course is all existentialist perception but it helps the mind to understand what is currently facing the western world.

The next major shift in consciousness is already happening. This shift has been triggered by the speeding up of the western scientific. The momentum has gathered to such an extent that each new discovery is becoming obsolete virtually the moment it is being discovered. The belief structures serving the western, business ethic are unable to match such momentum. There now exists an erratic uncertainty in values. They are failing to sustain their relative credibility as they become openly threatened through this speed of scientific revelation.

This is resulting in the gradual collapse of societal structures. The flimsy, religious ethos having lost its supports is leaving the retarded, spiritual side of western humanity openly exposed to its own harsh reality. This is the spiritual dilemma arising. It is bringing western humanity to a psychological precipice where one is now coming face to face with the ugliness that one has become. One can go on denying it, but one cannot deny it forever. All rail journeys comes to an end and the West is rapidly approaching the end of this current epochal era through this major shift in human consciousness that is flooding the past to extinction.

We are a world of consumers living in a world created by the collective, acquired nature of the personal self. The urge for new discovery is driven by the mass energetic being geared to fulfil our endless desires. The dawning of a clearer awareness arising from these discoveries now seriously threatens to expose our acquired nature as we approach the point of de-railing ourselves.

But something else is happening. We are entering the breeding ground for new beliefs to replace the fading cloak of the old as the personal self becomes fearfully exposed to its own superficial reality.

The searching mind is driven to find temporary shelter for its hollowness and it sets about seeking this through alternative religions. This occurs because the religiosity of the collective of personal selves can no longer ease humankind's feelings of hopelessness within. The mental dis-ease is triggering the ingrained mechanisms of western humanity's acquired nature and the beacons are being sent out to pull in alternative clouds rather than facing the actual truth.

This is creating a shift in the fundamental religious formation as can be understood in terms of the familiar law of physics that states, 'to every action there is an equal and opposite reaction'. Thus, we can see the shift in consciousness that spurns us into a clearer understanding calling up a counter shift in our world of illusion that is called *maya* in eastern religions. The despondency of our acquired nature rises again about us, like the seed falling among thorns and the thorns growing with it and choking it. This is our ignorance driven by fear, the fear of facing the truth.

This fear inevitably causes a change to occur in the religious structures of the masses brought about by the rising clouds of anxiety. Again we miss our true reality. How is this so?

Logically we can understand that space is all pervasive and the clouds that occasionally appear do not cause a division in space. Even when clouds blot out the sky, the mountains, the seas, nonetheless, space remains ever itself. Akin to space, awareness is the ground of the manifested universe, that appears and disappears as the clouds in the turbulent skies. Still, the awareness of western man, as in man and woman, remains obscured by the clouds of the limited known in the field of self-enquiry. Fear of the unknown and the truth it may bring is one of the greater concerns. Through lack of right discernment the western self chooses to remain in these clouds.

When the spiritual poverty of western humanity is exposed through reason the exposure is usually met with a sharp reaction. The ineffectual beliefs are hurriedly replaced by other beliefs of convenience, such as *reincarnation*. The acquired nature of the self thus finds its own continuity by changing the outer face of its mask even to the extreme of assuming its own enlightenment. Again ignorance prevails. The cunning, western ego again sustains its outer shell. This self-enlightened, western self perceives its position as other again from the age of mistaken enlightenment passed through the minds of previous centuries, western man. This is self fooling self. Its position regained, it can continue with its wilful play through the emotional strings of the human psyche. The train is back on its rails.

Such is the ingenious, western ego of our acquired nature which is not an integrated part of the eastern experience. It would therefore be frivolous to expect that the western mind could be comprehensively challenged by eastern philosophies, seeing it is not an intrinsic part of eastern consciousness. The subtleties of its cunningness out-manoeuvres eastern understanding that is part of another world of evolving consciousness that we can only assume is closer to the heart of conscious man and woman, whereas, we in the West are totally outside of ourselves. We need to be aware of this lest the wisdom of the East when interpreted through the western mind should spill on abusive ground. Mixing the modes of cognisance without first understanding the acquired nature of this cunning, western self only gives rise to confusion and leads one further astray.

The West is an evolution of consciousness by the scientific unfolding of knowledge through matter while the inner, spiritual realm is being discarded through evolving belief systems courting an external reality. Thus knowledge expands while wisdom contracts. The inherent desires and emotions of our acquired nature obscures.

The spiritual side of western humanity has remained engrossed in dogmas that were a deformation of truth even as they began to take root in our minds. These beliefs of convenience grew over and suffocated our true nature like the seeds of the sower being smothered when they fell through the brambles and weeds.

The mind-weed is our acquired nature that is our denial of the truth. This denial is the unawareness we defend even to the point of equating it to the eastern, higher self. Such interpretation can only be an expression of higher ignorance of the polished, western mind. Surely, this is what reincarnates. Well, it certainly does in our day to day living, as we can clearly see when we honestly look at ourselves.

But western humanity cannot honestly look at itself for it is centre-less en-masse. This is the existentialist nature of the West. One cannot truly look until one first tastes that place of stillness within and re-discovers one's source. It is only then that one can expect to transcend the subtlety of one's acquired nature that usually does all the looking and all the interpreting from within the confines of its own limitations.

Our acquired nature is this imprisoned plight where we objectify life through our scientific minds. This is the external thrust of the West where one is forever seeking fulfilment outside of oneself. This is our societal conditioning where all of our perceiving and all of our assimilations are part of our acquired nature and this can never transcend the objective, it can only play with the notion of it. The only way of coming into the oneness, to the understanding of the eastern philosophy of non-duality, is by transcending the objective through the objective mind. This is our excursion and there can be no other way, for western humanity for it is the road of discovery that the western mind has imposed on itself. It is the western evolution of human consciousness relative to the acquired nature of the West. By choosing another philosophy of understanding, without first coming to realise the extent of our own acquired nature, can only lead to desecrating such a philosophy.

How is this so? When the western mind commences to earnestly question the purpose of life, when it begins to seek a *'raison d'etre'*, its search inevitably brings it into the field of eastern mysticism, particularly in the philosophical field of non-dualism. The curiosity of the western seeker revels in the delight of this new-found understanding, for usually the seeker has already come to acknowledge his or her own previous mental confinements.

But the subtlety of the western mind is the expressive of the acquired nature of western humanity. All its personal ambitions, having been finely tuned for such an excursion to begin, would now suddenly find what appears to be a door through the wall of ignorance that it has tentatively seen in itself. The mind then believes that it has at last found freedom of mind. Many serious works prematurely refer to this state as that of self-realisation.

However, the subtle, acquired nature of the western mind is cunningly resilient. It may even profess to let go of its previous beliefs that evolved through its institutionalised religions allowing its wilfulness to flourish. But it will only do so once it has locked onto an alternative source to conditionally support its wilful domain. This is the western *'avidya'*, the veil of ignorance that covers one's true nature within. One needs to assiduously question this that enters the vein of *Vedanta* self-seeking its own continuity.

One needs to be aware of the deep-rooted characteristics of the refined, western self. It is a delicate task and nigh impossible for the unobservant. Indeed, one must carefully question if it is really the truth one is seeking. Perhaps, one is merely trying to close the perforated gap in the psyche so one can continue in one's own relative comforts. Perhaps, one is still cosseting one's bounty of new attachments, as one again outmanoeuvres the incoming tide of awareness that the philosophical interpretation of the Vedas may have brought to one's door. It is only within oneself that this can be honestly answered.

You the individual, as I the individual, can only be aware from within. If we were truly in harmony with the philosophy of *Vedanta* and opened to its inner meaning would we not be ready right now to totally let go of all our beliefs and opinions without seeking alternatives? Would we not be prepared to do so, unfettered from fear and desire? Would we not be open and free to *be* life instead of endeavouring to 'become' something better as is usually the case of the western seeker?

But the western mind, that is the expressive of the acquired nature of western humanity, does not have the ears to hear what is being asked. It can only hear through its conditioning and this is the illusion it serves.

Freedom of mind can never bring about a true understanding of the eastern, mystical state of enlightenment, for all mind is bondage and all suffering is mind. The western mind can only equate through its bondage and suffering. Hence it misses the message of Christ by focusing on the sufferings of Christ. By its very nature it cannot raise itself to the joyous level of Christ, so it pulls Christ down to its own level of suffering. This is how it expresses itself in the religiosity of the West as the religion of crucifixion or that of a notional, appeasing god being the comforter to the sufferings of western humanity's existentialist nature.

True religion is intrinsically rebellious. Jesus was rebellious, whom the priests of that time could not tolerate. When religion becomes the established order then it is no longer religion, it becomes part of the world expression. This is the mind-weed.

Mind is forever contrary to freedom. Enlightenment can only be present when the quantum leap is taken. This quantum leap is not freedom of mind, it is freedom from mind.

The mind cannot do this, even if one should sit for a thousand years in meditation serving the notion of it. Meditation as such is merely the building of another wall that again is mistaken for a door. It is this inability to face the truth in oneself that creates the space for the self-professed, westernised gurus to take advantage of one's infantile, spiritual state. We, in the West, are raw to such through our spiritual poverty.

Western humanity has outwardly indulged in mastering the science of matter while the eastern philosophies speak to have a deeper understanding of the spiritual within. In our world of 'becoming' we appear to have become poles apart. So let us be practical by asking ourselves if a religious synthesis between East and West could possibly regain our own lost wisdom from this place where we are looking. We live the superficial reality of our acquired nature. We have become lost to this. We weigh, we measure, we judge, we fret and we die accordingly.

Surely, we in the West must first acknowledge our spiritual poverty, we must first acknowledge the truth of our own situation rather than intellectually forcing a spiritual synthesis upon our ignorance, for this is what we seem to be doing. We set out to try to subjectively understand the nature of eastern mysticism as we interpret objectively through our scientific minds. Perhaps, it is only through a synthesis between that in which we each excel, that is a coming together of the western scientific and the eastern spiritual, that transcendence beyond the visible and hidden limitations of both might truly take place. This is an open proposition for us to explore.

Discoveries through scientific research are causing the scientists to question if matter really exists in the manner through which it is normally perceived. Scientifically, it can be stated that we are merely light particles of pure energy. The world of science seems to be coming to acknowledge that ultimately there is no matter, there is only energy or light. In this realisation through the unfolding of the scientific we are experiencing the object of matter being partially surpassed. We are gradually coming to the understanding through science that matter is merely a projection of light through the energetic field of consciousness.

Those who have experienced the soundlessness of the inner silence are already knowledgeable of this from the dimension of inner awareness. In deep meditation there is only the matterless state. Through stillness one experiences the state of oneness in the inner light that the western mystics and eastern masters also affirm. Should this be in your experience then you know it only occurs when the self as subject of matter and all pertaining to self as the object of matter is simultaneously transcended.

When the deeper implosion occurs and nothing is left to experience, when the experiencer dissolves through the experience and the experiencer, the experiencing and what is being experienced are one, then there is neither light nor darkness, there is neither East nor West, there is only fathomless nothingness. This is the true synthesis, the transcendence of both the subjective and objective and all that matters to the mind disappears. It is the state of no-mind.

Anything short of this cannot be a synthesis, it can only be a compromise, a mutual appeasement to sustain what is mutually pleasant and agreeable. This is how one tends to cosset oneself with the relative comforts of the known and this seems to be the current trend of the western seeker. It is so how one deprives one-self of the wondrous unfolding of the unknown as one misses the goal by attempting to understand the truth of the Vedas through the objective mind. Instead of reaching the state of self-realisation, that surely must come about before enlightenment, the western mind tends to lock itself up in its own sentimentalities.

But the religiosity of the West feeds these sentimentalities, so one seems to keep missing the mark as one fails to truly understand one's own acquired nature. One is again and again reminded through reason that the dogmatic beliefs of the western forefathers are nothing near what they set out to behold. Still many remain bound through superstition to a particular church even though one can see that organised religion is little more than a business arrangement with God. To be truly religious one must drop this business arrangement and *be* the spontaneity of the play that is life.

Some turn their backs on it all and set out to escape through atheism. But atheism is also a religion for it is supported by the belief of not believing. This usually lasts until some crisis occurs, such as a terminal illness when death becomes imminent, having ignored the fact that living itself is a terminal case! Then one hastens through one's grossly, undeveloped spiritual state. One gropes in the darkness speeding towards the wall of imminent death. Denying reason one tries to find comfort in the discarded beliefs that one had previously come to realise were purposely made to serve the living illusion. But there can be no comfort one finds, there can be no Santa Claus, for once it is known to be untrue it can never again be unknown. One cannot go back, one is obliged to move on.

It is a pitiful sight to see the integrity of man and woman reduced to such grovelling. The true atheist suffers not from such. The true atheist is the courageous one refusing to compromise the truth of his or her being. The true atheist sees life exactly as it is and takes it exactly as it comes. Such a one is honest for the sake of honesty alone. As an atheist one may not appear to have found the truth in oneself but at least one can exit in honesty.

Then there are the ones who refuse to relinquish their ignorance. When their religious beliefs are demolished through reason they expediently replace the vacuum created through knowledge unveiling by scattering the seeds of another religion in the making in order to alleviate their fears. It is so how one seems to blindly ignore the subtle extent of one's acquired nature. This is the western ignorance that dances its dance beyond the parameters of eastern understanding. Now the acquired nature of western humanity in its search for convenient enlightenment has discovered a partner for its own shadow-dancing and it takes to the eastern philosophies by loading all of its own shortcomings onto this shadow.

It is true that the eastern philosophies can help to bring the scientifically, evolving mind pertaining to matter to the threshold of looking into itself. This must be the end of its journey for beyond the point of awakening this western mind to the realisation of its own superficiality the mystical East can no further be heard, for the mystical cannot be heard by the mind. Indeed, it can never be heard through the solidity of the acquired nature of western humanity. Some additional assistance is required to crack open the density of ignorance that the acquired nature of the western mind has constructed about itself. This is particularly so when this density of ignorance is now evolving into the contemporary religion of the West where the new priests are the western scientists.

The western, egotistical shell is proving to be quite capable of absorbing the eastern philosophies to further reinforce its own beliefs of convenience. When it is threatened through the light of awareness challenging its flimsy, belief structures it grabs at a more conducive belief-system in its exertions to shield itself from its own, harsh unreality. One needs to examine if this is how *reincarnation* has become the western buzz-word. One needs to be astutely alert in order to truly understand what is actually happening. For this, in fact, is the acquired nature of western humanity again at its play in adopting another belief of convenience as the ideological support for its ongoing materialism, or should we say, 'physicalism'.

When the subtle, western ego embraces this new belief through the eye of its own established order it gives western humanity the extended opportunity to continue building its glass towers of fortitude to the sky, to continue making its world an even better material place for its transient, physical comforts, this being its main priority. Now western humanity can religiously perceive itself to be around again and again to reap the enjoyment of its personal desires. The acquired nature feels it has now discovered its own nirvana as it locks on to this conceptual continuity of perfecting itself in its own good time should the need arise. The concept of reincarnation can be made to complement the ideology behind our current economic system as well as being easily adopted as a convenient interpretation of purgatory for the disenchanted Catholics falling from the periphery of the hard-core Catholic expression. Here it can be seen how two icons of the acquired nature of the western self are being neatly reinforced by one.

Conveniently, western humanity can again indulge what it sees as the imperfect side of its nature and shed it only when it loses its flavour to its personal tastes. One is again on one's journey of gradual perfection in accordance with one's measure while one continues the play re-vitalising the taste-buds with extended sensual indulgence. This is another postponement, it seems, as one clings onto one's attachments. The light may flicker through the darkness of the western mind but the eyes seem to squeeze tighter refusing to acknowledge the cold reality. When one is truly aware then one can see it exactly as it is, then nothing more is required.

But those unable to see because of their unwillingness to face reality are the ones who are trying to manufacture a new religiosity. One might set out to devote the rest of one's days to the promotion of good karma still not realising that all karma, good bad or indifferent, is karma, nonetheless.

The 'do-gooders' may look upon themselves as the good karma-producers but they can be more dangerous, for their badness hides in their goodness. The baddies know they are bad and they have no place to hide. In them there is the possibility for transformation for they know and acknowledge their plight. But the ones who think they are good are the ones who lay down the conditions and the criteria for their type of morality. This is the societal expression that is keeping us stagnant. The moralists blind themselves with notions that they are the saviours and protectors of the social good. But they are the protectors of the old, the protectors of the established order, the established religion reshaping itself, the preservers of past. There is no place for the new among them.

Socrates came and Jesus came as revolutionists for the new but they were rejected. Socrates was charged for challenging the established order, for corrupting the youth with new ideas and questioning the societal beliefs in the gods. He was a revolutionist against the established order. He was not a 'do-gooder'. He was new, totally new. The old could not tolerate the new so he had to be silenced, he had to be killed.

"Likewise, no one pours new wine into old wineskins. Otherwise, the new wine will burst the skins, and it will be spilled, and the skins will be ruined. Rather, new wine must be poured into fresh wineskins. And no one who has been drinking old wine

desires the new. 'The old is better,' he says." (Luke,5,37).

Jesus pushed humanity to a higher level of consciousness. But the old established order, the old religion could not tolerate. The priests, the social moralists, became obliged through their morality to crucify him. They killed him because of their religious goodness. These were the 'do-gooders'. This religious goodness is the same religious goodness in western humanity today. The wineskins are old and the contents, the old beliefs, are turning to vinegar, this being the static nature of institutionalised religion. The concept of *reincarnation*, as the new wine being mixed with the old, is to sweeten the taste of the old going sour for the declining taste-buds of the acquired nature of the western self.

It is the 'concept' of reincarnation that is the problem for the western mind, or its application, interpretation or understanding by persons or groups. When interpreted through the conditioned mind there can be nothing enlightening in this as it only lends itself to the ignorance. But the acquired nature of western humanity thinks otherwise. It has it philosophically sussed as the mind issues another adjournment to some distant future before making itself ready for its final departure into the ivory tower of its conceptual, eastern *Absolute*.

One comes to accept this through the mind as the absolute perfection, then wrapping it up in the old wineskins the mind believes it will keep, for it is not quite ready in itself for transcendence. The new wine becomes part of the old. The mind has discovered the way and it sets out to do it all by itself. It indulges its perceived imperfections according to its desires and when it desires these imperfections no more it will condemn them as hideous. Then the conceptual mind will make religious laws banning their play as happened for centuries before, thus restructuring the walls of the institutionalised self, all of it being the acquired nature having its way.

It is so that I, as western man or woman, make it a linear journey in time in a mind that can never quite fully understand that
absolute perfection must be inclusive of all imperfection.
Wholeness is totalness. Seekers of perfection choose on polarity.
The imperfect is rejected. Therefore they can never find wholeness. They become stuck in the web of their own making, the web
of philosophising about wholeness but never knowing it, never in
the *being* of it, never open to the new.

Thus the personal self continues in its circular motion of ratio-
nality while it wilfully dodges its immediate truth. It courts the
play on the sensual periphery believing it to be the reality. Fear of
the unknown denies it the inward implosion, it denies it access to
the source, to the witness within. It seems as such that true understanding, the food of consciousness, is utterly denied. It is so how
we are locked in the repetitive past with our stories of woe recurring and recurring like the rusting wheels of the train locked
between two parallels. The denier of truth continues its journey
on its merry-go-round and such is the mental anguish of the western mind.

How odd it all seems, this acquired nature having turned the
message of Christ into static institutions divorced from the
essence of love and with each particular one ideologically opposing the others. How odder still are these institutions in their con-
demnation of violence when they themselves are part of the seed
thereof. Now, through mindful interpretation, this acquired nature
seems to be taking suitable meaning from the philosophies of the
East. It delights these changing taste-buds of time with eastern
concepts. In the wilfulness of this acquired nature one further
indulges the notion of one's own personal continuity as one still
clings onto one's personal world of 'becoming' through one's own

subtle attachments.

Some may take to meditation and this is not to deny meditation its enormous potential for it is, indeed, the first step towards transcendence, but one needs to look at one's reasons, one needs to challenge the deeper layers of one's acquired nature replanting the seeds of its weeds.

The mind must be free of the known. This is being with the silence. It is not the induced silence through the application of some method or other. When one becomes dependent on some method one is again allowing the self to fall under another form of self-hypnosis as the body sits rigid on the chair, stunned to a partial reality in meditative pose. The mind continues its dance through the distant flashes of wisdom finding its partial continuity through its new belief in *reincarnation*, that allows it beyond the only reality of the *now* where it has no place to hide.

But the mind-weed refuses through fear to look into its situation. Should the acquired nature of western humanity face the truth of what it has become then it would surely see there is no mind, no self, no personality to reincarnate. Indeed, there is nothing to reincarnate but the ignorance itself. When we look at it clearly is this not a basic fact? Ignorance is the recurring story.

The western mind is an emotional mind. It is in a spiritual mess. One needs to honestly look at the self and to question if one is replacing one's Christian heaven that is notched together with faltering beliefs by now becoming a 'believer' in *reincarnation*. Should one look at it honestly one surely can see this being the current play of the western mind scrambling for self-assurance so it can continue its part in this world of humankind insanely outside of itself. One needs to see the truth in the false and the false in what one perceives as the truth before one can hope to transcend this state of recurring ignorance. Some may foolishly go as far as trying to discover their past incarnations while still oblivious of the immediate present. For surely this moment of *now* can be the only flash in existence where life actually is, or where 'I' am life. This I re-cognise as the lungs of this body breathe in and breathe out. All one needs to do to discover this in one's own experience is to come to stillness within and allow the awareness to focus on the breathing that spontaneously occurs through the natural intelligence of the body that is free from the thought-ravished mind.

But this may be too fine for the thinking mind to behold in its darkness through conceptualization of knowledge that is the fodder of the mind-weed in its quest for its own continuity, in its quest for its own perfection. Is it not so how this thinking self is the living debility of an ego possessed outside the truth of its being? This is the hideous nature of the subtle, western intellect. Surely, overcoming this chronic condition of ignorance should be the immediate task rather than condoning it with a further concept such as *reincarnation*, for such can never be more than a concept to the acquired nature of the western self. It is extremely difficult to understand. Indeed, it can never be truly understood by the discursive mind that is the instrument of one's acquired nature.

The ego by its very nature can never be perfect. Through some concept or other it always hankers perfection but it is forever imperfect. Should one let go of all this hankering, let all of it drop and stand naked to the unknown, then there is a tremendous beauty where there is no ego, no self, just a deep nothingness and out of the nothingness arises an unimaginable bliss. This is *being* of no-mind, this is freedom from mind, the transcendental consciousness.

Stillness is the way. The mind of one's acquired nature that achieves silence as the outcome of some applied action is a forced, superficial silence. Such a mind is not a still mind. It may seem to work for some time on the surface of itself, but it will always return to its mental confusion. Stillness arises only when the entire process of thought is understood. When one truly understands the process then one comes to the end of thought and this is the beginning of stillness. This is the perennial silence and the transcendence to the statelessness of no-mind where the meaning of reincarnation can be clearly understood. Experiencing the new dissolves the old, but only when it is being received as new and not being interpreted through the old as is the recurring problem of one's acquired nature.

Because one interprets through the old, then each new confrontation in one's life, each new crisis occurring, is usually similar to some other that one failed to previously address. The world of psychology is based on this repetitive story. One seems forever to be seeking the answer to one's repetitive problems from somewhere in the distant past that has no real significance to the actuality of life. One fails to grasp that everything past is being expressed in this moment's occurrence. This is the moment of *now*, the only moment of reality. It is the moment of all beginnings and endings and this is the door to eternity.

Existence gives substance to eternity. But, in one's panic flight into existence one has gone away from eternity and one fails to see it being reflected each moment through one's body, one's space-suit, as the timelessness of undifferentiated life. One fails to recognise eternity in the ceaseless moment of *now*. As the space between objects is the reflection of eternity in existence so the inner space between thoughts is the one, eternal mind. Eternity is without past and free. But this is missed when one continues living in the memory of past experience always expired, this being one's acquired nature.

You refill yourself with obsolete information cramming the mind with useless data. It is true that knowledge is food for the mind particularly through your current deity of information technology. But can knowledge as such help you to break through the pattern of your cyclical behaviour? Can you see the repetitiveness in the ongoing situations of your own personal life? When you are still enough it is possible to perceive that your immediate obstacles are the hard, granite walls of the personal self repetitively being challenged by your living experiences. Surely this must be the truth endeavouring to enter your understanding. You must come to this cognisance of yourself before you can truly transcend your condition.

Understanding is the food of human consciousness. Once the level of consciousness is raised then that part of the ignorance in relative knowledge of mind loses its erroneous foundation and it automatically dissolves. Is this not the transcendental realisation being sought, this moving along from what seems to be true for now? But what is true for now is not the immortal truth as one can see from historical development in one's own experience. Therefore what can be the substance of recurrence but ignorance itself. This is the actual story of our day to day living.

All you need to do to confirm this is to look closely at your opinions. You know those opinions you had about something or other and how those specific opinions caused you to behave in a particular fashion. Then knowledge eventually brought a partial truth to your door showing you that all those opinions were untrue. You notice how your behaviour changed. It no longer supported those specific opinions once the truth had entered your understanding. The truth had brought the recurrence to an end. But as long as truth was not perceived the validity of those opinions continued to reincarnate through the situations of your life.

Is this not exactly how it is? Is this not the rhythm to the levels pertaining to consciousness being slowly transcended? But transcending what by whom when one alone exists? When the awareness is focused on the source of the self one knows. You can see there can be nothing to reincarnate other than ignorance. Truth is in the *now*, always in this moment of *now* and whatever is true in your relative world is only true until it is dissolved by the next incoming wave of knowledge, thus refining your level of consciousness.

But those lacking the courage to face the truth of the personal self will cling onto the concept of *reincarnation*. This is the limited self that believes it is going to be enlightened through self-realisation, while the truth of the matter remains that there can be no such thing as enlightened ignorance. For enlightenment to occur, the person, who is ignorance personified, must truly vanish. This is the death of the personal self, even as spiritual seeker, its function as seeker being served. Is reason not telling us so? Therefore, what is there left to re-embody, what is left to return to its repetitive condition, its recurring state of blindness cascading from withering, toothless flesh to suckling, toothless infant? What can there be left to reincarnate but the play of ignorance itself?

Is it not possible for you to let go, let all of it go, all your beliefs and all of this searching for the salvation of the soul of the personal self and stand naked to face the actual truth? Whether you can let it go or not, the fact of the matter surely remains, there can be no reincarnation, no salvation, no heaven hereafter, no God to save this pitiful soul of western humanity's acquired nature, for there cannot be truth in illusion.

This illusion has manifested itself through the fears of I, as western man or western woman, being this psychological wreck that I have become. I have locked myself outside the blissful garden of life with my personal beliefs of convenience, and particularly with this mental concept of being the possessor of a soul to be saved. As long as I cling to these notions I can never fully realise that 'I' am the soulless, 'I' am the way, 'I' am the life, 'I' am the truth. This is *now,* the perennial *now,* and there can be no 'becoming', there can be no *reincarnation,* in this.

But one is ensnared with the old. One has bound oneself up with the past in the mass hysteria of common denial. The masses chant mantras in their minds to deaden their vision as they cringe in dread of the truth. While endeavouring to transcend their vices they cling onto their virtues in their assumptions that such a one-sided affair can be their salvation. Such is the rational logic of their relative world. They fail to realise that virtue like vice is part of their karmic recurrence. It is so how the so-called 'good' people deny themselves access to universal intelligence that is the door to transcendental consciousness.

The masses are the current expression of this farcical dancing. They are still clinging on for dear life as their institutionalised notions are unceasingly being challenged by a blazing fire that is about to melt down their crumbling walls of ignorance. This blazing fire is the massive shift in consciousness already occurring through the western scientific. Whether one's acquired nature accepts it or not, one's time is done. The mass consensus as past expression is being dissolved. It is already happening in each and everyone in accordance with their lights. The ones whose inner eye has opened are fully aware of this. Should it be new to you then receive it as the 'cosmic' new, for it is not part of the old, nor is it in any way associated with it from anyone's level of perception. If you try to understand it through the old then you completely miss as it passes you by and you remain as the living dead, as one of the masses doomed.

But what about Christ? What about Buddha? What about Krishna? Are they not part of the past?

No, they are not. The human being is of time and all time is past, whereas *being* is the timeless and the timeless has nothing to do with the chronological order. The human mind-weed, that is but the shadow of existence, is of time. It was present during the manifestations of the indivisible Christ, Buddha, Krishna, as the mind-weed is present this day, whereas, the enlightened ones are timeless and the timeless is *now*. Christ is now, Buddha is now, Krishna is now.

Individual means indivisible. When the individual faces the truth of the situation then the level of consciousness reflecting the mind-weed is transcended by the sharper awareness arising. The truth of one's situation can only be faced when one lets go of all one's supports. This is not done by seeking alternative concepts to delusively patch over the crumbling walls of one's old beliefs. Reincarnation, whatever way it is being perceived in the East, is nothing more than conceptual to the western mind. It is merely a concept relative to a particular level of consciousness. When this level of consciousness is transcended through the shift occurring in the western scientific, then the truth of reincarnation is known and this truth in turn is made known to the East. This is the gestalt of East and West.

It is the way to self-realisation that is always present, always here in the *now*. Self-realisation is not a state to be attained, or a state to be eventually reached, self-realisation is in allowing oneself the statelessness of *being* one's true nature rather than seeking out some other manifestation of the Supreme Reality to further appease the acquired. All one needs to do is relinquish the ignorance and this is not done through finding new ways to sustain it.

But the concept of *reincarnation* seems too good to be missed by the acquired nature of the masses whose impoverished spirituality suffers from the exposure arising from the crumbling belief structures of the old established order. This is becoming the current beguilement as these western belief-structures are losing their hold. The blasphemy finds continuity through the fearful mind implanting such notions of alternative beliefs, both consciously and subconsciously, thus re-condemning itself to remain stuck on this train forever.

One needs to understand the process of thought and one needs to understand the meaning of silence. When the mind experiences anything but silence it is merely experiencing a projection arising from its memory of past and this past is memory both on the conscious and the subconscious level. Memory is time. There is no memory in the timeless. When there is freedom from mind then there is spontaneity. The still mind is free of the past, is free from all movement of thoughts. In this stillness one experiences the silence of the timeless. This silence is not the result of anything done by the self for there is no self to remember, no self to experience, there is no past to reincarnate.

The door to the timeless is through the source and to enter through this door one must relinquish one's acquired nature by seeing it exactly as it is. But where is the source? One can only know it through one's own experience. The source is before the first thought which is always 'I' followed by something. This something, in whatever process it takes, is the movement of thoughts in accord to one's acquired nature. This is the movement away from the silence of no-mind, shutting off the freedom, the spontaneity, the perennial truth. There is but one 'I' in one's own experience so let us question from that. Can 'I', the all-pervading, universal 'I', that I am and you are, have a voice to be heard? Can I let all of it go, even this temporary faculty of reason that got me this far, the 'Me' that you are, and be totally empty within to allow to come what may?

When one sees oneself through the personal ego, moved out from the source, out from the permanent into the temporal, then one should ask: Must I continue to wallow in darkness as I refuse to face the reality of my conceptual and limited self? But the mind condemns itself to the darkness. Should the lights be suddenly switched on in the cinema the images would disappear from the screen. So, too, the mind disappears in the light of pure awareness. This awareness is forever denied by the acquired nature of the personal self.

The spiritual teachers of the East, at best, can be expected to awaken the West from its sleep, but it seems that something more than this is required to crack open the shell of the cunning, western mind. Its train of personified existence obliges itself to the end of the line. It is here the journey begins for the one who is just re-awakening from madness. The goose is out of the bottle, for it never was in the bottle other than being in the mind.

Spinning round the point of now
Are all our yesterdays
All our tomorrows
While
Now
"I' always am

The final hour
Doth leave the body cold
Yet, mind holds on
Up to the final breath
Of flesh again to hold
Beyond death
Some other cage
On life's unending stage.
Mind
Mind
Wilful mind
Countless thoughts but all the same
In humankind's unending game
As clear blue sky the clouds doth blight
Blotting out the light.

CHAPTER 5

Looking! Is It Possible To really Look?

Let us speak universally, you and I, by allowing our minds to meet in the realm of the one consciousness. If we are not of similar understanding then true communication cannot occur. Conflict will arise between us where opposing opinions will be subtly used as missiles of subjugation. This is the world-weary turmoil that is the discursive nature of the mind.

Even when a relative consensus develops from such discursiveness it is delicately hinged on some form or other of compromise. This compromise usually only lasts until the time arrives when one body of opinions edges an advantage over the others. This is the raw imperiousness of our acquired nature. It keeps us transfixed, always in suspicion of the conceptual other, always in defense and with a rigid unwillingness to let go of our relative positions. Should we look at it clearly and see ourselves exactly as we are, then surely this is the state we must endeavour to transcend.

We are living in a world with multiple methods of communication while we are still struggling inwardly through our opinionated selves to communicate with one another. Surely we must put aside all our opinions for an intimate communion to take place. We need to mentally pause and re-enter the inner silence, this silence most feared, and to re-discover all that we are behind all the noise, behind the confusion. We argue, we debate, we

139

appease, while the fact remains that our minds can only truly come together in stillness. But stillness makes us uneasy in ourselves. It is contrary to our acquired nature. So we are driven to move, driven to war, driven to do something else, driven to become something else in our conceptual world of 'becoming'.

When I was working as a financial adviser I had occasion to be appointed as mediator to a business group whose partnership arrangements had broken down. They were no longer able to communicate without conflict arising. Their separate lawyers had been called in and a costly legal battle appeared imminent. There seemed to be no other way as their personal egos were heated to that critical point where their entire business was at the precarious brink of total melt-down. The battle raged and each one was right according to himself or herself.

The meeting commenced and opened a long and laborious day. I had been hired as the neutral chairperson. I listened to each of the partners, their lawyers and accountants, each telling their story relating to financial loss, personal fears and personal aspirations being unattentively denied. In the course of the unfolding it became clear to me that some of those present had even aban-doned their spouses and children in their relentless pursuit of this business. Now this business had become the monster selectively swallowing their remaining integrities as they set about flagrantly slandering each other.

It was a forlorn situation as I tried to keep order by allowing just one to speak at a time. Still, no one was listening as each one could only listen to himself or herself. The lawyers and accoun-tants did exactly what they were instructed to do by each partner present, thus increasing the force of the separate divisions. As the day rolled along I could see why I had been appointed. They needed a neutral presence. This was their last resort. Indeed, is this not an example of how typical we are in most of our precarious arrangements with others when we look upon others as separate and to be overcome.

There can be no real communication when all are personally serving their own vested ends. There can be no caring, no real understanding of others frustrations, not even the willingness to care. This is the reality. The evening eventually arrived, then cold, inconsiderate night. Lamentations continued right up to the midnight hour for time had become imperative. A decision had to be reached relating to an offer being made from a larger company wishing to purchase them outright.

I could see that their problem was due to the fact that they had no appointed leadership in their current, haphazard arrangement. Everything had been working on compromise and uneasy, mutual appeasement where all previous problems were buried rather than being painfully faced at their time of arising. They were running their business as they were living their lives and now the end was suddenly upon them. Some wanted to hang on, even though this was now impossible. One way or another, the larger company was about to absorb their entire market space. If their business could not be amicably taken then it was about to be taken by subtle coercion. They had two choices, to either go quietly or go screaming in anguish. This was the truth of the situation which I was obliged to put bluntly before them on the morning of the second day. When your time is up then your time is up, this is the way of the creation and it certainly is the way of the mercenary world that was but the reflection of their own encumbrance now menacingly bearing upon them.

The whipping into action was about to commence. After all, they had engaged my services to bring their crisis to a conclusion. Past is past. Previous problems which had been unattended for years were about to be instantly burned in this final bonfire. In the course of such action one can take no prisoners. Should one insist on holding on then one is obliged to die into the problem being held. All must toe the line according to one's measure for better or for worse. When the end is imminent then one is obliged to wake up to the actuality. All worn-out opinions must be tossed in the trash-bin. This had to be cleared out of the way before communication between them could be re-established. It was, indeed, a turbulent morning, but gradually the affairs reached an acceptable conclusion for all but one who was finally obliged to accept through a majority decision. Then he, too, was contented being relieved from the pressure of personal accountability.

At last it was over, the job had found its completion to everyone's satisfaction. We all retired to the nearby pub for a late afternoon lunch, this being the custom in Ireland. Tea and sandwiches were ordered with the complements of the partnership about to be dissolved. Now everyone chatted exuberantly as they gathered around the clustered tables. Their severed lines of communication had been re-connected for their final adventure together, for now they were seeing it as an adventure into the exciting unknown. They had allowed their problems to be finally burned as they had come to realise that all their old, unattended problems were merely excess baggage. Should these problems have been faced as they arose, then all would have gained through increased understanding. But such opportunity had passed and this is how past accumulates that causes death, or the end, to be feared.

My job was done for this is all I had been appointed to do and I quietly savoured my sandwiches in the midst of the noisy melee rising to its next crescendo. This noise is the communication of the relative world that one foolishly takes to be real, for real it remains until the next dilemma arises. It is like bashing one's head off the wall, being told to stop, enjoying for a while the release from the pain, then starting all over again. It is so how the world of the self is cascaded from crisis to crisis. All one has to do to verify this is to look at one's own personal situation. This is the way of the world and the world is as I am.

Then suddenly I felt a radiant presence and raising my eyes over the tumultuous crowd *She* entered my vision. *She* was quietly sitting alone with her child. *She* was open and free in Gypsy attire and I was in my closed, business suit as one among many at the shadowy side of the worldly expression. *Her* dazzling eyes smiled into mine, flashing life's exuberance right through me like a magical fragrance. It was instant and in that instant we both entered life's probabilities of *being* all that we are as one together. This is real communion, the absolute communion in life. Nobody noticed for nobody could notice, this cannot be seen through the noisy communication of the world where blindness prevails. The worldly are far too busy bashing their heads with all their ideas and opinions and then seeking cures for the pain.

There is no escape from this blindness other than coming to stillness. Stillness is a stepping out of the mayhem where communication is usually distorted as it passes through the modes of each one's particular interpretation in accord with one's particular conditioning and one's own vested interests. This mental conditioning leaves one in the unnatural state of not being able to listen as one can only listen through the mental confusion of one's racing thoughts where nothing can truly be heard, nothing can be understood and this is the cause of one's problems. Does it not make sense? How can one really hear when one's mind is conditioned to a particular frequency? Or when it is frozen to some narrow band of coarse interpretation?

One needs to look through the silence at oneself when in the midst of excessive commentary. This is bringing one's inner attention to focus. One can notice how the mind endeavours to hold onto the flooding thoughts. It endeavours to continue its incessant thinking to the imaginary end of its story. But all of it is nothing other than mind-weed when it is seen by the unengaged eye of one's inner awareness. This inner awareness guides one into a deeper consciousness where communion is ever present. The lady in Gypsy attire was fully there in the present, spontaneous and free, *being* life as it is, while the others around me were again being lost to their minds. She was in freedom to give and receive without interpretation while the others were again imprisoning themselves. It took a day and a half to empty them out so they could have space to see and understand what was needed to be seen and understood. Then having reached a conclusion to their previous mess they were eagerly filling themselves up to high-tension capacity again.

It is as though they are scared to death of the silence. It is so how the great beauty is missed. Should one have the will to *be* the silent observer, should one come to rest in the inner silence, should one allow all thinking to cease in the middle of its flow without waiting for the imaginary conclusion, then one will probably find the ongoing echo of the mind-weed will be, at first, unbearably deafening. But, staying with the silence as the impartial observer, this echo recedes and the inner realm unfolds according to one's level of receptivity. One only sees as according to one's lights and the mind is forever in darkness.

When one comes to absolute stillness, where no thoughts whatsoever are arising, then it may initially seem that one is taking new information on board but the opposite is actually occurring. The light from the stillness dissolves the mind-weed. This is the clearing out of the mental dis-ease, allowing an emptiness within. It is freedom from the opinionated self, freedom from the force of mental exertion and the first step back into the actuality of *being* life. This comes about when one looks from the inner seat as the impartial observer, being totally unmoved by this mental commentary of that which is being observed. This is looking behind the shadow of mind, it is looking into and out through the silence.

Then it is possible for one to see the limitations one is ceaselessly placing upon oneself. In order to do so one must first acknowledge the prerequisite that there is but one 'I', and there can never be more than one. One needs to focus on the source of 'I'. Could this source be the universal observer, the one without another that is seated in each and everyone alike? This can only be realised in oneself. The acquired nature of the discursive mind can never get a hold of this, it appears to be too simple and it is immediately slotted into a particular, ready-made box. Again and again the depth of its meaning is missed as it becomes mentally conceptualised through placing an interpretation upon it.

The 'I' is the portal to the inner realm, the inner space that is equally as vast as the outer space that appears as infinite to the human mind. It is the awesomeness of all that 'I' am. This 'I' is not just me, the speaker. I am merely one body of infinite bodies transmitting through communication the key to the inner communion between you and I of all that we really are in this great oneness. It is known to each and every one of us through *being* life as it is, but we forget because it cannot be known through the mind. This 'I' is the first personal pronoun that one always uses when addressing oneself. There is no one else but oneself that one addresses as 'I', not even one's nearest and dearest. This is a basic fact. There is no other 'I', nor no other 'Me', other than the 'I' and the 'Me' of oneself.

When entering the depths of the 'I' through one's inner awareness one is to discover that 'I' am forever alone. This aloneness one can know through one's own experience of the 'I' should one enter its stillness. It can even be perceived through one's sensory world that is teeming with billions and billions of 'you's' struggling through shadowy, external systems of communication, adding confusion to confusion trying to please, trying to understand, trying to find the perfect solution for existentialist living where no perfect solution can ever be found.

There is no communication necessary in 'actual' life, the need for communication only arises between life forms. Here the misunderstanding occurs that causes the mind to mis-interpret reality. In truth there is only life. Life is what one is as 'I'. Everyone else is but a form of life, whereas, 'I' am 'actual' life in the *being* of life. This is the primary fact where the realisation of the 'I' must be allowed to blossom as one faces into oneself to accept and acknowledge the awesome aloneness of it all. It is through the universal 'I' that communion is re-attained, the communion that is being lost through sensory communication between the outer forms of life when one forgets that all forms of life are but a reflection of the oneness of life that 'I' eternally am.

The imperishable truth of this primal fact exploded within me when I had the privilege of being in the presence of one whose door had opened to inner space. The power of the grace emanating through his presence combined with my earnestness as a seeker imploded me inwards. My eyes were suddenly opened to see and my ears were opened to hear. These are not the eyes and the ears of the discursive mind that I speak of but the perennial eye and perennial ear of the inner 'I', where 'I' am the eternal aloneness. It is truth speaking to itself, the destruction of the mind where it can never again create a personal self as being apart from the whole. The initial realisation of this is ecstatic, filling the body with tears of joy, but when it is permanent then one rests in the silent humming of its perpetual presence.

It is from this seat of absolute aloneness within one, immediately behind what one normally takes as oneself without even considering the awesomeness of all that one really is, it is from this seat within one that 'I' am universally speaking, both to you the listener and to me the speaker right now. It is only through the 'I' that you and I can totally converge and converse. This is the fact of the matter. It is immediate to awakened consciousness.

All forms of apparent communication outside of the immediacy of this can have no real foundation in truth. This is a fact that is known to one from within and all must unfold once the nut of the personal self is cracked open. But nothing happens before its time, and if this is your time, then let us enter through this 'I', from where 'I' am speaking to you now. If we are truly to commune, you and I, then you must not put your 'I' on to me now speaking, you must keep it within you, as emanating from your heart-centre, this one 'I', as this one 'Me' within all the creation and beyond. This key I give as it was given to me while I was still spinning through worldly confusion. This key unlocks the prison of mind and through this realisation the freedom can be found that had never really been lost but only obscured by the personal self.

All one needs to do is seek the source of 'I' within oneself. In order to do this one must first cease all mental activity, one must first taste the pause from the continuous juggling and striving through all the thoughts flooding through the mind. One must be still and allow the awareness to focus on whoever, or whatever, is looking out through the eyes. This is looking inwards, to that place where there is no personal self. And where there is no personal self there are no personal problems. In fact, there are no problems, whatsoever. When one discovers this place within then one is totally at peace. Resting in this peace one enters the 'I', one enters the source. It is only then that one can truly be responsible and one can truly serve all that is life through *being* life instead of being the nuisance of one's pitiful self.

This pitiful self, with all its accumulation of problems and unending desires, even its desire for a heaven hereafter, or a nirvana here now through self-realisation, is usually what one wastes one's energy by religiously serving. This is the self, the problem-maker, screaming for a direction to find some way through its own inevitable end. Can one honestly assume that this pitiful self can find place in a heaven herewith or hereafter? Can one hear what is being asked? I mean really and truly hear the depth of the question being posed? When one hears through the perennial silence that is immediately behind the discursive mind then the answer can immediately be heard. It can be instantly seen, there can be no salvation, whatever, for the personal self. It must be dissolved.

Should one for a moment connect with the awesome vastness of all that 'I' am in Oneself then surely one would instantly transcend one's world of postponement. One would be ready, right now, to surrender all of this notional self to its inescapable death. One would be ready, at this very moment, to let all of it go, for one would fully understand the actual meaning of *now*. One would live each moment in *being* this oneness.

But somehow or other this does not seem to be the normal case. The self does not want to hear such profundity. It is too preoccupied with all of its worrying problems. When you are challenged as to why you do not allow all of your mental activity to immediately cease you can seldom reply. Indeed, you can hardly hear the question being posed, for there is always some worry being served and you have come to accept that this is quite normal. But what is normal is not necessarily natural. When examined closely it can be seen that all worry is thinking and nothing more or nothing less. Is this not a fact? Should the argumentative mind not see it as such then let us inquire if it is possible for you to be worried without thinking? You find that you cannot. Worry only has presence in thought.

When you look through stillness of no-mind you discover there are no problems in the perennial moment of *now*. The unruly mind creates the problems leading to the psychological tension tightening the nerves resulting in the functional disorder of the body. The mind is the cause, being pertinent only to your acquired nature. Even if you have an incurable illness in the body, still, as you come to rest, accepting the physical discomfort, can there be the added distress of worrying yourself to death without first thinking about it?

Should you be bound up in self-pity, is it not through the thought of the inevitable loss of your personal something or other? Therefore, is not all worry rooted in thought? Is this not the pitiful fact of self-consideration? Nonetheless, your ongoing support of the personal self is your ongoing denial of the truth. What a farcical dance you engage with that which is not even a shadow of reality!

There is no strife when you are harmoniously *being* the 'I' in existence. In this stillness of mind there are no problems. You are being the radiant presence. But if you should impose this truth on your fretful mentality in order to give it some temporary relief, then you are again fooling oneself. There can be no relief for the acquired nature of your reactionary way while living through the circular motion of the discursive mind. This is your living hell, your own self-condemnation and relief can only come through dissolution.

Still, you fail to really look at your troublesome state. How wasteful it is that you only seem to be aware of the self when the body seriously malfunctions. It is then that you are shocked into acknowledging the temporary state of this form of matter as you scramble through your pain in search of something more permanent. But, is this not again the wilful side of the self now seeking a mental cure for its unanticipated shock? The mind clutches to the belief in a heaven hereafter in the hope of hopes for some other form of continuity.

It is all self-consideration, self deceiving self. When you struggle to hold the body and mind together in the midst of your worrying and fretting then it is usually this self that is serving itself. You condemn yourself to suffer when you are out of contact with your true essence. You become isolated as the personal self and this self then becomes your wretched lot. You remain stuck to the illusion of this mind-weed, even as the body passes through physical death. Your own self-consideration steals your allotted time, depriving you the realisation of truth. What a waste of space! What a wasteful re-occurrence!

There is but one 'I' and one 'Me'. Then what, may we ask, is the distinction between 'Me' and 'myself'? What, pray tell, is causing such loss of sight?

'Myself' is force, be it subtle or crude. This is the force you put upon the world when you are driven by your personal desires. Collectively it is the force of the masses that imposes itself on natural life. This is the acquired nature that you are groomed by your immediate society to support. It is precisely 'myself', as society is merely the outer expression of the collective, acquired nature of innumerable selves. It is so that you are fooled by your own reflection as you unquestionably take the societal expression to be the true reality that you oblige yourself to automatically appease. One is thus caught up in this circular state of reacting to one's own resemblance. This is how the illusion is sustained and how ignorance each moment re-births.

We are collectively locking ourselves outside the garden of life, so to speak, as apart from our truth within. There are myriad levels of consciousness, as in the seed, the tree, the vegetable, the flower, the animal, the fish, the bird, the rock, the human. Each level has its place in the creation in accord with its own true nature. Humanity however, has superimposed its acquired nature of its own emotional world upon the creation. This imposition is the force of the wilful self. It is our world of feelings, of opinions and notions, attractions and repulsions, fears and desires, envy and greed, an emotional world of mental disorder. This is what one has become as man and woman through the misuse of one's mind as one becomes lost in servitude to one's collective wretchedness.

The abundance of nature and all that is life is open to woman and man who use their minds rightly. The right use of the mind is in service to love, to life, to truth, to all that is God. This is the dissolving of the personal self and the opening of the heart to receive the hidden treasures of infinite wisdom where the secrets of your true nature can be revealed. Then you instantly know the distinction between 'Me' and 'myself' as it enters your understanding. 'Me' is the universality of all that 'I' am. Understanding is the food of consciousness and through right understanding you transcend the grossness of the human condition as expressed through erroneous mind. You can *be* your true nature by knowing what you are not when looking at yourself through stillness. Then your world of 'becoming' loses it hold as you are *being* the radiant presence.

'I' am the power that is divined in *being* life. 'Myself' is the endless force of 'becoming' something or other. This endless 'becoming' is your recurring volcanic convulsion that creates the unending anguish of an uncaring world. Why then must you cling to this force of a whimsical nature? Why must you foolishly endeavour to sustain your blindness to the omnipresence, the power and the beauty of all that 'I' am in the *oneself?* Why must you ignore the *absolute reality?* Why do you seem to stand aloof to the truth of this divine presence so immediate, even more immediate than your very own breath? Can you answer yourself why?

The world about you can be so convincing to the turbulent mind that seems to be programmed as part of its havoc, even before it was risen to be part of its service. It must be absurdly so as you worry and strive through each day of your life. You can see yourself as being ceaselessly possessed with thoughts that are one moment happy and the next moment sad. From this limited state it is nigh impossible to see yourself as anything different. There cannot be comprehensible looking through such clouds of mental activity.

Then how, may we ask, are you to get your life right? How are you to break free from the circles of ongoing thoughts that seem to be continuously crowding your mind?

The answer is clear and simple. I, the individual, get my life right by aligning 'myself' with 'Me'. This is being straight.

However, can you be straight in a consensual world that is dishonest to itself through unanimity of intent? This is the make-believe world of the psychological self. It is your actual creation. 'Myself' is the discursiveness of mind that is ever going round and round creating problems and more problems with the solutions. It is an endless spinning, is it not? This is the world of chaos, the world of 'myself' in endless conflict with a similar world of countless others pushing and grabbing for self-satisfaction.

You may try to disguise it all in a wilful politeness with all of your striving, even in what you assume to be love, for your own particular taste of the cherry. But being polite is being political and being political you are living the lie. This does not even need to be expanded upon. We are mostly democratic in our personal service to our collective acquired nature where democracy itself means abdicating responsibility to the unaccountable masses.

How can there be love in this world with the wolfing of wants as one opens one's gullet to swallow? Even behind the gentlest touch, is this not the hidden contrivance? Let us look at it openly. One finds a partner to one's own particular suiting in the force of the sexual drive prevailing, or of the loneliness one feels deep within. One even declares that one's love for this partner will last forever. Nonetheless, it usually only lasts as long as the want. Then one will probably find acceptable cause to divorce one's wayward self from the love-nest as one indulges in projects of work, or takes to the flesh of another to gratify one's changing taste-buds, while the loved one discarded is tossed on the dump awaiting some other gullet. This may sound a little extreme. But is this not how it continues?

You change your car and wonder machines while extending your credit beyond the bounds of endurance in your service to this insatiable hunger. It is as if you have been in a queue for millennia waiting to get into this life and psychically knowing that everything for tasting is gone in a fleeting instant of time so all must be devoured as quickly as possible. You promise yourself that tomorrow will do for change, tomorrow you will start acting responsibly while today you go along with the masses. It is so how the deception continues.

This tomorrow of psychological time never arrives and so the depredation goes on. Nothing is real as one inwardly feels in this changing world of perpetual changing. But you seem to deny the truth of this as you continue to shelter behind your consensual beliefs of temporal convenience in this psychological world of self-justification for your actions pertaining to such antipathy.

Therefore, how is one to overcome this condition which one has placed on oneself? How are you to awaken from this nightmare in believing that the next want about to be filled will be the one to bring the illusive happiness that you desperately seek? How are you to break free from the cyclical nature of your self-made deceptive world?

When you pause and silently look, then you can clearly see your world being driven by the multitude's fuel of countless selves gathering momentum and collectively approaching the edge of another abyss. Nonetheless, this world is but a reflection of 'myself'. When you clearly understand this, then you realise that you must focus not on the reflection but on your own mental state that causes it to manifest about your presence. What are you then to do with your condition if, perchance, this pause be allowed and you are suddenly faced with the truth of yourself?

When looking in stillness of mind you can see that 'myself' is the force creating this world of mayhem. This is your mental world of ideas, emotions and feelings, of rights and wrongs, all in self-justification of your own self-inflicting abuse and ongoing pretension. The solution is clear when you begin to see reality. The house of 'myself' must be put in order through right action if you are to get out of the circles of confusion that you are endlessly creating.

How can you bring this about? Well the answer arising right now is to allow the mental pause to occur in the midst of the confusion. By doing so you allow yourself the opportunity of coming to realise who or what is really looking out through your eyes. You then allow yourself the opportunity to listen through the silence. Stillness is the way, the only way out of the chaos.

But, alas, the discursive mind starts spinning in fury, for this coming to stillness through silent looking must inevitably signal its own inescapable end. It is logical to expect the wilfulness of self to do all in its power to hold onto its seat of indulgence. It will ludicrously find ways to reject the truth of its own unreality. It will rationalise through its clotting intelligence and seek its support from like minds of its own outer reflection.

This is the automated reaction driven by fear. The light of self-realisation is thus denied by this fear embedded in the acquired nature of humanity. It is what you become through your own self-consideration, thus being a prisoner to your own emotional disturbance. The fear is collectively condensed through the systems of communication circumventing the globe. It is the affliction pertinent to the human condition and the solidified voice of the spiritually impoverished.

Stillness is the key to the truth. Such a consideration is a fearful one, is it not? Rather than facing into your fears you will rationalise life back into the confusion of living the untruth of yourself. This is the re-occurrence when you are lacking the earnestness to go beyond. Again and again you will slip into your limited world of rational assumptions from within the confines of your mental tendencies.

Is this how you fail to realise your own true nature?

The answer, it seems, must surely be seen through silently looking at the wantonness of your condition. This calls for a fearlessness of intent so you can escape from these circles of mayhem by getting your life straight in aligning yourself with the stillness. Then, in accord with your lights, you may discover the reality of 'Me', the only 'Me' as the only 'I' in all of this play of existence.

You will see like you have never seen before, for all will be new, each moment new. Your nearest and dearest, spouse, lover, parent, child, will be freed from your previously fixed notions of them. Everyone about you will be given freedom to bloom, for no longer will they have to waste their precious energies in trying to break down your ignorance. This is the great liberation. You will taste the ecstatic dance of love for all will be known to you as love. It will be continuously experienced as the rapture of life that is forever present, forever *now*. Indeed, this is only denied to you by your assumptions that you are other than this.

Should you be wondering, how is one to reach this state? How is one to taste such liberation? How is one to be even aware of the presence of such bliss? All you need do is to ask yourself if you are ready to die right now to all that you see as your own wretched self?

You should honestly ask; Am I ready to come out of this hell of 'myself' so I may *be* all that is life immediate to all that 'I' am?

Should you really desire to know your true nature, should you really desire freedom, then you must take control of your mind by earnestly focusing on this mess that you take as yourself. You must honestly look, without judgement. You must honestly look through the eyes of the looker. Then, perchance, you will surely discover what you are not. Like peeling the onion, one needs to observe each layer of the self being peeled off and discarded through observation until nothing is left. One needs to stay looking in silence.

I seem to go on and on about all this unwarranted strife we seem to be placing upon ourselves. But I cannot be silent. The great wonder of life obliges me to speak out. *Love* is the most extraordinary experience of all. There is no communion other than *love*. This cannot be known to the self that needs to love someone or something. There can be no *truth* to such self or no *being* to such love. There can only be continual, emotional turbulence, happy today and miserable again tomorrow. Such is one's acquired nature. It is exclusively through the ultimate death of this personal self that *love* can be realised. This is the absolute communion when the darkness is dispelled by the wondrous dawn.

We seem to waste so much of our energy trying to enlighten our darkness while darkness cannot become light as self cannot become *love*. Where light is, darkness is not. Where *love* is, self is not. *Love* is the state of *being*. It is the ultimate state of God. Once this is known, truly known, then the illusion of this superficial reality can be no more.

Looking! Truly looking, then the bubble pops and all is there to be revealed. It is as it is.

It is so that I love you.

Looking from a still mind
All problems dissolve

CHAPTER 6

Meditation? Well, Let's Go Beyond

What is meditation? If one is a meditator then what is one striving to accomplish? Who is doing the meditating? Could it possibly be one's acquired nature further trying to polish itself? Is one now seeking some further experience, having become tired with the experiences of the flesh? Is this not the inner poverty of the self? Meditation! Who is being fooled?

Experiences are conditioned by what we are and the desire for a particular satisfaction prescribes the experience. When there is a meditator present in the act of meditation then some particular satisfaction is usually being sought. One needs to question the nature of the entity behind the act. One needs to look impartially at oneself. One needs to question one's motives.

Is some kind of discipline being applied?

This is a very subtle challenge. Discipline is conforming to action with a certain end in view. It is working towards a result. This might be acknowledged as meditation but it cannot bring freedom. It is conditional. The result is pre-supposed by the entity behind the practice. This can only lead to a consolidation of one's acquired nature rather than bringing about a dissolution of it and it is quite possible that the result might even leave the meditator in a worse condition than before.

It brings a story to mind. Once upon a time there were two old cronies, Jack and Frederick, who drank together in their local pub. Jack was a hunchback and Frederick had a gammy leg. On one particular occasion after the pub had closed and Jack had said goodnight to his friend he decided to take a short-cut through the local cemetery. There was a full moon and he felt that he could easily make his way through the gravestones, thus saving himself the trouble of walking all the way around by the road. However, as he was just about halfway across, a ghost suddenly jumped out in his path. Poor Jack was frozen to the ground in shock. He had never seen a ghost before. He could not even move a muscle as he stood in his stooped and worn-out frame. Then the ghost demanded, "What is that on your back?"

Jack could just about find his voice as he feebly replied, "It's my hump, 'Tis always been with me".

"Well it's not anymore for I am taking it off you right now", so retorted the ghost while reaching out and swiping the hump from the back of Jack. Then in a flash the ghost was gone.

Jack was astonished. He could hardly believe what had just happened. To his utter amazement he felt like a new man. For the first time in his life he was free. He could walk straight. He could lay down flat, roll over, even stand on his head. He could hardly wait to tell the news to his friend.

The following night in the pub Frederick was also amazed. "Be gob, I'll go home myself through the graveyard tonight, this is my chance to get rid of this gammy leg", he eagerly spoke. So off Frederick hobbled hoping for a miraculous cure and sure enough, as he was crossing through the tombstones the ghost, as expected, suddenly appeared.

Although Frederick was desiring it to happen, still he found himself frozen in fear and he could feel the hair standing on the back of his neck. But he braved it out, as he anticipated the freedom to be gained. He had suffered his leg for most of his life and he was overtly anxious to have it put right. With two good legs his world was going to be a wonderful place and he was already measuring his chances of getting a woman for himself at the local dance. Yes, life was going to be better and he could hardly keep up with the speed of the wants flooding into his mind. But now in the graveyard while facing this ghost of deliverance, he was frozen to the ground both in terror and awe.

"Hey, what's that on your back?" demanded the ghost.

"Nothing," Frederick muttered in a croaky reply.

"Well here's a hump for you then," said the ghost and therewith he was gone, swifter than he had appeared.

Frederick had been expecting something and, sure enough, he got his reward.

Should one be expecting something out of meditation then one will get something, although it may not be what one expects. Should any expectation be present, then the tremors of anxiety move out as waves of disturbance through the conditioned mind trying to sustain a relative comfort, a relative ease. One again projects, still seeking fulfilment in some relative continuity as the mind measures success through its deeply-cut groove. One does not wish to see oneself still trapped in thought, still trapped in a notional reality. There can never be validity in this, not even if one is meditatively stiffened for the entire duration of a lifetime through some prescribed methodology.

A seeking mind lives and gauges through its memories of accumulative past. Here it remains stuck within the confines of its own affirmations as it endeavours to hold firm only to that which is pleasing. It selectively seeks out the good in accordance with its own particular measure. Such a narrow perception fails to clearly acknowledge that everything affirmed must also contain its opposite. It is all contentious. There cannot be goodies alone. In order for goodies to be there must also be baddies. Each is dependent on the co-existence of the other. Right affirms wrong. Good affirms evil. Such duality is the unending battle between whatever is being currently desired and whatever is being currently discarded. The conditioned mind is still seeking out a cure where meditation becomes just some other mechanical method for appeasing the acquired nature of the self in fear of losing its hold as it rejects the world while seeking some other.

The still mind says no, for all methods are utterly habitual and this is where many place their attachments. Although, focusing can be most beneficial, whether on the breathing, a lighted candle, some object of worship, a repetitive word, or whatever can be of assistance in bringing the discursive mind to a singular point of attention, nonetheless, this is merely concentration. It has a function to begin with through helping the mind to know stillness, but it is never meditation, not even if one keeps it up for a lifetime.

True, there are moments when an experience occurs in the midst of such concentration. It might even be a flashing experience of ecstasy where everything may seem to dissolve into an all-consuming vastness. But they are seldom more than flashes and they become an addiction when one's polished, acquired nature rigidly seeks more and more of the same. This only leads to mind stagnation, a dullness arresting the natural spontaneity of life, and serving only the acquired nature that can never be one with the whole. Such cannot be true meditation.

Meditation is alertness, as in the understanding of the totality of life in which all fragmentation has ceased. It is in *being* the awareness of thought without inference, without dissecting, and out of this awareness an understanding comes through which one is conscious of the perennial silence out of which all action, all thought, arise and recede. This is the silence that can only be experienced through knowing and understanding the source of thought, when one sees that thought is never free, is always old, always past, always missing the *being* of life.

Should one sit for an hour or longer in concentrated effort one may attain to silence, but even so, it is a temporary silence for when the effort is dropped then the thoughts come flooding back in. True silence is being without thought as in the statelessness of no-mind. This is meditation where there is no meditator, no concentration, no trying, just *being* the totality. When one realises this then every moment of one's life is meditation. There is no expectancy in this. There is no result being sought, for there is no entity seeking a result.

Fear is the hindrance, fear of being impersonal, for a truly meditative mind is an impersonal mind. When one truly turns away from the thoughts created by one's desires and fears then one is instantly in one's natural state. Indeed, there is no such thing as mind apart from thoughts. When one looks, earnestly looks, this is obvious. One is one's thoughts, nothing more or nothing less, and thoughts come and go obeying their own laws, but never one's own. Thoughts, whether pleasing or unpleasing, oneself is always the one being used. When one truly turns away from these, particularly from the pleasing thoughts that sow the seeds of attachment, then one is one's own true nature. This is *being* the no-mind.

It is beyond what is normally understood as meditation practice. Meditation, as interpreted through methods of application, is a stilling of the mind, a temporary ending, so to speak, of the endless chatter of thoughts and inner conversations that seem to continually occupy every moment of one's life, from the time one awakens each morning until the time one again goes to sleep.

This chattering mind seems to continue as the normal day to day living that one has come to accept, even while sleeping, with its ongoing barrage of dreams sending shock waves of disturbance through the finer nerves of one's body. Without question, and the realisation of knowing better, one takes this to be normal while failing to see that normal is not necessarily natural, for the normal is part of the acquired nature of the self while the natural as one's true nature is being denied.

It is usually from this state one comes to see one's wretched condition of peaceless existence that eventually causes one to search for a temporary rest, a reprieve, one might say, from this ongoing hell of oneself. This search can only commence when one finally arrives at a place in one's life where one is momentarily ready to receive the signal, that is the inner pulse permeating all existence and always present even when one is outside of oneself. But nothing happens before its time and this seems painfully obvious to the ones who feel that they are unable to see, unable to hear, unable to receive without first undertaking a long and tedious journey of self-preparation.

For every one who has come to stillness in this relative world there seems to be countless others encaged in the prisons of their own creation in violent pursuit of sensory ease. Then, the pursuit becomes chronically selective as one sets out to shun the unpleasant through some applied morality. The thought-infested mind is set upon as some fiend, some arch enemy, and one takes hold of the psychic whip to scourge it out of existence. It is seen as evil, as the hindrance to self-realisation or to some other notional concept. The vicious circle continues, for resisting what is perceived as evil merely strengthens it by intensifying its assumed character. So the chaff churns the chaff, all of it mind-weed, good, bad and indifferent.

It is difficult for such a mind to understand there is nothing to oppose, nothing to fight, nothing to renounce. All one needs to do is to stop acquiring and particularly from the 'spiritual' markets of chopping, changing and choosing. Renunciation? One can only renounce what one has already taken, so even the notion of renunciation becomes a spiritual pride, it is still acquiring, still part of one's acquired nature. Is this not the actual case?

This chaff from the seeds of the mind-weed can never be one with the timeless, for the timeless is the infinitude of the seed within itself. Neither one's religious beliefs nor one's imaginary soul have a significance of truth as one's life is passed through in less than a blink of an eyelid. Dust unto dust, one is being endlessly dissolved back into the one, worldly block of unconscious density as the creation, preservation and dissolution of existence breathes in and breathes out one's perpetual beginnings and endings. It is all but a dream, this piercing scream of all that one feverishly takes to be real.

The bitter-sweet harmony of living the dream is endlessly disturbed by the relative world of thoughts pushing one into some action or other as one resides by probability alone on the edgy abyss. One lives by one's existentialist nature while chasing transient objects for temporary ease until the first flickering of the inner light brings one crashing back in through the senses.

Then the indulgence changes direction when it has to be accepted that the body must inevitably be left as temporary food for the worms. Conceptually one may know this, but the actual acknowledgement of it usually only occurs when the mirror on the wall proves to be too painfully honest as it shows up the temporality of one's facial make-up. The human being cannot escape from time. Time can be one's prison depending on how one perceives.

Self? Each day lived is another day closer to death.

Death? Can there be a heaven or a hell to follow? When one is obliged by the challenge of fleeting time to really look deeper, to really look into one's faltering supports for appeasing the self, then one is likely to see through these notions of a life hereafter that one may have been harbouring for most of one's life without seriously questioning. While one is absorbed by the artificial reality one does not give any serious consideration to these false psychological pillars. But when one becomes suddenly aware of one's temporal state, when it is confirmed in one's own experience by undiscerning time, then one knows that one must search, must seek, for some other type of continuity.

What can one do?

One might faithfully try to re-establish a continuity through the imaginary soul of one's acquired nature, as previously adopted within the restrictive bounds of one's mental conditioning. But there is no such escape for one still in the fear of facing the truth of oneself. In honesty one is inevitably obliged to acknowledge the cold reality that there is no Santa Claus, no external god, no saviour to save the soul, not even a soul as such to be saved.

Still, the wilfulness of one's acquired nature is persistent and especially so when it takes to meditation in the hope of attaining the eternal for its own wretched self. One needs to question deeply, not through the mind, but rather through impartial observation. One needs to understand that such behaviour is still that of one's acquired nature clinging onto the ghost in its efforts to pull the corpse of itself through all one's conceptual eternity.

This is not to deny the significance of meditation, for the stilling of mental activity must surely lead to a deeper consciousness, particularly when there is no specific expectation creating the additional barrier of projected conditioning. But one must be conscious of one's motives. Should you be attempting to achieve something or other through meditation then you are further fooling yourself, for there can be nothing to achieve other than the death of this personal self still seeking its own continuity.

This personal self is the manipulator of its immediate world of personal attachments as it enters the dawning of light through the force of its new discovery. When you look at it closely you may see this self still reasoning a way to sustain its own image as the personal wilfulness of your acquired nature continues. Meditation as such becomes another attachment.

So how are you to escape from such a dilemma? Or must you be obliged to accept there is no escape from this disturbing existence of your own creation?

Indeed, if one really wishes to escape, then one should be seeking to discover who is this wretched entity who is actually trying to escape. This calls for impartial observation through silence. There comes enormous clarity when one observes from a mind that is absolutely still, when there are no value judgements, whatsoever, to impair or distort. Then one can understand and acknowledge the necessity to free the world from one's acquired nature. One can let all of it die, not only one's imaginary god but even one's imaginary soul.

This is the real challenge. When one looks in through one's personal condition and sees it exactly as it is then it is possible for one to see that the god being created is but another shadow of one's notional self, another appeasement for one's acquired nature that one fails to relinquish. This must be seen, must be realised, before meditation commences. If this is not first realised then one is merely fortifying one's ignorance when indulging the self in some meditative practice for some particular result.

One should seek the one who is striving to attain and question oneself as to who or what is looking out through one's eyes. One should earnestly enquire into who one really is, as to what is one's source, then, perhaps, the penny might drop. One might then come to the realisation that one must face into the inevitable death of this notional self. Therewith, in all one's previous looking upon this world as a pitiful place that needs to be saved, one would surely come to realise that the only saving it needs is to be saved from this notional 'me', even this 'me' now taking up its posture of meditation in the hope of attaining to something better for its own unacceptable condition.

Meditation is really a coming to stillness within, with no thoughts arising, or at least allowing the ones that seem to arise to pass, without engaging or entertaining them. Then the stillness should be allowed to extend beyond the periods of meditating, into the activity of one's daily life. The stillness within can permeate a speed of cognition beyond that ever imagined and cognition only comes through silence. Such silence is in knowing, through understanding, the source of thought, in knowing that thought is always old, always past and can never be one with the *now*. Through silence the great awakening occurs.

This is not a cultivated silence. When silence is cultivated it becomes a repression. This is merely putting a lid on the subconscious and such is futile, for the accumulating subconscious is all of humanity's accumulated repression. All of the subconscious is no more than this. It is humankind's accumulated ignorance as the accumulating past where all one's denials are amassing as the one, gross mind driving one deeper into one's anguish. It is utterly impossible to repress.

Repression occurs when one is angry with oneself, when one fails to understand. Such is the nature of the self-perpetuating, subconscious mind. When the subconscious is truly understood then nothing is repressed. Everything is consciously faced and dissolved through right understanding. Then there is no pile-up beneath the surface. One is in the immediacy of *now*.

Divine silence is not achieved by repressing the mind. The mind must be understood and should one be truly earnest about transcending one's state then one should open one's closet, allowing everything to come to the surface, as one silently watches, without prejudice, without value-judgements, without attachment. True silence is when one looks sympathetically at one's mind, not to judge, change or improve, but solely to understand it. Understanding is the fire, the purifier of the subconscious. When everything arising enters the fire without being repressed or ignored then one is free of the subconscious, one ceases accumulating past and one is illumined to life. This is the freedom.

There must be stillness for illumination to arise. Through the illumination one's true essence and the source of one's true, cosmic nature is realised. The phenomenal speed of such consciousness completely dissolves the seeker. This can only be known through one's own experience when all is given up, the good as well as the bad, the perception of virtue as well as the perception of vice, where no result whatsoever is sought. When the seeker totally dissolves then the fragmented world ceases to be and it never again arises. Stillness is the way, the only way, to the absolute reality.

But we tend to take meditation as an end in its own, whereas, in truth it is but a means to an end. This end is the end to the personal self that must inevitably be faced. One must be ready to pass through one's personal death, by letting go of all one's props and supports, for this personal self can never transcend beyond the limitations of mind. Therefore one must die, totally die. This is not the death of the body but the death of all that one upholds as the self in one's continuous struggle to satisfy some immediate desire, even this personal desire for the attainment of some grandiose self-realisation to illumine one's unconscious state.

True meditation is entering the lightness when pausing from the mayhem of psychological existence. It is coming to the stillness that arises within from the inner source of illumination. When illumination occurs then all that is self dissolves in the light. Therewith, each moment of one's life is meditation as one is connected to the permanent stillness behind all action. It is the blessed statelessness of *being* life. This cannot be scientifically or intellectually understood, it cannot even be understood through the meditative mind, it can only be known through one's own dying into the stillness, into the divine silence that is perpetually dancing, singing and throbbing with all that is life.

The ecstatic experiences occurring through moments of meditation are merely intonations of this absolute reality, but nothing more. These flashing experiences of ecstasy where everything may appear to dissolve into an all-consuming vastness are seldom more than mere experiences arising in the state of one's acquired nature. Experiences, no matter how ecstatic they appear, cannot be one's true, cosmic nature, for experience is always relative to time, always relative to something or other, whereas, *being* is absolute and timeless.

Meditation, as usually perceived, is akin to a crutch being used as support for an injured leg. It may be helpful and necessary at the beginning but then the tendency arises to hold on to the crutch long after the leg has healed. Meditation becomes a condition, an applied repression of one's mental tendencies as such. But when the witness within is pure awareness then one is conscious of the subtlety of one's acquired nature restructuring itself, one is conscious of one's subconscious nature as being that of all humanity's and one no longer tries to sustain it.

While consciousness is partial and changeable awareness is total and unchangeable. Awareness is the silent witness within the trilogy of observer observing the observed. This is the divine silence, not the calculated and superimposed silence of the self when applying some meditative method for stilling the mind. Methodologies dull the mind and a dull mind cannot know stillness. The dull mind clings on to the crutch of meditation for dear life itself, refusing to see through this new attachment that the leg can stand on its own and the crutch is no longer required. Meditation, as such, is merely reconstituting the self and therefore it is little more than a form of perpetuation for the old.

How can one find freedom from this wretched condition of clinging?

One needs to be honest when one imposes a calculated stillness on oneself at appointed times each day, in stiffness rather than ease and momentarily frozen while awaiting in hope for another taste of the timeless. One needs to be honest in order to impartially look at one's sensitive addiction where meditation becomes another impediment to the self-realisation of one's own ignorance. In pure awareness one can see one's condition as being part and parcel of the worldly wise, still being the acquired nature of the self trying to retain its own continuity.

It is difficult for the acquired nature of the personal self to be honest. It is more than difficult, it is an impossibility. Meditation can be one's first step to this realisation. One must be earnest, one must persevere through silently looking. It takes great and silent sympathy with oneself. It takes love, silent unconditional love, as one's heart seeks. A teacher is necessary to show the way when taking the first step out of the darkness. One needs to be guided through the vast emptiness when one faces into one's absolute aloneness.

How wondrous it is to discover it all from within, from the fearlessness and desirelessness of one's true nature. How wondrous it is to *be* this freedom, to *be* this life, to *be* this love.

When one drops all one's supports one can clearly see one's immediate teacher in whatever is manifesting immediately before one. Be it a magnificent tree, or an insignificant weed pushing its way to the light between concrete kerbs on a busy sidewalk, be it one who is enlightened, or a cat awaiting to pounce on a chirping bird unaware of the danger, be it a tin of worms with each one wriggling and twisting in its own importance, be it whatever it is, once one totally lets go, then one's teacher is seen as immediate.

One's direct situation, whatever it may be, is one's immediate teacher reflecting to one the illumination of all that is love, of all that is the one, omnipresent 'Me' in every heart. Here in the *now* there is nothing to fix, nothing to change, just to see, acknowledge and *be* life as it is.

But some impediment remains when there is a meditator present doing the meditation. One is still clinging to one's personal crutch, not realising there is no longer an injured leg in need of support. When one honestly looks through one's attachments then one can see there is not even a leg to restrict one, never mind a leg to be mended, or a pitiful self to be gradually healed. When one steps out of the time of the personal self into the *being* of Oneself then one clearly sees that all things relative to time must come to an end, as must the personified self that one may still be supporting, even through the appointed moments of meditation. One needs to be extraordinarily alert to see and understand this anomaly.

It is the nature of time to put an end to everything of time and within the bounds of time the personal self tries to grasp, to gain, to attain to some divine state or other. One's interest is aroused, one's curiosity, then the wilfulness follows, for excessive interest leads to self-identification and further reinforcement of one's acquired nature. When the truth of it all is seen and understood exactly as it is, only then can it come to its end. This end is the ending of all psychological time within. It is the door to the time-less.

Meditation is but a means to this end, for when the transcendence occurs then every moment of one's life rests in the undying stillness. Be it in serenity or swallowed in noise, it remains, nonetheless, in that stillness emanating from the perennial silence as the illumined essence of one's true nature. So what is beyond meditation is a life that is totally absorbed by that alone which is permanent. This is the freedom. This is the great celebration.

Where are they, the ones who have awakened?

By their actions you can know them and the ones still clinging to specific methods, to doctrines of some form or other, you can know to be sleeping. You do not need to believe me, or anyone else, for the truth of it all is within you, within your heart-centre, that is your true, radiant presence of love.

You are this life, you are the poetry of love in motion. Let this be your perpetual meditation, truth acknowledging truth, in gratitude for all that you are.

Stillness
Nothing needing to be known
Oneness
Other than which nothing exists to be known.

CHAPTER 7

The Dark Night of the Soul. Have You Been There?

It is the winter solstice, the end of another circumference, a day without sun on this the shortest day of the year. I face the longest night, alone, totally alone. The streets are crowded with people in frantic and weary wind, trying to pack everything into their shopping, presents, the endless wrapping of presents for the moment of unwrapping on a stilled, Christmas morning.

What is to follow?

The mounting piles of the discarded when pleasures fade, when assumed happiness can no longer be derived and the temporary appeasement is flooded again by the incoming tide of raw, nauseated emptiness. This, we make claim, is our way of appreciation, our way of celebrating the birth of a saviour whom we were so eager to crucify. I ask my solstitial soul;

Can I still not see this present madness as being the ongoing crucifixion?

The world is out of its tree, insane, the insatiable hunger, the fear of the beast within relentlessly driving one on, consumer wantonness, consuming pain, in absolute terror of coming to stillness; noise, unrelenting noise, within and without. Christmas is the annual climactic of one's day to day disturbance, wants piling high upon wants, a crescendo of noise, for the silence must not be allowed. How long more must one continue? How long more must this madness be expressed before man and woman return through their senses to their own divine presence?

But it is a time for merriment, a time to be happy through the force of societal expression. The bells are loudly ringing and the albedo from all lighted cities shimmers through nature's night blotting out the starry skies. It is the time of humankind's glory, humankind's self-declared excellence, as one's gaze becomes totally absorbed in this glittering image of what the self has become.

Fulfilment? Consuming, consuming beyond the bloated limits of the belly's physical capacity! How much more can one consume before one returns to one's centre? How long more must one be swallowed in this multitudinous madness?

This is the demonstrative face of our world. It is all this world can offer, with nothing but blindness and deep, inner torment through the force of itself. How sad, how terribly sad as I enter to be with you and allow its torment to flood right through me. This sadness I embrace, I ride upon it like surfing on the crest of a wave, for much I know can be revealed in the sadness as I dwell here in silence just looking, silently looking at this long, dark night of the soul.

Our children are fed with the terrible deception. We create a make-belief world of love and paint it with the chemical blood flowing through the veins of our static selves. In our chronic condition of blindness we force our denials upon our young lest one child's vision might get through this pitiful expression of hell and point out our folly. No, no, this we cannot allow. For what if one did? Another saviour born for another crucifixion! This is humankind's insanity, humankind's utter denial, as it raises the seasonal altar to feast upon its despair in homage to the god of its own acquired nature. It is the perpetual abyss as the beast of humanity's world consuming the endless souls cascading into its fathomless depths. It is you and I as humankind's madness reducing humanity to this. For you and I are this world. We are the custodians of hell.

Can there ever be hope for this exhibit we are?

Can there ever be love?

Will this madness ever dissolve?

When I look into their eyes, the mothers and children, the men and women, they are all caught up in themselves in their own particular worlds, indifference to each other's inner conflicts. Each one is bent on his own or her own particular want, even to the point of forcing their pain on each other with presents wrapped up in tinsel trying to compensate for the terrible, terrible emptiness within.

Is this my reflection, I ask?

There is no love present, only hunger, cold reaching hunger, while every heart is aching for the love that cannot be found. Where can it be found when it is denied by this forceful hand of the human condition, this raw-bellied emptiness, screaming, grabbing, clutching?

I notice a demented mother with whining children, sickened through want, pushing her laden trolley over the legs of a begging cripple. In her torment she is denied the eyes to even notice. The cripple recoils from his sprawling position on the sidewalk and with blood oozing from his shin he huddles in foetus posture in an unused doorway. Feet, countless feet pound by him. Waves and waves of shoes of varying shapes and sizes pen his worn-out blanket to the ground as he struggles in vain against the relentless weight of humanity to retrieve his only possession. But there is no love in the faceless multitudes to even notice his struggle, there is no one present, not even one loving human, for this is humankind's glory, this is humankind's solstitial altar to hell.

It is the festive season of forced joy, forced wonderment. The well-to-do, old folk need not venture outside. They do not have to unnecessarily suffer this rising flood of mayhem swallowing the pavements. They can sit it out in their relative comforts, having had the opportunity to earn the right. But the begging cripple has no such choice. His home is the open street and his home is the place being oppressively invaded where his presence is perceived as being an unacceptable nuisance to the relentless invaders. This is the message on the countenance of the many as they push and seek through their personal pain.

Today the begging cripple is valueless to this societal expression. But on Christmas morning he may be one of the few serving a moment's importance when some self-inflicted conscience might endeavour to release itself by serving him a plastic dinner. Nonetheless, such paltry action cannot bring permanent release when one remains in denial, when one is unwilling to face the truth of the self. Surely, the beggar-man knows. But whether he knows or not, he is obliged to accept without comment for hunger speaks louder than words. One dinner a year being served on a plastic plate is better than none for him.

I see angry faces, all of similar expression, engulfed in fumes appearing as snarling traffic, pushing, swearing and spitting, in fear of losing one inch. With all of this self-centred caring there is no one who cares for Oneself. What madness, what utter, all-consuming madness, and all because we need to buy each other some presents! Who are we fooling?

Is this my madness? Is this what I am being obliged to support?

The glorious mother earth gently edges her way around her orbital curve and we enter this longest night of the year. This cyclical hour of solemn proclamation recurs again and again, reminding us of a greater reality, of the wondrous ways of the creation. Still the artificial sheen from the corridor of mirrors sends out its erroneous distraction. This is the seasonal cheer, so one is being told. It is Christmas time. The bells are ringing. We must honour the birth of our saviour.

Get with it! Be happy! Drink in the spirit! Please join in the panic!

All I can do is rest in the present, in whatever is present, for *now* is all that there is while all these faces furiously spin their confusion about me. It is my mirror, my dream, my delusion, for I am man, I am this life, I am this madness. I have entered this night, this long, dark night of the soul. The frenzy and the mayhem spinning and spinning I see as my own reflection. What utter darkness! What calamity! This madness is my own unrelenting recurrence. I am this humanity. I am the flesh of this moment.

Humankind walks with unseeing eyes on this bounteous earth dazed by this make-believe world of projection that has grown like fungi upon it. Where now is the natural beauty, I ask? Where now is the love, the life, the truth? Where now is the light to dissolve this darkness?

There are glittering automobiles in their millions and houses of wonder that are stately mansions to those who have nought. There are cities piled upon cities of the most extraordinary architectural shapes with each one endeavouring to outshine the imaginative pulse put into the competitive draft of the other. There are the catwalks of fashion with strutting young women all looking alike. There are businessmen of assuming importance befitted with similar suits tailored to the latest cut and design. The footpaths of concrete continue expanding as nature's green carpet is impetuously rolled up and dumped over the edge of a quarry. Nature is perceived as a thing to be conquered.

The grandfather's clock keeps ticking its way through the chronological calendar in the midst of all the razzmatazz and urgent endeavours of reactionary force. Urgency prevails for we cannot be still. We cannot allow ourselves to listen to the natural order repetitively reminding us how we are being washed away by this unrelenting force of ourselves.

The lambs of springtime playfully dance on the fields turning green. Then the swallows arrive to hatch out their young. I watch as the creation gives them their wings and I watch as they learn to fly and dart through the air midst outbursts of song filling the long summer days with delight. The gentle perfume of the honeysuckle gives way to the autumn colours as the migrating birds of this universal intelligence intuitively gather for their long journey South. They are in tune with this great, undivided play. Time continues its whirlpool of spinning round the centre point of all beginnings and endings to bring me back into this one, longest night. I pause and ponder as I enter the darkness of humanity's soul.

This is the winter solstice, as yin is to yang so must be this darkness to light. One holds presence relative to the other. The demon of both lurks in the shadows for the shadows arise as they both intermingle. "Eat, drink and be merry", I am tentatively enticed by the blaze of frenzied activity as the multitudes endeavour to drown themselves from their repetitive sorrows. But alas! the sorrows also take part in the pungent melee. Try and try as it does, humanity cannot escape from its own wilful wretchedness.

But this time is different, I am being told as I am invited to partake in the festivities.

"Come in and join us, come, taste our liqueurs".

I enter a stately room with tapestry curtains and matching sofas. There are ornaments of solid silver and others of ivory on top of the rosewood cabinet that is pregnant for decades with shelves of embellished china awaiting rebirth, all being the baggage of a bygone generation whose eye for beauty had so been consumed.

A group of pretty young ladies are seated around a large, wooden table reflecting each other in their physical prime. Their bags of Christmas shopping are scattered before them. I notice a bottle of wine standing almost empty among the many objects about to be wrapped as presents. The smoke from their lighted cigarettes curls up to the ceiling thus filling the room with a shimmering haze. The scene is energetically charged with their presence.

I notice the old table of pine still holding pride in the scars of its years. The young ladies jovially laugh as they each relay their most recent encounters in their group interpretation of stirring events endlessly flooding about them. Their youthful exuberance is a joy in itself to behold. This is their pause, pregnant with life, their coming together for natural communion.

Standing apart with a dust-cloth in hand is the grandmother of one, her wisdom amused by their tales, and when meeting my eyes she radiantly smiles. I am instantly enchanted by her deep, inner beauty, so much so that the ornamented room disappears, as do the lovely young ladies who had grabbed my attention as I entered their space. All that remains is the all-knowing radiance from the eyes of the grandmother shimmering through me. This woman knows. She has passed through the inner door. Her radiance is coming from inner space. How awesome it is to receive such a smile from the mystical eyes of immortality.

I pause for a moment to receive through my mind the depth of the beauty I see. But the mind is forever one step behind where life actually is in the moment of receiving. The mind can never get hold of such illumination. Still this world that one frantically serves, particularly during this festive endurance, is nothing other than mind-weed that is the unrelenting barrier to such light of the soul. The world tries and tries to reassert its importance. Nonetheless, its very nature disallows it to perceive, to know, to truly understand.

"We are beautiful young women in our prime," is the group expression I receive through the sudden dismay on the faces of the young ladies gathered around the old, wooden table. They intuitively know that they are instantly downgraded by the luminosity of *She* shining through the countenance of the much older woman. Reasserting their physical wealth of sweet, bodily curves they try to compete for the attention of this man who has entered their space. Each inwardly knowing their abdication to this surface expression of matter, they need their continued reassurance. Indeed, they may have dazzled me so, as they would surely have become accustomed to dazzling all grovelling men, if it was not for *her* presence silently standing with gentleness and ease and radiating natural beauty. The illumination emanating from *her* countenance fills not only the room but all that I am through my senses. In this dark hour I thank the creation for allowing me to see and so dispelling this moment of darkness.

This wondrous woman had too been the possessor of physical youth as now appear these fine, young women momentarily lost through this brief recognition by time. The light of the grandmother's presence is openly aglow for even the blinded from birth to be conscious of her mystical depth. This woman is exuberantly alive to life as my eyes fall upon hers. All the creation flashes in the radiance immediately within and about her as she lights up the room with her smile. The ornate objects of apparent beauty instantly fade out of sight, no longer aglow, like the moon being diminished by the brilliance of the morning sun.

Moments like this may come and go but the radiance of the inner light is always here, always ready to shine out through the eyes of the one who knows. But it is particularly brilliant, particularly dazzling, when it suddenly illumines the darkest night of one's soul. Like Saul on the road to Damascus luminosity has the greatest effect in darkness. When one is in permanent darkness then one can never know that one is in darkness. One has nothing to compare. But when the light suddenly flashes across one's bow it is only then that one can realise, it is only then that one can see and know one's darkness.

In the awesome privilege of it all, in this moment of *now,* I am stilled into the reality that 'I' am here to receive, 'I' am here to feel the wonder of *She* within this body. *She* is the exuberant child at magical play, the princess so pretty in her bodily bloom, the passionate lover with ecstatic eyes from the mist, this beautiful woman matured as the goddess of all in her all-knowing smile. *She* discards all past in this vision of beholding, openly shining through this beauty of all that is life, of all that is love. *She* dispels my darkness.

When I look into the flower of fragrance in bloom, when I look into the eyes of the one I love, when I look into the numerous stars of the brilliant night sky, what do I see but this reflection of 'I' as instantly seen in *her* smile. This is the beauty of all that is real, of all that is always present behind this notional self of myself going through its own darkest night.

It is the inner space reflecting its luminosity through all the confusion dancing about this temporary body in time. When I am privileged for a moment to receive the beauty emanating from *her* all-seeing eyes then all of this clustering world of seeming importance is instantly dissolved. The darkness is gone. What service, what great, great service there is in a smile.

Like the solstice, this is the turning point. It is, indeed, a moment so special when all time dissolves as this vision of beauty suddenly appears in the omnipresence of all through your eyes, your heart, your acknowledged aloneness. Gratitude sweeps over me. It is more than word can explain. Such moments are the natural flashes of light guiding me through these reflections of anguish as I journey through my own darkest night in the burning aloneness within.

When you smile from your heart-centre you shine the light of love through my darkness, you ease my burden of self and lighten my load. Such is the beauty of life. Such is the beauty of your love, your essence, whoever you are, wherever you are, such is the beauty of you.

CHAPTER 8

Money! So You Think It's Not Your God!

Enlightenment shines through the mind but the mind knows it not. It shines through consciousness but humanity buries it under the weight of its own self-made subconscious. This is the cemetery for the souls of the living dead, spinning and spinning through the unending recurrences of the self-perpetuating ignorance that is the human condition.

When I was working as a financial adviser I found that I was conversing with the inner souls of the ones who sat down to enter serious discussion. We were talking about god, the absolute god of the world, 'money'. This is the sacred and the secret. I had entered humankind's most holy and most venerable ground.

Those who were not only partners in business but also in marriage did not disclose the innermost nature of their besottedness to money so openly to one another as they directly did with me, being an impartial player.

Personally, I have no special talents for opening one's closets. My relative success was due to the fact that the ground before me has been over-prepared. We are a confessional society as part of our mental processing. This is the psychic implant in all connotations of Christianity through which the mind of western humanity consciously or subconsciously functions, for all thinking comes through the psyche as the manifestation of this relative world.

This is the fact of the matter.

Our thinking is the grossness emanating through relative con-sciousness that is our acquired nature and our ongoing retardation denying us the truth of ourselves. This truth we refuse to acknowledge. Through our rational minds we create a god of con-venience so we can reprieve ourselves from our own self-decep-tions, be this god of convenience the priestly god of institutional religiosity or the rational, appeasing god of the overburdened, 'could-not-really-give-a-damn' psychiatrist.

As an independent financial adviser I could afford to be impar-tial, I could be their listening ear, for I was the stranger who seemed to bring ease to their troubles and I was outside that net of emotional involvement that people seem to place on each other. Even some priests engaged my so-called, financial expertise as to how they should invest their hoard. I could see first-hand how many were totally absorbed by money. I experienced people in business placing it before the love they displayed for their spous-es and children. Some, I encountered, were even prepared to mur-der for it without blinking an eyelid.

I was dined and bartered by senior executives of financial cor-porations in London, Dublin and off-shore money-havens in their efforts to bite into my tiny share of the market. One particular embassy invited me to the business launch of one of their home-based financial corporations then spreading its wings. They had, it appeared, the investment fund to outshine all funds and they had appointed a nuclear physicist as manager. This man was from India and he was one of the few who happened to be at the right side of the fence during the October, Eighty-Seven, stockmarket fiasco. He was introduced to me in the grand dining-hall of the embassy as the wizard, the great magical guru, who had tapped into the secret forces driving the markets. We all gathered round in our eagerness to avail of his secret formula.

Why should we disbelieve him? We had been sorely disappointed by the dismal performance of the investment funds of the life-assurance houses we were already representing. Indeed, many investors were suffering considerable losses. Here was a light presenting itself in the presence of this nuclear physicist with all the appearances of an Indian guru through which the forces of greed could flourish. Of course, none of us present could see at the time that these were the only forces being represented among everyone gathered as part of the energetic drive to partake in the forthcoming venture.

This man at the helm knew how to split the atom and now we were about to partake in an explosion of another kind. The wine was exquisite as were the promises of financial reward from the immediate future. Nonetheless, the future came and passed, as did the nuclear physicist, with no such promises fulfilled, but the wine at least, well, it tasted delicious.

This was one of many such dances in my own particular search for the comparative edge over others and there were always others presenting themselves as the ones qualified to lead the particular way. We are all both leaders and followers. Whenever I looked over my shoulder there was my entire collection of people following my direction, my instructions, and I was merely following the shadows of the ones who claimed they knew.

This is how it is, everyone tries, but no one can succeed in making it different as long as one is captive to the same old repetitive system. Gradually I came to realise, after many years being enchanted by the empty promises of the world's financial wizards, that no one really knew and that empty vessels make the most sound.

Everyone caught up in the self-perpetuating system is driven by this want to profit. It is the economic pulse of the world, sell-ing, selling and more selling. I even sold one of those life-assur-ance savings policies to a Jehovah's Witness who claimed he did not personally believe in such things. The nature displayed was always the same with whomever I seemed to be dealing. The outer expression of devotion to a religiously-perceived god was always secondary, for the ways of the religious god were always obliged to bless and condone the worldly 'money-god' which showed itself to me as being humankind's foremost veneration.

It was my personal trip into the actuality of what man of the western world has become and the dust of it all got into my eyes. I became a little sanctimonious for a time as I began to consider that I was merely partaking in all of it as a detached observer.

Then it suddenly dawned on me that the utter ugliness of humankind's acquired nature which I was now experiencing first-hand was also that of my own. This cold realisation occurred when I made a chance encounter with a woman who was avidly seeking the truth. She led me out of the world of the 'money-god' and slowly but surely to a spiritual master who was to guide me back home. Oh boy! what a shock to the system.

This master split me wide open with greater impact than an atomic explosion, thus exposing all that I had become in my per-sonal service to humankind's most venerable passion. I saw the psychological chains I had placed on my hands and feet when I was suddenly made aware of his freedom. Then I realised that I had never before met anyone who is actually free. I had nothing of substance to compare with before this encounter, only the mul-titudes, and they are insane. In the open-air asylum of this world I could not have been expected to realise my own utter insanity. Few, if anyone can. But encountering a spiritual master is a rare privilege. This was my challenge, this was my death. Now these are the questions;

Are you a slave to the 'money-god'?

What really governs your thinking?

What comes first in your life?

Can you see how the personal self is enslaved to money through the programmed and rationally, conditioned mind?

Is this the actual truth of your current situation?

Do you really know who or what you are?

Has the whole of humanity gone mad?

Before one hastens to defend one's position, let us impartially endeavour to examine these questions together. Let us look at this world that has been superimposed on the beautiful earth, this world of man's making, and let our awareness fall upon the ever-increasing momentum of consumerism circumventing the globe. Let us take stock of the crazed, advertising bombardment polluting the airways and invading every aspect of our lives. This electro-magnetic phenomenon is now polluting the brain just like humankind's excessive use of fossil fuels is polluting the body.

The far-reaching effects of this is not fully acknowledged, that is, if it's being acknowledged at all. The human brain is being unceasingly blitzed with radio waves, not only silently damaging but additionally damaging through auto-suggestion and accumulating consensus of global ignorance escalating at a phenomenal pace. One can witness it in one's day to day living through people's impatience, unexplainable road-rage and the general build-up of anger causing the astonishing escalation of violence wherever one looks. And this electro-magnetic net is being cast over the entire world in service to humankind's 'money-god' as an accepted part of western culture!

But opinions may start to rise up in arms, opinions defending one's wayward world in which we all are a part, and again I ask to let us be open to the extraordinary depth of the challenge being posed, a depth that reaches beyond the permitted parameters of societal mind from within which is one's usual place of response. In order to proceed any further one needs to be humble by admitting one's ignorance as one takes courage of heart so one can have some clearance to face into the actual truth.

Once this first step of seeking out wisdom is taken, when one acknowledges how little one really knows, then one has some chance of discovering the nature of what may or may not unfold as one challenges this system of things that one, through one's conditioning, emphatically considers to be the reality. One takes so much for granted without question solely on the grounds that it poses itself as the societal norm. This assumed reality needs to be seriously examined and not by one's usual conditioning but rather by an open mind where clear intellect from one's deeper intuitive side has some chance of beaming its light.

Nonetheless, it may be argued that we are all in the world and we are all part of it. Accepting that, then let us further inquire. Let us look deeply into ourselves, in through the psyche. Let us search for the force that is relentlessly driving humanity en-masse in the guise of this western expression. Let us look at the nature of commerce and the nature of the mind that is so conditioned.

When one really looks through silence then one can see the psychic entity taking over one's space as this self-made world expressing its hunger from all its personal thrones of our conceptual and personal selves. This psychic entity masquerades as the 'money-god' which we are obliged through the wants of the self to venerate. It takes up the primal position in one's life and it is sweeping the world through all the self-made systems giving it support. We are so chronically possessed that we cannot even imagine an existence without it.

But money is necessary to fulfil one's wants and one can be selective while one avails of the societal morality to shelter oneself. But one should look deeper than this for the actual reality. Whether they are apparently good or apparently bad, wants are wants, nonetheless. One may be working for money so one can buy food for one's child. This can be seen as a good want, but one's job through extension in this exploiting world may be depriving some other child of its natural rights. This is on the surface side of one's actions as part of one's external world. But should one look inward, I mean really look inward, then one may discover the fact that one is so attached to one's child one cannot allow it to die of starvation because it would be too painful for oneself to endure. This may sound a little extreme but it is merely meant to highlight the subtle levels of self-consideration. One feels for one's own, one looks after one's own while ignoring the countless mothers and children who are hungry and homeless. Such is one's societal morality.

This is not to question whether or not one should look after one's child, rather it is using the example to allow one to look deeper into one's motives. One needs to be extremely honest if one wishes to enter the core of oneself. Entering the core is meeting with one's psychic double, the inner possessor, the unacceptable anguish, the unspoken hell. It is going right in to one's inner depths, behind all the facades, even the most inner facade where one's self-deception initially starts. When one is prepared to have all the facades dissolved, when one has been sufficiently burned, then one is ready to listen. One can then genuinely ask;

Am I ready to honestly look at the subtleness of my acquired nature?

Am I ready to acknowledge my own self-deception?

Am I ready to impartially look into that place within from

where all my sad, sad stories originate?

Am I ready to question my personal ego should I have abdicated my seat in existence to this acquired nature?

Is this the sad truth of myself?

Well, it is either true or not. But it is not easy to measure when we have nothing better to compare with and the pace of living is seemingly too fast. One cannot stop for a moment for all one's energy is being absorbed in just keeping up to the multitude's speed. There seems to be no time to pause and examine, no time to seriously question the senseless nature of it all. One is forced to take on extra work so one can keep abreast with the mounting costs. Then some new object of temporary wonder arrives on the scene and again one is obliged to have it. It becomes another necessity in one's accumulating world while the spare room and loft are filled to capacity with yesterday's junk. Everything is speed, cold, relentless speed while one's heart is silently aching.

One's lover whimpers in pain, "Let us make love."

"Love?" one replies, "Where do you expect me to find the energy for love? Can you not see I am all washed out keeping up to the masses!"

Well, material comforts are not to be had for nothing. We must work and work in order to keep pace with our wants. The mortgage has to be paid for we have signed over our sweat to the mortgage-house men. There is not even space for babies to be born against the speed of ourselves pushing back the biological clock calling time. We are selling humanity's probabilities to feed the unrelenting hunger and the plastic money-lenders have their feet firmly embedded in the honeymoon suite with their thumbs on our watered down sperm!

Love? Another quick bout of sex, perhaps, but love, we have lost contact with that while jumping from one physical or mental liaison to another. We seek and we seek and we cannot stop running. One must keep up with the mob displaying one's worth with the accumulative possession of material goodies lest the others might see one's sagging libido.

Is this not the story of our lives? Is this not one's living hell? The good news is, everyone dies. Thank goodness for that! The absolute hell it would be should one be condemned to live such a life forever! How wasteful it is should it take a lifetime to discover, should it take a lifetime to awaken from this living nightmare, this utter madness.

How wondrous it is when one can *be* life to the full, when one is working in service to *love*, for the love and the fulfilment of *being* life, when one is fully in the present and each moment in tune with the natural order. In such a blessed state money is obliged to take its respectful place, its presence is obliged to be of service to humanity rather than being used as a means for exploitation by the 'money-god' taking possession of the sacred space between lovers.

Should movement be necessary in this state of love then one is moving in freedom towards freedom, and away from the curse of want that seems to have become the energetic surge of the human condition en-masse. One can then be the bearer of clarity to those imprisoned in hell, punch-drunk, saturated with wants and desperately trying to find partial fulfilment through feverish devotion to this worldly god called 'money'.

But one needs a clearer awareness in order to focus on how one's energy is being sucked by the psychic pulse of the misguided masses. One needs to understand how money has moved from its original function as a measure of exchange for goods and services to have currently become an energy possessed by itself. We have actually lost sight of the truth by serving the illusion we now take to be real as our energies spill out towards the illusive crock of gold at the end of each shifting rainbow, this being our psychological need.

We are now living in a world of plastic money that one precisely believes to be one's real world. It is all very prim and secure and even more profoundly convincing to the unawakened consciousness. But it is also the age of technological warfare where one's apparent security can be undermined by cyber attacks reaping havoc in the computer networks that one takes for granted as being safe, relative to one's worldly understanding.

One fails to realise that one's wealth is little more than digits in some computer memory-bank and life's energy is being given to this, while the only money one can be partially sure of is the money in one's own pocket! Everything else is exposed to cybernetic intruders where password protection is just about as effective as a child with a toy gun facing an armed battalion! Still the trustful feed it their energy and give it their foremost veneration as it is put before love, before life, even before the necessity of discovering the truth of oneself.

This world, as we know it, is but a hiccup in time. Nonetheless, we in the so-called, developed West relentlessly serve our belief in the 'money-god', even to the extreme of hypnotising the inhabitants of poorer countries to believing in it also. We lend them our digital money and then convince them to buy our products, even products of warfare to kill one another. In return for this service they are obligated to give us their energy which is rarely enough just to pay us the interest.

So the electro-magnetic net expands and expands under the wilful guise of making it better for all, while voluntary workers wade through the mounting debris of human bodies forsaken to a living hell in discarded ghettos. Who is there to look? Who is there to listen?

These are our times and this is our expression. Forests are turned into wasteland as we fill the innocent with material wants while our hidden interest is in sapping their energies to feed the insatiable hunger of our 'money-god'. We do not, of course, purposely set out to do this, we do not have to, for the intent is already established. Our own energies are being sufficiently absorbed in keeping the accounts and setting up nice clubs and societies to distance ourselves from the truth of what we have become in our relentless pursuit. We have seldom the time or the inclination to pause and to genuinely question. Indeed, how can we seriously pause when the truth of it all is too fearful to face?

This is the era where humankind is enslaving itself in the automated system while there is no one in particular accountable. Democracy gives autonomy to the masses. The faceless entity possessing humanity has free reign to exert its wilfulness on all forms of life. Although, deep down, we may actually know this, nevertheless, we seem to have given up as our energy is being drained into serving the illusion. The 'money-god' grows larger and larger as it feeds off the collective energy of the masses. The individual grows weaker and weaker in autonomy and further away from the truth. This is the sad reality.

How does one escape?

Well, apart from the scourge of desire, fear is the driving force of the system. One is subtly being driven by fear, the fear of losing one's image, one's possessions, one's partner or whoever one is trying to impress, to name but a few. Should one really wish for freedom then one must face into one's fears and the greatest fear is the fear of personally dying. This is the big one being denied, so this is the first one needing to be addressed. Most other fears originate from this unacceptable fear of death which is one of the roots of our acquired nature.

The moment of death is inevitable and when we truly understand death then we know that death is a celebration, for death is intrinsic to life. When one is truly conscious of death then one is in the fullness of life, one is ready to die this moment right now without attachment to the next want or next moment arising. This is freedom, the greatest freedom, for each moment can then be lived to the full with each moment being fully served with one's vitality, thus giving joy back into life instead of wasting one's energy spinning through the circles of exploitation.

Then the presence of money is seen as nothing more than a medium for commercial exchange, this being its only relative function. The 'money-god' has no power over such freedom when the psychic implant for venerating greed is honestly severed.

But this is not acknowledged by the masses for it cannot be known through the masses. The thought of death is pushed out of the mind that is totally absorbed by its devotion to money. We delude ourselves of the unavoidable fact that the death of this body and mind is imminent. We refuse to accept that when death occurs it can only occur in the moment of *now*. This is the fact of the matter. *Now* is going to be the moment of death whether one likes it or not. Will one be present to embrace it as it occurs or will one still be in this dilemma of trying to fulfil some immediate want? Sooner of later it is going to be necessary to face this unavoidable question. Sooner or later the realisation is going to occur that the moment is *now*.

Is this not how it is?

When the moment of death is suddenly upon one then all this stupidity of frantically living one's life as a slave to one's wants suddenly appears through the momentous flash of clear intellect in that one split second of time. This occurs when the mind is stunned into permanent silence as one's body flounders on its very last breath. Suddenly all becomes clear in that split-second state of no-mind.

Believe it or not, you are right here in the present when that moment occurs. And that moment is *now*. Yes, it is *now* and you are about to pass through. You are instantly aware there is nothing you can take, particularly the self as it is stunned into silence in its final acknowledgement of its own blind ignorance.

The great beauty of this realisation is missed as one's lights go out through a mind still clinging to a notional continuity in something or other hereafter through some deal one may have being doing with one's 'money-god'. What a wasted opportunity in missing this ultimate joy, this great climacteric where all life and death is instantaneously cognised as being one and the same.

Here, you quite suddenly know the meaning of intrinsic. But, alas, too late! You are gone!

Most of us are absolutely terrified of dying because we are ignorant of death. The moment you know your true nature then all such fears are instantly dissolved, for then it is known that death gives immediate freedom. In order to be free in the world, one must die to the world, one must die to every moment so one can be always spontaneous and free to *be* each moment arising. This is the great awakening, the great realisation, once you totally die to all your acquired nature and to all of its supporting beliefs.

You can do it right *now* for this is the moment of death, forever the moment of death. If you do not know this then you cannot *be* life, you can only be one of the masses, a corpse of the living dead.

Living is dying. Without death life cannot be. This is the universal law. Once you truly are this, once you have totally passed through, then the universe is your own, it is your body.

When the seed of the tree enters the earth its universal intelligence knows it must die. It is not possessed with an idea of the new form awaiting. The seed must vanish completely and out of the seed the new tree comes into being to eventually shed millions and millions of seeds down through the infinite line of the new, as life flows through in abundance. And from the seeds of each tree just a few will connect with more fertile ground, just sufficient for life to continue its perennial flow. Nonetheless, all seeds must perish, whether germinating or not. We are not different. The law is universal, even in the esoteric nature of oneself.

While billions and billions are born, still only a few re-enter the light. This is the way of the creation. It is a great beauty and a great blessing that is ever present in the *now*. It is here to be eternally savoured once one lets go of one's blind hold to the personality of oneself and realises that the self is really nothing more than just one of those billions of seeds. All self must die, totally die. When one realises this, truly realises this, then one can *be* life, one can be the joy and the fullness and one can sing and dance forever through the wondrous creation.

This personality is what the societal collective supports as one's acquired nature even to the point of constructing a conceptual hereafter for its assumed continuity. It is utterly impossible to know the awesomeness of life while one clings onto this. It is utterly impossible to understand what is meant by *now*. It can never be known while one suffers one's existence in this world of one's own making as an hypnotised disciple of the 'money-god'.

Does one really have to wait for the final moment of body and mind in existence before the truth of oneself can be clearly understood?

Where is it then, one's service to the 'money-god' perceived as one's wealth, as one's body and mind returns to oblivion?

The entire world being driven by the consumer machine of the West is eating into the very core of the earth. This world of humankind's making is ruled by the concept of profit, for profit is the worldly measure of progress. In service to this concept our entire educational systems are programmed. Even the foetus is receiving the conditioning through the veins of the mother who allows herself to be sold into the slavery of this conditional, profit-seeking world.

Religious institutions have established their base within its root. Through it the human mind has become the mass saturation of want. Most of the western, economic structures for bringing improvement to impoverished countries is subtly geared towards the expansion of this apparently, contagious growth in the conceptual mind of humanity. Even the ones who set out to do good, who see themselves in service to humanity, more often than not find themselves being used as pawns to the 'money-god' through some extension or other. This is the world exactly as it is. For better or worse, can one really tell? We in the West are in service to profit. This is our godly symbol, our idol of adoration, 'money', the golden calf being worshipped.

Where are you, Moses, to smash the tablet of truth on our heads?

Is there just one who can come to stillness within and be free from the subtle depths of this mass conditioning? Is it possible to awaken from this nightmare that is spinning the globe from Wall Street to Tokyo to London and back? Is it possible to bring to a halt this human destruction of life?

It cannot be expected that everyone will quite suddenly awaken, for this world of money veneration is the imaginary tree that has grown from the seed of ourselves. But it is possible to examine the seed, to examine, even with our infested minds, the wilful destruction being done to the harmonious chain of life in itself. We need to really look at how we allow ourselves to become the slaves to this 'money-god' through this concept of profit that we venerably hold dearer than life.

Even if we have been slaves for all of our lives that is known to us, even if it may seem to be nigh impossible to see the condition we are in, let us endeavour to see through our blindness, to see how we are negating love, negating life, negating all that is good. Let us pause for an extra moment before we kill off the next seed bearing the light as we killed off the man, Jesus, and desecrated his essence through our religions of societal convenience. That pause, that extra moment may bring us closer to this venerable moment of *now*, as the only moment where we can truly take stock of ourselves.

Our world may be entering its final phase as it is, and maybe there are ones who are ready to listen, and listening through stillness the clarity must come. Clarity is the saviour. When one can truly see one's pitiful condition exactly as it is, only then can it cease to be, only then can this pitiful state be transcended when it is flooded out of existence through the raising of one's consciousness. This is how one is gradually absorbed by the light of awareness. It is the dissolving of one's acquired nature back into the wondrous universality of all that is life. Then the real awakening occurs and one is re-born.

It is what Jesus has said through the words, "I am the way, the truth and the life". When the self totally dissolves, as willingly as the seed on the ground, then one enters Jesus, one enters Buddha, Allah, Krishna, or 'I'. This one 'I' is the heart of one's being in the *being* of all that one really is. Then the self is no more, for it is clearly seen that it is nothing but an illusionary shadow.

Where there is no self there is no soul of self to be saved on behalf of the 'money-god', there is no impoverishment. There is only bliss and this is one's true nature, ever present, behind this madness of the living hell. This bliss cannot be achieved through human effort, for it is a grace, not an achievement. Bliss is only realised by the one who is not seeking, not searching, it is realised by the one who is receptive, by the one who can totally let go of the world.

But society encourages the achieving mind to be aggressive towards life, to get what it wants and the worldly religious condone it. This is a moving away from one's true essence, a moving away from the truth and is one's recurring anguish. It is the manipulative wilfulness of one seeking to control, one seeking to purchase bliss through one's worldly efforts, even one's so-called religious efforts where a business deal is being struck with one's god. This is the bliss-less hell as one's veneration to one's worldly wealth, like the crock of gold at the end of the rainbow, always envisaged but never achieved.

One's subtle aggression denies one perpetual bliss while self is the victim of self as one's acquired nature being served. The truth of this cannot come from outside, for all that comes from outside is part and parcel of the infected world, it can only come from within, from within each and every one of us going in through the seed to the source. The source is the awesome discovery. It is the seat of universal wisdom deep within oneself that is being denied by the self-created frontiers of one's own ignorance. Stillness is the way. In stillness one can free oneself from all one's gods of conceptualization, particularly this business-god most immediate to one's world that one blindly serves through one's personal devotion to money.

Great energy is required to transcend the frontiers of one's deep entrenchments. It takes extraordinary courage to let go, but let go one inevitably must, sooner or later, for one is bound by the universal law. One cannot fully understand this from one's relative position, particularly so when one gives oneself up to the belief that one's salvation is in the 'money-god' that one so eagerly serves in the foolish assumption that through it one can buy oneself happiness, even salvation itself. This is the mental anarchy clouding the consciousness of humanity.

In truth there can be no salvation for self, there can only be dissolution. Should one silently pause for a moment from all the conditioning, from all the noise of the mind, then it might be possible to stop losing one's precious energy to the madness of hell. It might even be possible to come to the realisation that the soul one might be trying to save is merely that of one's 'money-god'. This is nothing more than the psychic entity of the worldly possessed.

But do not believe me. Indeed, you do not have to believe me, for deep within your heart you know it yourself. It is your life, your only life. It is precious. It is *now*. You are conditioned by the masses to waste it in service to madness.

No matter how far this madness may seem to have taken you away from your true essence do not be alarmed. It is always *now* and *now* is the moment to stop.

Man's god
In man's image
The Christian god
The Muslim god
The Hindu god
All the gods of man
Are but his money-god.

202

CHAPTER 9

UFOs. Who Is Kidding Who?

U fos are ourselves in time coming back. How about that for a wild statement! "Now, he has really lost it", you are probably saying. This guy is totally out of his tree!" Nonetheless, this is the proposition being made. You and I are these Ufos. This is a statement of fact. It is not speculation. Listen to your silence. Discover the statelessness of no-mind. Then you will know. Should the truth of this statement not be known from within then you can only hear it through the discursive mind, so we will accommodate by examining its validity through reason.

Are you ready to come on this journey?

Well, why not? You will either discover that I am totally mad or, perhaps, what I am proposing might, in all probability, be true. One way or another there is nothing to lose and, possibly, something to be gained. It does not make a penny's worth of difference to me. Sane or insane, I am that I am.

We can surmise from what we are told that there are two bodies of knowledge available to us, relative and absolute. This may sound a little confusing, but let us continue. Relative knowledge, that is the basis for our rational logic, is within the confines of our thinking process. On this I am sure we can agree, for all of our thinking is in fixed proportions. There can be nothing absolute about that. Now, I consider these rationing confines to be the bounds of our acquired nature and within these parameters such a proposition being made about Ufos would be too bizarre by far to accept.

Therefore, in order to test this hypothesis we are being asked to expand our understanding from the relative to the universal which is as near as we can hope to get to the absolute without disappearing from existence. But we need not be unduly perturbed, for reason should hold us somewhere in the realm of perceivable sanity. So, let us continue.

This is not an easy assignment as it must remain but a hypothesis to the discursive mind, itself being the product of time, that we are hereby endeavouring to transcend. This may seem to be rather unusual for we are setting out to transcend the mind through using the mind as our means of proving the hypothesis. Nonetheless, we are about to partake in this exercise of mental gymnastics for those who are possessed with the articulate need for such unusual activity.

Now is the door to the timeless. The mind by its very nature cannot know the meaning of *now,* even should the actual realisation of the *now* occur as an explosive experience, still, experiential life is not the absolute truth. Experience denotes duality and this is divisive where there is an experiencer experiencing something or other, so we need to look deeper. We need to be able to see beyond the mind, beyond this circular recurrence of merely hypothesizing reason that is nothing more than an exercising of our rational logic. This may seem to be a difficult assignment, but we must not be discouraged for Rome was not built in a day.

Ours in the West is a scientific world where mind is envisaged as a function of matter, so, perhaps, we should probe our discursiveness through the scientific. This is an acceptable road to the western mind where scientific research places the stepping stones of conclusion upon conclusion for reason, as we know it, to follow. Here we can feel relatively safe as we tentatively probe the unknown. We will be carrying extra passengers, no doubt. These are one's fears and they are going to seriously impede our progress.

Nonetheless, provision must be made for should one be requested to discard them, then one will be unlikely to come on the journey. So, with all our baggage attached, we can slowly edge our way through the darkness while still holding onto the bounds of relative consciousness sustaining ourselves as part of the masses. Fear stops us from stepping too far, not just the fear of the unknown but the fear of losing the self. So we can offer this self a relative security by adopting the proven scientific as the carrot of curiosity to tease it out of its own limitations.

We need not be alarmed for we are still in the familiar realm of rational logic that sustains the illusion by putting second things first. These are our relative attachments, our assumed consistency, that we endeavour to hold onto while denying nature's unchanging message that the only thing constant in the entire creation is continuous change.

We are bound by our attachments, just like the monkey being trapped when it grabs the bait that is specially placed in an open jar secured to the ground and then is unable to retrieve its clinched fist back through the narrow rim of the jar. The misfortunate monkey hangs on to the bait, screaming in mounting frustration and because of its unwillingness to let go it is soon bundled up in a net and on its way to the zoo. There is no real effort required when catching monkeys for they oblige the catcher by catching themselves. It is an easy business so long as there are zoos to need them.

But, I assure you, there are no zoos where we are heading and our attachments are our extra passengers, our extra baggage. These are our fixed opinions, our beliefs and our fears. Should we still bring them along? Or, perhaps, with a little bit of courage dump them right now? Surely, one must travel light if one is to enter the light.

The explosiveness of scientific discoveries occurring as we turn the second millennium is astounding to relative consciousness spinning through the vortex of time. Everything is caught up in the expanding spiral from the infinitesimal point of all beginnings and endings to the farthest reaches of the outer heavens. Humanity is being cascaded through the walls of ignorance at a phenomenal speed. The coarse and subtle elements are all in circular motion where nothing is static and what may appear to be static to the perceiving eye is not really static at all but is merely part of a much larger circle.

While all is circular motion, humankind's incursion is linear time and so one continues to miss the greater reality, for linear time gives rise to one's psychological world. This is the world of the self, the amassing subconscious of the human condition.

The mental tendencies cannot get a hold on this so let us remain with the rational. One can easily notice in one's own experience how one's interest drops when something moves beyond one's relative understanding. So let us be grounded as we move into the hypothesis.

We have instruments devised to measure the scale and density of pressure at the central point of an earthquake by recording the shock waves sent out through the crust of the earth. Indeed, many thousands of miles from the actual scene of occurrence the extent of movement can be measured to an acceptable accuracy. Likewise, the disturbances occurring on planets that are billions of miles away are being accurately recorded by special instruments of scientific measure. Indeed, we accept all of this and much, much more, without question, as established scientific fact.

Now let us come closer to personal experience. The effects from throwing a stone into a still lake is something more simple to understand. Most of us have done this at some time or other in our lives. One can visibly see the rippling circles of disturbance going outward from the point where the stone enters through the surface of the water. One can pause and enjoy the effect in silent amusement or one can put the imagination to work. Through the mathematical calculation arising from the circumference and diameter of these circular waves of disturbance one can determine the moment of the initial happening relative to the moment the calculation is being made by the researcher.

I am sure that something in the nature of this principle is being used by scientists who are still struggling in their efforts to determine the beginning of time, while not being able to realise that time as we perceive it from our rational minds is nothing more than illusion. We can expand upon this, should we later return, but it is not our direction of enquiry for now.

As we proceed let us shift our relative position from looking out to looking across these occurrences, to a place, so to speak, where one can observe oneself being the observer looking. In other words, instead of one being the subject one is now going to be the object of the observation. It is like taking a step away from the mind where one is now observing oneself in the oneness of the inter-relational trilogy of observer observing the observed. This is asking one to step into the 'I', into the void of the vast nothingness. One need not be concerned if nothing happens, for nothing can happen while one is still holding on to one's baggage. All one needs to do is to keep letting go until the state of the no-mind is reached. This is the stillness, the pure awareness, from where the laws of the creation can be more clearly understood.

The stone breaking through the surface of the still waters creates a circular motion. Likewise, the disturbance we are constantly making with this world of ourselves being created on the face of the earth also goes outwards, out into the vastness of space. When the instruments of ascertainment being created by the scientist are sufficiently subtle, they too will be able to measure through actually seeing and eventually re-entering this world of the past, that is our world of the present. This present is from where we are now looking, be it looking out or looking across. The understanding of this will occur when scientific discovery breaks through the conceptual barrier of time, that is when the scientist will come to realise the fallacy of there having to be a beginning.

We cannot discard such instrumental discovery that may not have yet entered our consciousness, no more than we can discard the fact that the current scientific discoveries were hardly in the consciousness of the state of ourselves some few hundred years past. Therefore, we can acknowledge through reason, when we examine ourselves within this limitation of mind that has always been present, that we are still legions away from scientifically knowing the fuller story of all that we are in our wholeness. Through the use of reason we can understand our ignorance, we can acknowledge our limitations of perception from where we perceive en-masse at this moment in time. This, we can accept, even while holding on to our baggage.

Our limitations are becoming clearer to us through the volumes of information increasingly flooding our way in this current, scientific world. Indeed, the dissolution of the frontiers of the known in this technological age has already become swifter than the responsiveness of our recipient selves, for we are still pitifully entangled in our turgid economic systems trying to sustain the dissolving and still binding ourselves hand and foot to the past. This is the 'money-god' as the distorted head of humankind's greed screaming to hold onto its place of comparative advantage. We don't need to elaborate on this, as it is painfully obvious. New technological discoveries are continuously being shelved or silenced in order to accommodate the vested interests of the market controllers.

When we look at it openly, with no opinions or conjecturing of thought, it is obvious that our scientific discoveries are seriously penetrating the walls of ignorance that we have been endlessly constructing about ourselves. We can easily see the massive shift in the consciousness of all humankind that is now taking place, even in defiance to the subtle controls of the 'money-god', still trying to hold on, still trying to control the energetic flow in its unwillingness to face the reality of its inevitable end. Believe it or not, the psychological supports of this 'money-god' are about to collapse under the sheer pressure of revelations already upon us.

We are now at the edge of this epochal time and at the dawning of a vast realisation. The quality and quantity of scientific knowledge now flooding the human mind through the energetic field of the universe unfolding its secrets has had no precedent in the level of relative consciousness we hold. In the new transparance, even the history as we know it is about to be suddenly dissolved.

There has already been mention of photonic power opening the possibilities for exceeding the speed of light. This is not solar related but more in the nature of cosmic consciousness. Nonetheless, these are but infantile days to what lies immediately before us in the world of the relative scientific that is merely beginning to open this way. Humanity is beginning to see, beginning to catch the flicker of light. We are this journey, as the speed of consciousness evolving through matter.

Scientifically, we can now reasonably assume that the time is upon us where we can examine the data of events that took place in the past as at the actual moment of happening. It is so that history is about to become immediate in this world of 'becoming' before we come to the fuller realisation of all that we immediately are in the greater reality. This is coming about as humankind scientifically succeeds to break free from its current understanding of time. History is about to disappear when our interest totally drops after we examine, re-examine and finally exhaust it.

Our reservoirs of relative knowledge have got us this far and now the accumulating mass of the subconscious, that is our sub-active waste, is at the point of being totally discarded. It is about to be dissolved back into the nothingness. This is the extraordinary shift in consciousness, the ripples of which are now being experienced. We are now rapidly approaching the end of this epoch and the next break-through is imminent.

Human consciousness en-masse is edging this way, homeward bound so to say, like the prodigal son having made up his mind to return to his source after burning through all his illusory desires. We are but the same, being as one humankind returning to light. When the prodigal son drew near his original home his father came out to meet him, so the parable tells us. We can use the significance of this to help us to understand our true nature. We, as one humankind, are nearing the final stage of our own journey home.

Human consciousness is coming nearer to its source in each step it takes in transcending its own limitations. Reason qualifies this when we look back on our more recent discoveries. Each moment brings new unfolding and a speeding up of consciousness. We are lesser and lesser bound by our old beliefs and our old superstitions. Our source as pure consciousness is our true essence coming from inner space to meet us as we are nearing our journey's end, or what appears as an end but is really the simultanuous ending and beginning of all that is time.

Those of us with extra-sensory perception are experiencing the outer ripples from the stone that has entered the waters of the future ahead. In the timelessness and spacelessness of the *now* we are the stone entering the waters of the absolute reality. We can see this more clearly when we transcend our confinements of conceptual and chronological time. There is nothing extraordinary about this for this knowledge is immediate once the ignorance imposed by the defined, societal parameters on reason is transcended, that is when the duplicity of our rational, logical world is exposed. This may sound to be presumptuous to the societally conditioned mind so let us examine it more closely together.

In the beginning is the word as so we are told by the ancient books of wisdom. The word is the vibration through which 'I' arrive. Do not run away. It is futile to try for this is your 'I' that you are now observing, so you cannot escape. 'I' am the vibration of the ripple at hand, which is time. Existence appears about 'Me'. 'I' am the centre, the eye of the vortex, the way, the life and the truth. There is nothing other than 'I'. This is the 'I' whom you instantly realise you eternally are at the moment of death. If you cannot accept it now, do not be too concerned, for as sure as you are reading these words you are going to accept it then. So, one way or another you are going to know it.

Let us continue.

Whatever occurs or does not occur, 'I' am here to observe it. This is the universal law. It is how it is. Reason can bring one to this knowledge but to enter it and *be* it one has to transcend the mind, one has to be in the statelessness of no-mind. No-mind is where the personified wilfulness dissolves and the personal will is aligned to the universal will, as relative knowledge being aligned to universal knowledge. In this statelessness nothing is thought or imagined for whatever needs to be known is instantly known. Everyone experiences this when all of one's life flashes before one at the moment of death. This final experience is the relative re-aligning with the universal as the final all-consuming thought of existence dissolving back into the void.

A tree falls. Does it make a sound if no one is present? Can there be a tree, or, indeed, anything other than 'I', the observer observing the observed? Therefore, 'I' must be the door to the source. The 'I' within you is always the first thought through which all other thoughts arise. Everything and anything can only have presence relative to 'I'. 'I' appear through this first thought. Should 'I' not appear then nothing appears. Through 'I' the world about me manifests. What comes before 'I' is inner space, as vast if not vaster than all that is scientifically perceived as outer space. This knowledge is within each and everyone, although few, if any, can realise it through the discursiveness of the conditioned mind.

As persons we suffer the torment of our own misconceptions. We take our bodies and minds to be the only reality. Each of us sees ourselves as one among many. Of course this is true in the relative world, but we lose it completely when we consider that the relative world is the basis for wisdom. Then we are back on the journey of improving ourselves, of improving our relative comforts, as we sever our connection to our deeper universal intelligence.

This is how we have become since the original flooding of ignorance alienated us from our cosmic essence that is this moment's occurrence. We deny ourselves our true nature by refusing to accept that the body is unreal in the sense that it has no independent existence. It can only exist by virtue of existence whereas existence is not independent of the body. This needs to be understood if we are to see beyond our self-imposed limitations. It is not easy for the entire world is frantically serving the body of matter in the narcotic belief that the body lasts for ever and ever. Such is matter-consciousness. Belief in the immortality of the body is an utter negation of truth and rank materialism that clouds the intellect and keeps us bound within our relative worlds.

The consciousness in all matter is turgid and slow, be it a tree at the end of its time or an eardrum receiving new sound. We surmise through reason but one binds oneself by the limitations of the known. From within these confines one tends to rationalise anything beyond one's limited understanding. This, being our acquired nature, is the logic one uses when thinking in fixed proportions and so one starts out on an erroneous footing. It is the way one has become in our world of 'becoming' and this is one's ignorance. This ignorance is the world of conflicting beliefs and total absorption of our energies en-masse.

The unknown, in a flash of expanded consciousness through relative existence, is only received by the occasional few. This is always unidentifiable to the many due to the vagueness of worldly understanding of the inner 'I' that each one is in oneself. Let us again be reminded, this is the 'I' that you are, the one, omnipresent omniscience. When one realises the Oneself then one does not need to know anything in particular, nothing needs to be worked out because it is then realised that one's true nature is the ever-present whole other than which nothing exists to be known.

So let us place the observer of it all, whether receiving through mystical story, physical sight or scientific device, let us place this observer within you at this time now reading into the proposition being made, as being the focal point of all occurrences. This can be directly known in *being* it which is the heart of oneself, or it can be relatively known through secondary knowledge which is the mind partaking in discursive gymnastics.

When one is *being* it then one is the centre point of the vortex and when one relatively understands it then one is a helix on the spiral either spinning towards or spinning away from the point. In the course of this spinning there are multiple co-existences simultaneously occurring as one travels in or out the spiral. Also, there are multiple numbers of vortices within the vortex itself, even the immediate vortex being one within another of multiple others. This is the infinitesimal point of the void going forever inwards and forever outwards from wherever it is being met by relative consciousness, like the multiple seeds within the one seed at any one given point.

Humankind lives by probability alone in this spinning vortex of time. This is exactly how it is even though one might foolishly believe that one is shaping existence. One might even foolishly believe that one can make it all better when one does not even fully understand the helix of one's immediate presence, being trapped to the partial by one's own personified ignorance. Here, we are obliged to make effort to overcome this ignorance if we are to progress any further in our search for the truth behind this phenomenon of Ufos. Our ignorance is our excess baggage that is bound and secured to the past while our hypothesis needs freedom to meet with the conceptual future here in the *now*.

In existence we are working through mind as mind. We are using reason to give ourselves light and reason has always been our friend in this relative world. This is existence, here in this moment of *now*. One enters existence as one projects out through the 'I', out through the first 'I' thought. One must first understand the 'I' as being the centre, or the point where one enters. Reason qualifies this. Whether it be through the doctrine of monism, or through the sight of a meteor crashing into the ocean, or an earthquake at the other side of the earth, it cannot be denied that all happenings can only be experienced relative to 'I' being the witness where life actually is in the *being* of life in this body.

Who is this 'I'? This must be one's first enquiry. When this is not first understood then nothing can be clearly understood. This is the problem with scientific research and why the greatest of minds are obliged to ignore, or belittle, unexplainable phenomena. The mind is logic but on its first movement away from the 'I' thought it becomes rational logic. This is the fall where immediate limitation occurs as one becomes severed from one's true nature. One moves from no-mind, or still mind, to rational mind, out into existence, putting second things first. The mind rationalises, dissects and proportionates as it creates its own objective reality and this becomes the world of humankind's existence.

Pure consciousness is the 'I' immediately before or behind the first 'I' thought arising. The 'I', as pure consciousness, enters through the mind. Human consciousness is pure consciousness being reflected through matter where the mind as the self becomes attached to its objective world. Then one comes to believe in the mind's creation, or sub-creation, as being the truth behind existence. Ideas arise, beliefs arise and one is in conflict. One has condemned oneself to search throughout existence for the greater reality. But no matter how far outward one might go, nevertheless, one is still no nearer to truth for all the disturbance is emanating from oneself. The self is the stone entering the still waters of pure consciousness. The mental tendencies are the circular ripples going outwards, out through the vortex of time that is time itself becoming part of the mind's objectified creation.

The 'I' is the first arising of awareness through the consciousness of matter in existence. This first is life in the *being* of life, then all other expressions of life appear. If there is no life in the *being* of life, then there can be no other forms, or expressions, of life. Should you see it as other than this, then you are being divisive, you are seeing yourself as separate from life and such cannot be true, for reason tells you in your bodily experience that the 'I' whom you take as yourself cannot be separate from life. Reason is still your companion.

You cannot experience life anywhere other than *being* life in the body where life actually is right now. This is an 'actual' truth. All life that is perceived outside of the body cannot be 'actual' life as known through the *being* of life. You cannot *be* life in any of the forms outside of yourself. All forms of life are but a reflection of life that can only be known in the *being* of life in your body. The life that you are, in *being* life, is the seed within the infinitesimal seeds of life at any given point in time. That point in existence is always *now,* for *now* is the only moment and place where life 'actually' is as life *being* life. This is logic, *now* is logic, and everything perceived as other than *now* is rational logic.

Now is the eternal, is it not? It does not require analytical research to discover this. *Now* is immediate. The realisation of this is in stillness. Absolute stillness is the needle passing in through the eye of itself. This is the paradox. One is the needle, existence is the needle, time is the needle. The mind cannot understand for the mind is nothing more than the thoughts that come after the first 'I' thought. But when there is no person, when there is no self-consideration whatsoever, just a silent nothingness, then such a realisation has space to flash through and whenever it does flash through human consciousness then one realises immortality.

'I', the observer, am the central point. All that is seen outside of 'I' is the reflection of all that is within, of all that 'I' am. Within and without are one and the same. It is from this central point that all is pertaining to the 'I' that is one's true nature. If we are to use the hour-glass as a simile, then this point of the 'I' in oneself would be like the central point of the glass where the grains of sand as particles, or bodies of matter, are passing through, and even that is but a poor example of what is beyond word, beyond time.

When it is understood that the 'I' is the central point of all that exists, and that is to say that existence has no true reality other than its relativity to 'I', then nothing can be other than 'I', this one universal 'I'. The 'I' is not alone the witness of all occurrences but the infinite line of witnessing within the witness itself. The 'I' is the observer, the observing and the observed. It is timelessness, mindlessness, perennial life, beyond word, before sound, beyond relative consciousness, yet being every facet of the relative as well.

This is but a partial explanation to what cannot be relayed through this written vibration of sound, for we are now speaking of the undefinable that is not only within and after but even before the vibration itself. This undefinable is beyond the world of scientific explanation, for should this existence have a scientific beginning such as the assumed 'big bang', then the nothingness before such an occurrence remains unexplained. Indeed, how can there be a 'big bang', even a nothingness, if 'I' am not here to observe it? It is not difficult to see that all such scientific rationale is less than a shadow projecting from a much deeper reality.

The world exists but its existence is phenomenal as an event that may be observed and those who know are not deluded by the play of events. Man and woman in existence abide in the body and the body is but a spacesuit, a capsule in time. But man and woman through the mind, project themselves outside of their spacesuits where, instead of truth they settle for beliefs and opinions and instead of life they settle for a better kind of living for their spacesuits. They discriminate between the pleasing and the not-so-pleasing life-forms immediately about them and they become lost to their true nature as they place all other forms of life as separate. They even see nature as separate and so they set out to control it.

They spill their energy developing a future and evolving the means of improving their spacesuits, thus entrapping themselves. It is almost unbelievable, but this is the fact of the matter. Everything man and woman serve in this world is an expression of this madness when everything perceivable by the human mind is tied up to some form of material comfort. Even their religions have become attached to this phenomenon through their mental concepts of soul to be saved, or reincarnation, while deep in their hearts they know they are not being true. They cannot be still, for in stillness they have to acknowledge their utter aloneness. They search for love, but they can never find love, they only find partial fulfilment. This is how man and woman have stepped out into time and out into their own bewilderment.

For a future to be there must simultaneously be a past. Thus man and woman enter linear time where past accumulates and overtakes them, this being the fundamental ignorance of their projected, human intelligence. Their acquired nature exploits the present through their own amassing recurrences. This is how man and woman have become divisive as they become lost into time. Now there is not only nature but human nature and the environment as nature controlled, as man and woman set out to replace the earth, and all that they object to, with their own humanoid world. Here they become stuck in the helix of their own rationale as they spin out through the spiral of the vortex seeing all other forms of life, never mind co-existences, as alien to their own.

Man and woman, through their rational logic, thus alienate themselves from their own true nature. They divorce themselves from perennial life through their minds. They have stepped out through the *now* into chronological and psychological time, the horizontal and perpendicular, as the cross for their own crucifixion. This cross they refuse to acknowledge so they put it onto the back of their world that they see as other than themselves. Here the source of their conflict arises. This is their human nature, the one they acquire, in eternal discord with the natural order of the creation. Thus, man and woman become lost through themselves as they cannot see beyond their own self-imposed limitations.

So what are these Ufos, which are beyond humankind's understanding? What are these unidentified objects manifesting to the occasional few?

Before we attempt to answer let us first have another look at our baggage for we may still be carrying a lot of unnecessary weight.

There is a story about a small aircraft being abandoned in a primeval island after the great war. Apparently it was forgotten by the evacuating army and it remained undisturbed for some time, until a primitive tribe suddenly chanced by it. It was an awesomely, spectacular find for they had never seen anything like it before. This particular tribe had not been part of humanity's evolutionary process through the narrow confines of scientific discovery. They had remained exactly as they were for some thousands of years living each day as it came.

They examined the aircraft with the greatest of wonder and

could only surmise that it was a certain type of bullock-cart, for this was all they had experienced that moved on wheels. It was a great novelty, indeed, and they could only assume that it was a gift from the gods for their chief. Then, hitching the bullocks up to the nose they used it as such for special occasions. The chief of the tribe felt that he had been specially favoured by the gods and so it helped to increase the penetration of his power on the minds of his subjects. All became more respectful of him, seated as high as an elephant's ears in the cockpit and being pulled along by the two hefty bullocks specially assigned for the privileged task.

Then, one day, a member of a distant tribe chanced by, having lost his direction. Although he had never encountered an aeroplane before, nonetheless, this man had experienced the war and he had been exposed to the presence of automobiles, jeeps and other such vehicles that moved on their own. He had even been shown the mechanical workings of some. This new information he had eagerly absorbed with his curious mind. Then the men of war departed as they had come, still in their own confusion. But this man had occasion to absorb a little of their scientific knowledge and this partial knowledge had gone to his head and congealed. He knew it all, of this he felt sure. When he encountered the tribe using this scientific invention as a bullock-cart he could hardly believe what he saw.

"Why! This is an automobile," he loudly declared, "This does not need bullocks to pull it along for it can move on its own."

The chief was angry with the new arrival, for he had no idea what this raving lunatic was trying to say. This could be dangerous to him. This man seemed to be speaking about a magical power that the chief knew nothing about. His position as chief could be seriously threatened as such. This he could never allow. The man had to be silenced.

"A bullock-cart moving on its own? What rubbish! This is utter nonsense, absolutely impossible. How could a bullock-cart move on its own? Kill this lunatic at once," the chief harshly commanded.

And rightly so according to our character, for no one human being likes to have its ignorance challenged. This is a fact, it is exactly how we are while living within the constraints of our acquired nature.

Am I making it up?

Well, all one needs to do is to check it out in one's own experience, to listen to oneself the next time one finds oneself defending some opinion or other, not to judge or to change but just to silently listen to whatever is flowing out through one's own mouth. Then it can be seen in one's own experience.

"I beg you," the poor man implored, "Just give me a chance to show you how it works and I will show you how to move it yourself".

"Come then and show me," demanded the chief in an air of brash superiority.

The man spent several hours explaining the works of the engine. He fumbled through the unusual controls as they seemed quite different to the few automobiles he had occasion to discover. But eventually he figured it out and the engine started with a terrible roar sending an enormous blast of black smoke up into the sky. Everyone ran for their lives into the thickness of the forest for they had never heard such a terrifying sound before.

No one remained but the chief for he was determined to get all the information he could cluster to himself from this unusual stranger. Indeed, the stranger, in his pride, was more than eager to display all of his new-found knowledge. So, the lesson and the experiments continued for the course of the day while the terrified members of the tribe hid behind their fears in the forest.

When the chief was eventually satisfied with himself, when he felt confident that he could move the bullock-cart all on his own, then he picked up a rock and bashed in the brains of the misfortunate mechanic. This is knowledge he cannot share, for all others he sees as other than he and he needs to personally rule, he needs to grab and hold onto the power for himself.

Indeed, can he be blamed when it all sounds so familiar. He is not too unlike the rest of us as we silently plunder our relative worlds. The rocks may have changed to computers but the intent is relatively the same. Adam is still being chucked out of the garden of life by this acquired nature of the self, so it appears!

The Ufo one might see through one's extrasensory perception is the self re-entering the self, like the prodigal son vaguely catching a glimpse of his father coming to meet him through the haze of himself as his journey is nearing its end. At this infinitesimal point the self of the future is coming to greet its own return, for this moment of *now* is pregnant with all past, all present and all future. *Now* is the point that infinitely stands between time and the timeless. Before you pick up that rock to bash in my brains, I would like to remind you that you may be the chief and I am merely the obliging, half-baked mechanic! Give me more time. There is much more to be realised.

Past, present and future are totally condensed in the *now* in existence. This is a fact. It is only in the moment of *now* that one is life in the actuality of *being* life. There cannot be actual life in the *being* of life other than *now*. This is the only moment in chronological time as we know it where life is actually happening. All our yesterdays and tomorrows are part of psychological time where our fears, our emotions, our desires and everything outside of ourselves abide. When one is absolutely still then it is possible to meet with the *now*, where there are no fears, no emotions, where there are no desires. This is the door to the realisation of immortality as has been mentioned before.

We have already explored the oneness of 'I' and discovered through reason that there cannot be 'actual' life other than 'I' where life is happening through this body right now in the *now*. This can be clearly understood when one checks it out in oneself, in the 'I' that is you in your immediate body. When we hold to this, of putting first what is first, then our hypothesis is on safe footing. This *now* is the point of the needle passing through the eye of itself, as the central point of the vortex, a fact not fully acknowledged by the scientist still seeking confirmation of extraterrestrial life, still chasing the conceptual shadow of the 'I' through the perpetually decaying eye of the living corpse of his or her spacesuit.

But let us not be critical of scientific discovery for such discovery is confirming our repetitive past as we endlessly try to establish the existence of life that is other than 'I'. This is humankind's wretchedness forever stretching outside of itself. In our current state it can hardly make any improvement to our worldly condition even if humanity should succeed to colonise another planet. Indeed, humanity may have already done it before in this past of ourselves. One alludes reality with such thinking that the next time it can be better, when even this future perceived is already the past through the eyes of the future self.

This future self is sceptically seen through the darkness of one's current vision as an extraterrestrial being.

But do not be confused as to what is being said. Rather let one depend on reason to bring oneself closer to home, for reason authenticates the proposition already being made. There is enough fuel in it all to burn deep into the discursive mind and the discursiveness needs to be burned. It is part of the relative process as the gradual road back to one's source. This is the slow procedure of gradually enlightening oneself. Eventually one is going to realise that the brilliant white light as the flying saucer, or in whatever shape it appears, is a reflection of 'I', in the universality of all that 'I' am.

Mind can be taken as a product of matter but matter is also a product of mind. This is not new for, indeed, many of the great gnostics would have already reminded us of this. Human consciousness is pure consciousness being reflected through the mind and matter of the self and casting its shadows into existence. The scientific mind sets about perfecting these shadows by using its human intelligence. While great feats of discovery may appear to have been achieved within the limitations of this human intelligence still little or nothing is known of the *absolute reality*. The reason for this is due to the fact that the *absolute* is the light of pure consciousness shining out through the 'I', whereas, human intelligence is the self of mind and matter creating the shadows that appear as existence.

When human consciousness turns towards the light then it starts to dissolve. In the course of this dissolution the self passes through the self as it passes through the subconscious and it becomes finer and finer until it eventually passes through the infinitesimal point of eternity. But the mind cannot take part, for the mind's relative existence is focused on the shadows.

Shadows can only travel out from the light and never towards the light. The mind is gazumped so we can leave it with the paradox of the needle passing in through the eye of itself. All that is mind must be let go. Stillness is the only way. When the statelessness of no-mind is realised then all is immediate according to one's lights.

The end is the beginning. One is a constellation within a constellation. Everything that is seen by human intelligence in outer space as one views it, and even within one's conceptualization of outer space, is all within one's first constellation. The next dilemma about to confront the human mind evolving through matter is the discovery of an actual boundary to outer space as currently perceived, if it has not already been discovered. This is the larger limitation surrounding the immediate limits we have currently placed on our minds. It is not too unlike the rippling circles going out from the stone from where it enters the still waters as the first disturbance geometrically travelling outwards.

When one is to transcend this outer limitation it can only occur through all of one's immediate constellation simultaneously transcending as the understanding of this takes root in one's mind. This brings the next awakening phase into the turgidity of human consciousness pulsing its way through the technological discoveries that are slowly dissolving one's apparitional walls of ignorance. This is the scientific journey of the western world unveiling the mystical message to be found in the scriptures and the wisdom of the ancients that is already within the minutest part of one's make-up. But it is still unknown when one has not discovered the key to unlock the secrets of the universal laws governing the entire creation.

One creates one's own limitations through one's attachments to the world of partial knowledge that is one's acquired nature, thus one is being continuously driven out into time. But when one actually awakens to the utter reality, when one is looking back in through matter, in *being* what one is, then one is re-entering one's true realm, behind matter so to speak, and here is discovered the gateway to transcending this first constellation. This transcendental occurrence is neither of mind nor of matter. Indeed, matter and the unflowering mind are always within the limitations of one's consciousness in which one is being endlessly placed by the ignorance pertaining to oneself.

When each new vision as knowledge is flashed through the intellect and it takes root in one's understanding then the previous ignorance immediately relating to this new flash of awareness is dissolved. This is the actual occurrence, for understanding is the food of consciousness within one's relative mind. New understanding is ignorance dissolving and one gradually comes to realise that this realm of matter that one is endlessly re-creating and placing at the other side of one's eyes is merely being re-created from shadows. This is the mistaken reality which one is placing outside of oneself.

When this new realisation takes root in one's understanding then one enters the next realm relative to outer space and a new system of journeying presents itself to human consciousness. The seeds of this are already being sown through the scientific discoveries that are taking one through the apparent shell after shell of the self. These are the gateways of the unknown unfolding through the evolving scientific as one passes through the variances of self-realisation.

Gradually one discovers through clearer understanding that none of these shadows are the shadow of truth as one comes closer to the light. Suddenly, the passing through is imminent where it is realised that there is nothing other than 'I', the 'I' at the point of existence where everything perceived instantaneously has its beginning and ending.

When the outer explosion and the inner implosion happens simultaneously, when the outer world is shattered and the inner psychological is forever gone, then realisation in its fullness occurs. This is the transcendental consciousness to the next constellation arising. But the explosion and implosion rarely occurs simultaneously, for when scientific discoveries cause a shattering effect on the societal, belief structures a psychological vacuum is produced that causes not an implosion but further imbalance.

This effect arises because western humanity did not take occasion to develop its spiritual side to co-ordinate with the western, scientific mind. This mind has left itself with no other communion other than its perceptions through its base as matter. The parallel occurrence of human endeavour via the gateway experienced by the relatively few mystics among us has all but gone unnoticed for such could not be scientifically valued. These are also Ufos to the scientist, in a manner of speaking, for they are not part of the scientist's rational intelligence.

One in the West pertains to the form in matter so it is only through bringing all of this knowledge to the outer boundary can one be enabled to crack through the shell of oneself. This is how one evolves as the western voyager towards one's own awakening. The imminent dilemma about to be presented is the discovery that all the constellations in outer space are within the shell of this one large constellation, that is in fact only the first constellation in the current understanding of the scientific mind. This new dawning happens when the knowledge of the existence of this ultimate, outer boundary of space is reached through scientific exploration. This is the actuality of the scientific realm reaching the end of its current shadow. Nonetheless, it is all in appearance.

Matter is of one mass that is dissected by the mind into myriad forms. All forms of matter consists of similar constellations of components. Be it the minutest particle of matter or that of a planet, such as the one on which we exist, or the entire universal matter of constellations that arises from mind of projection, matter is matter, no matter what. In one's mission of scientific discovery towards outer space it is in fact a journey of discovery into this matter of oneself. Let me explain.

The clay is matter, is it not? We take the clay through a process of spinning and shape it into a form that we call a cup. The clay has been changed from its previous form but it remains as clay, nonetheless. In the process of the creation of the cup the mind has entered into the matter perceived at the time as clay. Let us hold with this for the moment, for we have not realised through this hypothesis that the clay in its apparently original form is also but a creation of mind. Yet, we can acknowledge at this level that the human mind is the creator of the cup.

If we rapidly proceed from here we can acknowledge that all objects of matter, such as biomaterial is entering this creation through the human accumulative mind pertaining to the study of matter. This is the mind's endeavour for the ultimate knowledge of itself and this is the scientific journey through matter that has to take place in order to discover its truth. The mind obliges itself to come to its end.

When this scientific breakthrough inevitably takes place then the end and the beginning will be ultimately seen as the one. At that place in time, for all that is being said is still in its realm, at that place in time the realisation will occur that matter, being a product of mind, must instantly cease from being the manner it has been conceived. At that chronological moment, which actually is the moment of *now*, all knowledge being instantaneous in the absolute realm implodes this relative world of 'becoming'.

It is so one exits from matter into what can only be verbalised as the void when the knowledge of the limitation of all the stellar constellations will have been scientifically confirmed and will thus have raised one's level of consciousness through understanding on this particular route undertaken by the western, scientific

228

mind. This void is the absolute emptiness, an emptiness that is free from all connotations. Being absolutely empty it consists of all, even the limited mind that exists therein. This void is potently pregnant and limitless. It is timelessness.

But let us go back to the surface of the conceptual self, out into the mind with its turgidly slow, dissolving perimeters. From this surface of the self there are the few with extra sensory perception who are experiencing what can only be termed for the moment as Ufos when the knowledge of such objects has not yet been transmitted to one's level of consciousness through one's understanding at this particular point in chronological time.

But the void pertaining to the timelessness of all that one is holds that whatever be partaken in time, whatever is future as whatever is past, must already be contained in the timeless. Even the word containment is too narrow for that which is behind mind is also beyond word. It can only be entered through understanding, refining one's consciousness in the stillness of *being*, when there is absolute silence within.

Let us continue through observation as best can be continued in word while we set about unravelling the self from its own confinements. We need to realise that point of placelessness and timelessness beyond all our self-imposed limitations. Let us for the moment be free of all mental activity so we can enter that state of uniting with the ceaselessness of whatever it is that rests in the stillness at the core of who or what is doing the observing.

In order to make this a possibility one needs to hypothetically assume a point in the timeless as a hook for the mind. In truth that point is the *now*. From this point one is entering through immediate experience every moment in time that is past and one is also entering every moment in time that is future. We have already acknowledged that timelessness in order to be timeless would have to contain all one's mental concepts of time through extension of what is being said. So all that one mentally perceives to be past or future is right here at this point in the timeless that is this moment of *now*.

We must at this point acknowledge that we cannot proceed any further than this as a theoretical exercise lest we slip back into conceptualization and back into the state we are endeavouring to transcend. First-hand knowledge, that is beyond the theoretical, can only occur through experience. Therefore, what is being said can only enter the consciousness of mind by the experiencing of the timeless through the point in the void that is in the moment of *now*.

This is the point where all scientific intellectuality must be willingly and unconditionally let go, for the cup of the mind must be totally empty and sparkingly clear for the future as past to appear. This is the threshold of the dawning about to take place in the scientific evolution of knowledge unfolding. It is the unprecedented shift in consciousness that the world is bringing upon itself, this world of matter pertaining to matter, as it is evolving through the core of its ignorance to come to its inevitable end.

First-hand knowledge comes at one in waves from the depths of one's being, of all that has been and can be, through the cosmic super-consciousness in the infinitesimal *now*, this hook in timelessness immediate.

These waves entering the point as apparitions, or Ufos, eventually pass through one's consciousness through clearer understanding as one comes closer to the home of oneself. One in the future as one in the past can only be in sensory existence as experienced through the matter of oneself in this moment to moment of *now*.

This is a matter of fact, is it not? But do not believe me, for there is no truth in believing. The truth can only be known in the moment, as the manifestation occurs. The beginning is in the ending. Past is future as future is past. There is but one 'I' as observer observing the observed. This is the trilogy through which the unidentified flying objects seem to appear when I as the self objectify the universal 'I' through my own reflection in matter. Therefore, before I can understand the truth of Ufos entering time from the timeless I must first realise the 'I' in this body right now. I must first realise the timelessness of who 'I' am. Then the clairvoyance is immediate. We will leave it at that.

The chief with his newly-found bullock-cart held all his new knowledge to himself. It was his security for sustaining his power. He used it only on the festive occasions when its impact had most effect. Of course, he had no idea about the fuel situation, the energy required and the energy being used, nor did he care about such matters. His profit was immediately at hand in his new-found, power machine and this was his only interest. Today's festivity of man is rather similar as he sucks at the limited supply of fossil fuels from the great mother earth. Nothing has changed, apart from the costumes!

The heads and their subjects from the adjoining territories were now paying homage to our primitive man. They came with their armfuls of gifts as he sold them his blessings and his accumulating wealth piled higher and higher on old wealth fermenting. Everyone wished for a piece of the action. Women clamoured to join the melee as they set about out-performing the warrior men who were now becoming grossly weighed down by their excessive obesity. Mayhem ensued with the foetus being tossed from the womb. Soon, all were grabbing a share of the swelling pie as the rot took hold at the base. The accumulating matter could not be consumed, seeing that satisfaction through the belly's consumption is painfully limited.

The chief assumed that he had it all reasoned out. It was his privilege, his knowledge to dissect in accord with his own understanding. He had been given the keys to the kingdom. Now he made the rules and his subjects were obliged to honour and obey. Whatever he wished for himself or his clan he immediately received from the neighbouring tribes. It had to be so, for he had the honoured position of being the only possessor of a godly bullock-cart in all of their world. And he was the only possessor of the knowledge. Of course, the brain-bashed mechanic was totally forgotten!

Can we criticise? Can we judge and condemn? We use our knowledge to serve our desires. Don't tell me it's different. This is our acquired nature and our energy is being used for supporting our ignorance. Is this not our world as we scoff at the notion of Ufos, or anything unfitting to our limited perceptions?

Then a pilot happened by, riding on a donkey and carrying his spare container of gasoline that he had rescued from his own little plane that crash-landed and sunk in a lake some miles from the tribal village. He wished for a miracle and a miracle he suddenly received. He could hardly believe his eyes when he discovered the old, war relic just sitting there waiting for some pilot to come to its rescue. Quietly, he topped up the tank of his new discovery, started the engine and edged the plane out into a clearing. The chief hearing the noise jumped out of his deepest sleep and calling to his tribe they gave chase behind him of foot.

They ran and they ran like they had never run before, but their bullock-cart kept gathering speed, until eventually it seemed to take off the ground, and to their dismay, it kept rising and rising out over the trees, out over the mountains, and finally disappearing in through a dot in the sky to another dimension somewhere beyond their limited minds.

The chief kept running and running, his mystery gone and now he is running for dear life itself! With all of his new-found pomp and ceremony he had all of them fooled. He had the power, for it was his 'chiefmobile', for his use only, until it seemed to return on its own accord to the gods in the heavens. But now his weakness is exposed to the others who are right on his heels. Should he stop for one moment he will have to face the truth of himself.

This truth, alas! is instant death. And here you are, his Ufo looking on! With all our science we are much smarter now.

This could never happen to me. Really? Someone needs to wake up!

A dazzling light
Solidifying into time
Into matter.

Aliens?

Mind is the alien
It alienates Oneself.

CHAPTER 10

Self Realisation! So What!

"The self is the eternal witness, self-luminous, distinct from the physical and astral bodies, just as fire that burns and gives light is separate from the wood." Srimad Bhagavatam, XI, 5.

I had occasion to attend a lecture given by one who was aspiring to wisdom through the study of eastern philosophies. The speaker was a highly educated man of the West. He convincingly stated that he has never personally seen or met anyone who is self-realised. He made it as a statement of fact as he spoke from his appointed seat of authority on such matters. Indeed, he had studied the Bhagavad Gita, the tales from the Srimad Bhagavatam, Vedanta that is the metaphysical nature of the Upanishads and other books pertaining to wisdom in complementary tune to his own Christian base.

He seemed fully familiar with the Four Noble Truths and the Eightfold Path of Buddhism. Its Harmonies and Principles he had deliberated in depth. The Pillars of Islam were his to command. The Qur'an had unfolded its mystery to him in a way still unknown to its millions of followers, as so he ascertained. His life was in strict accord, meditating twice daily, adhering to the notion of *sat chit ananda,* that translates from Sanskrit to English as *being consciousness bliss.* These were the ingredients of his newly mixed pie.

This philosopher had it all worked out. This was his world, his established domain. He had, indeed, become an authority on the recipe. The subtlest dancing of man's acquired nature could not be more elegant. He was not to be challenged on anything he said for he had all the right answers stored in his memory and he knew that he knew from where he could intellectually see. This was the theosophical mind of this man performing its captivating dance before me with the greatest of agility, the greatest of ease.

This philosopher had become established rock solid in the truth, his truth as a western seeker, and he was not going to be shaken from this. When a listener asked if he had met anyone who is self-realised the notions this philosopher portrayed seemed to indicate that all the self-realised have been and are dead. The man convincingly knew as he gazed from the platform he had now chosen to seat himself rigidly upon. This was his rostrum, his place of current indulgence for his own acquired nature. He seemed to be firmly established in his own security from all the knowledge he had attained from his years of intensive study and then this knowledge being selectively applied in accord with his own conditioning. His audience were swallowed by this as they listened in awe to his words.

But such an encounter makes me feel a little mischievous, for ignorance is here to be challenged. The chief of the primitive tribe seems to be still running for his life as he agilely ducks in and ducks out of time! He could be forgiven for mistaking the aeroplane for a bullock-cart but could he be forgiven for using his new-found knowledge for his own, personal advantage? This ignorance is the crime he has been committing against himself. But, who is there to judge or to be judged? This philosophical platform of knowledge appears to be so convincingly real that it could not possibly be mistaken for another bullock-cart! Or, could it?

When a question arose relating to fear, the philosopher's vulnerability was there in his closest attachment. Between the lines of all that he said I listened to his most immediate fear of losing the love of his wife. Books of knowledge can burn very well but they will not show man how he is failing his woman. Only woman can impart such wisdom to him.

Woman is God, the only God there can be to man, as man is to woman. This is the way it is in existence and I dare not oppose, for opposing the universal law is not alone futile, it is nothing but ignorance. Still, man takes it unto himself and he philosophises love out of existence. Then he wonders in dismay why his wife has stopped loving him!

Man struggles to satisfy his own acquired nature under the shadows of such. Indeed, this man has come to acknowledge in himself that the personality of all that he has become can never, by its very nature, become self-realised. Perhaps, there is a deep realisation in this, even if it is not being openly expressed.

Socrates claimed that he knew nothing while others looked upon him as being the wisest of all. Apparently, he had realised that all knowledge claimed is only that of humanity's acquired nature and such is destined for hell that is but one's own immediate creation. This, the philosopher inwardly accepts, on this he is clear as he faces his own inner conflict between the philosopher and lover within, his intellectual mind being a front for his fears. The biggest of these is the raw, nauseating fear he is now being obliged to face, for all the knowledge and all the religiosity of the world cannot save him from the reality of life.

However, his philosophical nature has succeeded in carrying him unchallenged this far. Someone somewhere, perhaps his wife, had flashed him a light that sparked him off on his journey to seek out the meaning and purpose of life. But now, alas! his own research has become his devotion, his replacement and his current attachment. This again is the man's acquired nature still putting itself first as the impostor self-seeking its own continuity.

The philosopher of eloquence shone to his captive audience, while behind the closed doors of himself he had lost the love that he needs from woman. Nonetheless, while all of us come and go in life's never-ending flow, love is forever present.

When self-realisation is conceived as a grandiose, godly state, then the anguishing self is in terrible plight trying to bridge the distance created. But in reality, it is nothing more than the realisation of one's own appalling condition, for only then can it truly be dropped, only then can it be truly let go. Oddly enough, it is *love* that remains. This is not love for someone or from someone but actual *love* that stands on its own.

While fear lingers in the heart then *love* is not realised. God realisation is the realisation of *love.* This is the universality of one's radiant presence. Should the philosopher live for a billion years in service to his acquired nature he will still be unable to touch the philosopher's stone. When man totally surrenders himself to life, when he is freed in his heart from personal need for emotional love, then he is likely to realise that he *is* love in itself and not only his spouse but everyone in his presence can share in the joy. Woman cannot be fooled. She can *feel* the presence of man's hidden claw in intellectual or holy disguise.

This man is quite right in what he says. To him there cannot be any self-realised beings on the face of the earth, for accepting this would give it reality and then he would be obliged to face the truth of himself. While he wastes his energy supporting his denial it is not possible for him to see anything beyond his own limitations. Through the polished subtlety of his acquired nature he is being denied the opening of his own inner eye. All the accumulative books of wisdom in this world can be of no real assistance to him. The books of wisdom are meant to ignite the fire within, but the philosopher prohibits the fire. Self-realisation? Perhaps, all he really needs to do is to honestly inquire from his wife as to how he is failing to *be* love in her life.

It is the calamity of all humankind. Not alone do we live in denial, but we group together and form an intellectual society to support our mendacity. Then society protects itself from the truth as it forms a hard crust of rigidity over the macro-denial of the grouped, personal expression. These rigid structures refuse to give way to the new. They only reluctantly bend towards gradual change when they become chronically exposed to the light. This seems to be the way of things where it takes a massive shift in consciousness to break this dead man's grip hanging on for dear life through personal attachments.

But a shift in consciousness draws up the fears of the masses when old belief systems supporting the values and norms of society come under serious threat. This results in reshaping the situation where the societal institutions realign the old structures with the incoming new to refill the vacuum being created. It is so that the acquired nature of the personal self survives the transition. The blasphemy of the entire situation is when the rigid self not only sticks solid to its old beliefs realigned to the new but then sets out to impose them on others in an air of self-assumed, intellectual authority. This is how the stagnation re-roots and so perpetuating the damnation of humankind. Ignorance prevails where, again, the natural flow of life is being dammed. It would be better that a millstone be tied around our necks and we be cast into the depths of the sea!

But none of it is done intentionally, of course. It takes courage to ascend from the ground of our well-formulated opinions and away from our functional beliefs of temporal appeasement as we carry our clouds to a higher elevation in search of new food for our hungry minds. Such cloudy abandonment of our rigid position is like taking a leap across a deceptive ravine. The seeker with his old fermentation is quite suddenly clawing through empty handfuls of air while endeavouring to cling onto a dissolving fog that has again been mistaken for solid ground.

The mind can only perceive from within its own limitations. Should it be obliged to abandon its old familiar ground of past then it quickly restructures itself through its fears. This is the ongoing problem facing humanity in its attempts to absorb and understand the mystical new, for the new is always mystical and always being missed by a mind equating to the old.

In the midst of our notions of self-realisation we are still deluding ourselves through placing our heads in the clouds of what we convincingly believe to be the perpetual paradise. Then we fool ourselves into believing that we have discovered *ananda*, the ultimate state of bliss, while we quietly cling onto our personal attachments. We form clubs and societies of like-minded friends and we look upon our group as the good ones selected while we indiscriminately guard what we have from the rest of the world. In so serving our ignorance we foolishly consider this to be true service, until one's nearest and dearest may cause one to wonder.

Alas, when we really look closely at the western mind we can see how it subtly diverts the piercing arrow of *Vedanta* out over the edge of the cliff and back into the seas of oblivion. The western mind will accept and convert into theory, it will formulate new information into a new structural belief while it emphatically remains oblivious to the truth of its own acquired nature. Should it discard all its masks it would meet its inevitable end. But this is its subtle refusal.

Before this western mind can come to the fuller understanding of *sat chit ananda* it must first pass through the ultimate death of itself. This ultimate death is dying to all beliefs and the passing through all of one's fears. It is the actual rebirth through which arises the dawning of immortality where all self-consideration is transcended. It is only in this state that *Vedanta* can truly be known. Other than this one is merely hypothesizing through theories for the purpose of temporally appeasing one's own unacceptable denials.

The world of our acquired nature is fixated with pleasure in movement. This is the heedlessness that sustains the illusion. The shadow can never be the reality. If one has to move to give oneself bliss then it cannot be bliss, not even if such movement is in the seeking of self-realisation. Shadows are shadows. Bliss is the absence of wanting anything other than what is in the moment of *now*. For two thousand odd years the cold, hard fact of this has been buried beneath the animosity of western society, the truth having been swallowed and conveniently denied by institutionalised dogmas of societal convenience being specially designed by those wishing to retain psychological control.

As a result, the intellect of western humanity has been superimposed and is totally dependent on its body of matter, even to the extreme of wrapping itself up with the belief that the body and soul, that is mind, will re-formulate on some notional last day of judgement. This has been the western evolution of consciousness that is the sustenance of the acquired nature of the western self. The body of matter is the only host for the restless mind. So the mind defends its presence in or out of existence. It is the wilfulness that has to be faced in facing the truth.

But this is not usually the case of acceptance when the theoretical mind is confronted with the mystical. When it unexpectantly lands on a floating carpet of Sanskrit stitch it slips into an ease of aloofness by creating a rainbow jacket of eastern padding. Then, it can quite surreptitiously appear to have attained its own self-realisation as that elusive butterfly of wisdom flying over the hazy meadows of dreamland. So the clouds of illusion continue.

Quite true are the words of the good man spoken, there are no self-realised to be seen, particularly so if one be seated betwixt and between. It can, indeed, be difficult to get oneself out of this groove. Indeed, where can there be vision when we are locked in the maze of our insecure selves?

This may seem to be serious business when the word 'insecurity' is mentioned, for this may be the core of our faltering steps. When we are living in fear, however subtle it may seem to appear, then we are encaging ourselves in all these beliefs, the prison of old can only be discarded when the same prison of new takes root in the mind. So we serve the changing face of the illusion as we continue to imagine that we are keeping our feet on what we perceive to be the ground of reality. We may seem to be slowly evolving, while all that is really occurring is ignorance revolving through ignorance.

The intellect of western humanity is smudged with its conceptualizations of matter. It frantically tries to hold onto something that is perceivably concrete as it endeavours, from its level of clinging, to surround this eastern concept of *sat chit ananda*. The western mind cannot even hope to fully understand as long as the intellect is locked into serving only the acquired nature of this western expression. Nothing really can be done until it passes through the ultimate death of itself.

When this death occurs then one knows the universality in the *being* of life. This has nothing in common with the lower or higher self for the ones seeking self-realisation. As mentioned already, all self in western humanity is ignorance. Therefore if I, being this good man, cannot see anyone who is self-realised then, perhaps, there is something amiss with whatever is looking out through these eyes. Perhaps, I am still looking out through the latest opinions I am feverishly clinging onto for the security of this wretched self of myself.

I am still endeavouring to make permanently real this visualisation of myself as a higher self, while in truth there can be no higher self for me as I am, there can only be higher ignorance. Such is the play in motion. The fear of losing something, or someone, and ultimately the terrifying fear of death that western humanity sees through its partial intelligence as separate to life, all such fears prevents the western mind from acknowledging the fact that 'higher self' is nothing more than higher ignorance.

One needs to understand these notions of self being created by the mind. Such notions are only food for our acquired nature and one does not kill a monster by feeding it. There is only self, the one self-luminous witness that is one in all. Although this may be theoretically acknowledged by the western philosopher, nonetheless, it can never be known through the philosophical mind in the *being* of it. Such a mind can only philosophise about it, but it can never *be* it, for *being* is the statelessness of no-mind which is beyond the philosopher's self-imposed limitations. Notions, or concepts, are merely food for such limitations and a further extension to one's own self-denial.

To truly listen one must be still and one must relinquish trying to hear through what one already knows. When a question is posed to the philosopher the question is heard from the level of the mind and the philosopher answers the question to the mind. But this is not so with master consciousness. Wisdom hears the heart of the question and answers the heart which may or may not appear to relate to the question being posed. Wisdom immediately goes to the source of the question and in so doing brings the questioner to the source. This is what actually occurs.

The philosopher as a spectator will consider with his mind that the question is not being answered, but the one who poses the question will know that it has been fully answered. The philosopher answers the question, whereas, the one of wisdom answers the questioner. The questioner will have been taken to a depth of understanding that had never before been consciously known. The one of wisdom takes the questioner through the barriers of the discursive mind, beyond the questioner's self-imposed limitations to a deeper level of consciousness. This can instantly occur only when the questioner is fully open to the one who is self-realised.

But the philosopher hears it through the mind, he accesses it through the known and this is how he misses, this is how he can never know the meaning of self-realisation. He is trying to understand through the mind what can never be understood through the mind. It can only be interpreted through the mind according to the level of the mind. Self-realisation can only be in the statelessness of no-mind. The philosopher may seem to understand this, he may lecture on it, or hypothesize about it, but as a philosopher he can never *be* it. It cannot be *known* to him as an intrinsic part of his consciousness.

To know God is to *be* God, to live God in every aspect of one's life. This is not possible for the philosopher, he has to devise. He has to devise a god outside of himself, or within himself as a 'higher self'. The philosopher is in the mind and all mind is devised. It is not possible for the philosopher to realise his true nature. In truth one cannot realise one's true nature, one can only *be* one's true nature. The philosopher abides in the realm of the mind where he considers the truth can be realised.

The mind is the device, the devilling of the truth. This is the world that we philosophically support. The statelessness of *being* the truth is the statelessness of no-mind. This cannot be repeated enough.

We all have the seed within us. It is our great potential and our great anguish when the potential is never realised as the actual. The world of the philosopher, the world of 'becoming', even the notion of becoming self-realised, takes us the other way. The 'becoming' something or other is the mind-weed denying the actual. There is no 'becoming' to the essence of love. Still we foolishly endeavour to be loved while we unrelentingly cling onto our acquired nature. It is so how we lock ourselves outside the perennial garden of life.

The gardener is needed to nurture the seed, but the philosopher, by his very nature, can never be that gardener. We all endeavour to be philosophers in our assertions while so very few seek to be good gardeners. The seed, the potential, so seldom blooms and then when it does bloom into its fullness, into its full actuality, like Jesus bloomed, like Buddha bloomed, like Socrates bloomed, then the weeds of our acquired nature rise up again to smother it.

Jesus bloomed into the living Christ. Then the Christians arrived with their static beliefs and made a frozen decoration of him. The Buddhists believe that Gautama attained to enlightenment, whereas, Buddha *is* enlightenment, for there can be no attaining to what is always there, there is only the letting go of the clouds of one's own misconceptions, a total letting go to *be* the emptiness, the nothingness, that Buddha is. But there are Buddhists just like Christians making a veneration of stagnant notions, all of it mind-weed as support to one's acquired nature, with so very few gardeners and so many weeds.

One does not have to elaborate on what the philosophers are doing, for the philosopher is the mind-weed that prevents the actuality of *being* one's true nature. The philosopher philosophises the known and conceptualises the unknown through his fears of letting go the familiar. This is the philosophical mind as part of the evolutionary process of western thought that has been rattling along for the past two and a half thousand years in its brevity of recorded time from the schools of thinkers dissecting the world.

To mention but a few, Anaxagoras came up with the notion of mind being the force behind the creation as infinite seeds of life, all being part of an intelligent, rational order. His contemporary, Empedocles, argued that everything was composed of the four elements, fire, air, earth and water, while love and strife were the forces causing change, love bringing unity and strife calling up the force of destruction.

Then the Athenian Sophists arrived, peddling their wisdom on human rather than cosmic dissection. Protagoras is reported to have taught expediency as the way for manipulating traditional customs as he claimed that everything is relative to human subjectivity. Thrasymachus expounded that 'might is right' and many agreed as they still do today.

Socrates arrived on the scene, posing the greatest challenge to man's ignorance by claiming that he knew absolutely nothing. Then, his disciple, Plato, founded the first recorded university, and his student, Aristotle, founded the second, thus expanding the mind on multiple dissection.

Indeed, many philosophers have tried to unravel man's multiversity of ideas over this brief encounter with time, while few, if any, have touched the philosopher's stone. Most end up where they commence when failing to unravel their personal fears. The stone is the fire that is the dissolution of self and should the philosopher have the courage to touch it then he is a philosopher no more.

Such is the nature of the mind trapped in the fear of its inevitable death. Socrates had no such fear for he had discovered the deeper reality by holding to nothing. But western humanity is holding to something and fear is the bondage. This fear prevents the philosopher from attaining to self-realisation. Indeed, how can one attain to what one already is, except the realisation of knowing it!

We need to be brave to face into this fear, this fear of the truth to the inevitable death of the conceptual mind. Should we face into this fear and pass through this wall, then, perhaps, the dawning may have clearing to arise that everyone about one is self-realised, even if there are but the exceptional few, by the furnace of hell having so passed through to this understanding.

Self is ignorance
Ignoring the ever-real wholeness
Self-realisation is the realisation of this
It is nothing more
Nothing less.

CHAPTER 11

Who Or What Is Really In Charge?

Look at the body, not its outer reflection, for the outer reflection is in continual change, but look from deep, deep within, as deep as you can go. Look out at your body from the deepest, deepest inside of yourself looking out. Do it in an empty room where there are no outer distractions. Forget your outer image, put it completely out of your mind. Look at the palms of your hands. Look from the inside. Now close your eyelids, gently. Stay looking from the inside. Listen to the silence, the awesome silence within you, the stillness, absolute stillness, feel it, *be* it. It is here, forever here, directly beneath your surface expression.

Then noise, clattering noise! What is it? Suddenly you are aware of a thought having entered your mind. Let go of the thought, do not entertain it, let it go, immediately, once your awareness comes on it. Another thought arises. Let it go. Stay with the awareness. Tiredness overtakes you. Stay with the awareness, being aware of the tiredness for as long as you can hold. Do not be concerned. Rest for a while in whatever manner the body and mind has grown accustomed to resting. Then do it again as often and for as long as you can sustain without forcing. Build an ongoing relationship with it, wherever you are, whatever you happen to be doing. Allow yourself to fall into the stillness, even for a moment, when your body is in the midst of furious activity. Put no time on it, nor condition, nor expectation. Connect to it, *be* it, just for the moment whenever and wherever it enters your awareness.

This is not a meditation exercise. Meditation is most helpful in bringing temporary ease to the mind, in creating the inner space for greater insights to occur. But it can become as a drug, a daily fix for one's living disturbance.

I have sat in meditation with people who have been meditating on a regular basis for over twenty years and still many are unaware of the stillness. This stillness I speak of is not the applied stillness during meditation, rather it is the stillness in the midst of action that is always present but seldom known because one's awareness of it is absent. It is the stillness of no-mind where the speed of consciousness is so phenomenal that it is beyond all imagination, where all beginnings and endings are instantly seen and instantly known as one and the same.

Thoughts create a racket. This is a fact. Should one *be* the stillness of no-mind then one can know the cumbersome weight of even the gentlest thought. The coarseness of the vibrating sound can be almost unbearable. Even the thinking process of others around one are audible to the super-conscious mind through the vibrations grating the thought-waves of one's immediate space.

Thoughts are merely thoughts playing through the minds of each person, like millions of worms wriggling and twisting. Still, there are so many foolishly believing their thoughts to be personal when failing to understand that everything personal is but a momentary occurrence simultaneously happening to billions of personal minds.

My own awareness was first activated to this when I had the privilege to be in the presence of a spiritual master who was already resonating the inner stillness. I had suffered enough at the time, I was adequately numbed into silence and I had sufficiently died to myself for the vibrations of my being to be synchronized with his. It came out from inner space to meet me, from the inner space that is deep, deep within the 'I'. The vibrations coming through his presence were much finer and much faster than mine but an instant arose where they slowed down sufficiently for me to connect. Then having connected I irreversibly and irrevocably passed through. It was immediate and sudden. This is the realisation of immortality.

It is the meaning, the only meaning to me, of being in the world but not of the world. It is the great aloneness when one suddenly transcends to this finer state of resonance, but it is an aloneness that is pregnant with everything, for it is beyond all thought, all relativity, all restriction, it encompasses all. This was my experience of *being* the inner light as it occurred according to the circumstances of my life at that particular time. But each one's way is unique to one's own situation. It is your journey, your discovery according to what is right for you.

Consciousness is always relative to motion, physical and spiritual, and it can only be at the point of existence where spirit and matter entwine, as in one's body. Spirit and matter are one's changing nature, but transcendental consciousness is beyond spirit and matter, it is changelessness. Everyone lives according to one's lights and the variance as to the levels of consciousness in existence is enormous, but the transcendental realisation is always the same. What is permanent and changeless is beyond all the variances of consciousness.

Lydia, a rare and adventurous woman of Tibetan influence, keenly illustrated through her special gift that the entire creation is a manifestation through sound. When I was invited to be in her presence for a workshop weekend in the Wicklow mountains, she eagerly demonstrated the unifying consonance in matter, energy and light through the natural magnificence of her own vocal cords. The colours of the spectrum resonated through the vibrant in the inner depth of her voice aligning to the group energetic. When she entered the finer realms then all colour and sound seemed to resonate a deep silence through a shimmering whiteness. Most of the group were overcome by sleep, but the few who could still listen momentarily experienced a partial transcendence.

It is understandable why most fell into deep sleep. The whiteness, or nothingness, is the changelessness behind consciousness. When such an experience is being induced to one who is still bound by one's acquired nature then the mind immediately blanks out. It cannot tolerate, it cannot accept, for one cannot transcend through the mind.

One's body and mind are merely a movement in consciousness. Before one can transcend to the birthless and deathless state one must first die to the notion of personal self. When one is the impartial witness, only then can one withdraw beyond consciousness where there is no self in any physical or spiritual form whatsoever. This is *being* the statelessness of no-mind.

Lydia opened a channel leading to the point of transcendence. Such a privilege is a preview of what is immediately beyond. But it must not be taken lightly, for if one is not ready to relinquish one's acquired nature then such an experience can be quite devastating. Quite often madness ensues should something is forced to happen before its time.

When one has a special talent then one has a greater responsibility to the ones not knowing. Everything should happen in accord with the universal order and one must first be in the state of equilibrium before entering the finer realms. There are so many great wonders totally unnoticed and, indeed, impossible to see through the thought-infested mind that one foolishly serves, thus wasting the energy required for transcending the personal self.

When one's acquired nature forcefully takes access to the finer realms, then harmful distortions can occur, not only to oneself, but to others who may be innocently participating. The hidden tendencies of the personality become heinously excessive and the inner beauty becomes grossly distorted. This is the darkness usually surrounding the inner light. In one's own occurrence it is experienced as the guardian of the threshold, one's guardian within, not guarding oneself against danger but guarding the finer realms from one's acquired nature, this being the natural law. There is no passage through and there can be no passage through for the acquired nature of the self, nor can there be salvation for its imaginary soul. It must be dissolved, totally dissolved. There is no other way.

The acquired nature in a group expression forces itself upon the light as it wilfully endeavours to possess it for itself. This, of course, is an utter impossibility. It is like trying to catch hold of one's shadow. But the vitality of the light-bearer can be sucked to extinction in the process and usually by the ones in closest proximity. Black magic, white magic, the sinister one disguised as friend always lurks in the shadows. It all may sound strange, but it is not possible to explain colour to someone who never had sight. Our acquired nature is permanently blind. The message to be heeded is to walk away, do not look back, leave the darkness behind.

Who or what is in charge?

The witness deep within is always alone. That is how it always is. One enters life alone, one dies alone and each one is one's own witness in the river of life should one have the privilege of knowing it. We are all on a journey down-river. Time is the breeze.

The boat is the personal self starting afresh in the wind and finding its course in the flow, passing through rapids, still waters, relative peace, then rapids again, until its final encounter when it gives itself up through a sudden mishap or body wrinkled and worn with age.

The lone witness silently observes the relative world cascading along through its shadows of countless bodies coming and going with each one clinging for a fleeting instant, desperately trying to work it all out, desperately trying for personal continuity. But there can be no personal continuity, for everything personal dies. Logically, one is conscious of this. But, when one's consciousness is the object of observation rather than the subject observing then the realisation of one's true nature is possible.

All whom the witness encounters in the swift enactment upon the misty waters of time only have existence relative to the one perceiving on one's special voyage through this narrow passage. Should one lose contact with the witness then one loses his or her bearings before it is known who he or she is and the world about one falls into disorder. The boat overturns and gives itself up to the river. One becomes swallowed in darkness when starting all over again in another boat, another time with other faces, other problems arising to a personal self, yet all as the one enactment.

Again and again one is ensnared in events forever overtaking oneself, like the ball of accumulative past growing larger and larger cascading along and swelling the river of time. With each one it is a personal issue, some dark secret hidden. Every issue is relative no matter how frightful it seems, even causing the death of another, be it lover, spouse or one inflicting terror, it is all but partial truth as one battles with images of oneself when seeing all others as separate. This is the relative reality one believes to be all that there is when one is outside of oneself.

The battle of partial truths continues as man's inhumanity to man, like the lone lunatic battling with himself or herself while travelling alone in the only boat apparent among endless boats on the river. The inevitable journey's end is the open sea where the waters of all the rivers blend, but only to be spewed up again on this never-ending cycle as the sea becomes turbulent with the ghosts of the dead being tossed upon it. The dark, hidden secrets cry out in utter lament to be again re-addressed and again re-consumed. So it is destined to continue for as long as woman and man foolishly live in appeasement to shadows.

We have only one shot at freedom from the inner hell and that shot is this moment right *now*. This is the moment of release to the one who takes courage. What use can it be this denial while living in the fear of losing the love of one's dear ones, or the fear of losing one's societal face? Why are we so insecure? Why must we waste the great beauty in *being* life as we waste our sweet energies hiding ourselves from ourselves? What waste, what energy spilled when guarding these secret closets!

What freedom, release! When all one's closets are opened and no dark secrets left lurking within then one's authority is clear and one's integrity cannot be compromised. This is the freedom that is mine and yours when we let all of it go. This letting go is the releasing of oneself from the particular personality one had grown to support, be it good or not good, whatever that personality might try to impart. It is this personality, this bodyless entity, that is the free-rider making an over-laden donkey out of one's true essence. This is one's shadow, one's pain, this is one's anguish eating away at one's vitality.

This entity is one's acquired nature that the person is being societally conditioned to support, for society is merely the immediate reflection of the self. This self even projects beyond death with its conceptual soul being presumed by the conditional mind to have a continuity in some convenient heaven, or in some other life-form hereafter, in accordance with one's particular beliefs. It is self fooling self. Religious institutions exist in abundance to support such conditioning for this self-perpetuating ignorance as the souls of the dead being re-churned and re-churned.

As one breaks free from the conditioning then the density of ignorance is lessened. This is not a worldly freedom I speak of, for that is merely more wasted space. It is the freedom realised through a shift in consciousness. It is not intellectual discovery or mind-weed as such, for the mind is merely the modem through which pure consciousness can shine into existence. Insights occur through the still mind, whereas, the conditioned mind is the mind-weed that distorts consciousness to the level of its own mind-perceptions and such is one's intellectuality. Human intelligence is this distortion.

The social order is at the level of the conditional, for its structures are based on the accumulative past where rules and regulations pertain to a static idiom. This is our conflict. The struggling order of society is static while the natural order of the creation is continuous change. This is the blindness of humankind in endless discord. Therefore, the process of transcending societal ignorance in the consciousness of one's body is exceedingly slow.

Transcendental consciousness cannot be achieved through intellectual discourse, for such intellectualism is the accumulating mind-weed of the acquired nature of the self. This intellectual pursuit is merely an intensification in the polishing of the ignorance that reflects from the surface of the worldly as tinsel sophistication. This glittering reflection is an adulteration of truth and only leads to blinding one further in serving the static, societal idiom, thus perpetuating one's lack of true understanding. It is so one continues to miss one's true nature that cannot be seen, or understood, through such intellectual blindness.

Nonetheless, intellectual discourse is functional in the realm of scientific research and it certainly has value in devising means for one's creature comforts. Even when it is turned inward through the philosophical veins it has function in deriving the levels of societal ignorance, ignorance meaning the 'ignoring' of the fuller story. But before the intellectual mind can positively function in the field of inner inquiry it must first realise its own restrictions relative to its own conditioning.

Reason has been recognised by philosophers as the instrument of clear intellect and clear intellect is a pre-requisite for inner inquiry. Still, the age of reason came and went without humankind getting any wiser and in all probability going further away from the truth when one looks at the resulting catastrophic wars that engulfed this 'reasonable' world.

In any given situation one does not have to probe very deep to discover violence, even in the most holy it is close to the surface. Should one be bound to a religious persuasion of any kind whatsoever, then one is conditioned through its particular beliefs. Whatever one finds through intellectual discourse will be interpreted through this distortion. This is how ignorance sustains its continuity. One must acknowledge this as the first realisation and this takes extraordinary courage, for one is then obliged to step out of the masses.

Reason is distorted by the mind in accordance with its conditioning. Therefore, a journey of negation is necessary to attain to the state of clear intellect. One must step out of the norm, to take up the helm for oneself. One must be one's own helmsman lightening one's load. This is the letting go of all one's programming, of all one's static, societal beliefs. It is the only way possible to freedom. Through negation as such one pertains to the state of transcendental consciousness. Only then can one realise the true, undivided, cosmic nature of oneself.

I can speak of this state from my own experience in this body and it cannot be known to you by me or anyone telling it, it can only be known to you by you *being* it. But how does one know if one is it? There is nothing anyone can tell you or no way anyone can help you other than reflecting what is already yours within you. This I discovered several years ago when I openly sat in the presence of a spiritual master. Transcendental consciousness leaves no hidden secrets unexposed. I knew then that everything hidden through the acquired nature of my personal self was about to be flushed to the surface.

The master was the helmsman whom I, in myself, had allowed to come up before me. He was the first one I had encountered in the flesh in this life. I had the choice of staying or leaving. I chose to stay and I stepped onto his boat, for I had reached that state of dying to all I had become in my own personal world of 'becoming'. There I remained with him as we passed through the turbulent waters and jagged rocks of the inner dominion. Those jagged rocks tore away the skin, the flesh, the muscles and sinews of all the acquired nature of this personal self until I was eventually left with nothing as nothing. Then I was impartially tossed overboard. It was done, sweet freedom attained.

One cannot be released until the master releases. When this occurs then it is known to oneself that one is one's own master, one's own helmsman, sharper than the point of a spear. Then every other master, living and dead, dissolves into the nothingness, for their play is only pertinent to that part of consciousness relative to the acquired nature of the self. As the acquired nature fully dissolves so the master, that is the oneself, is fully realised as *being* all in one.

In transcendental consciousness, cosmic, or God consciousness, there is no acquired nature, there is no personal self. When one *is* this state then there are no secrets within or without. All secrets are spontaneously exposed, even the spiritual master's who came before me cloaking his secrets in what he expressed as the sacred while secretly partaking of the sacred flesh. A guru, or master, is no more than a crystal-clear mirror. He was positioned as thus for my release. It had to be so, for 'I' called him up as part of the worldly deception. This is the 'I', the one universal 'I', within me, within you, as the on-going play of existence.

The master imparts, the disciple imbibes. The master comes from inner space. He or she is centred and totally integrated. He or she is as one with the totality. The situation of one's life is one's teacher and the teacher knows about God, but the master knows God in the *being* of God. When one knows, then the knower and the known are one. Knowledge can be learned, *being* cannot be learned. When the dancer knows the dance then the dancer and the dance are one. Knowledge can never know the dance in the *being* of the dance. Even if one should dissect the dancer, as the mind dissects, still one will never discover the dance.

The philosopher dissects and examines. As such he or she can never know God in the *being* of God. The personality, the ego, prohibits. But the personality dissolves in the presence of the master, and the *being*, the essence, remains. This is the great tribulation, the great fear for the ego-oriented mind, and the great joy, the great exaltation, the coming home of one's essence. If it is not a part of one's experience then one can hear only words. But the words repeated over and over again will bring about the earnestness for the circumstances to allow it to happen. Nothing must be discarded as all is one with the whole.

This is the way it occurred in my experience, totally unexpected, for I had no idea before it occurred. Then, in passing through the master who is seated before me I am passing through the shadow of self. This is my death, the death of all which I have become in my world of 'becoming'. It is the transcendence from my acquired nature, the transcendence from the hell of my own creation. It is passing through the darkness of this netherworld and the realisation of God.

The Lord gave up the body to physical death thus showing us eternal life. This eternal life is as it is in this moment *now*. In existence the *now* is the eye to eternity. The inner implosion is the passing through the eye to the statelessness of immortality. This is when everything is dropped, when one allows oneself to be totally unsupported, totally undefined, unprotected, uncertain and alone. Only then can immortality be known through the *being* of oneself. Stillness is the way when one is as nothing, desiring nothing, remaining exposed and openly vulnerable to life as it happens.

Thinking? Thinking is never *being*. Good, bad or indifferent, all thinking is mind-weed. God cannot be known through the mind. But the mind can be guided. As one thinks intently, so does one become. One can rise above the tumult of the objective with a concentrated mind and then in the stillness one can rise above the subjective as well. This is the re-birth, this is the place where one enters the kingdom of God in *being* God in oneself.

But one must first die before one can be born again to enter the kingdom, so we are told by the scriptures. Where is this kingdom? Who is this God? Priests have taught us, teachers have taught us, all of it mind-weed, all of it in accordance with their particular beliefs, with their own vested interests. Their mind-god is good, never evil, so there is the necessity of a devil, for their god is a partial god and not god enough to encompass all. This is not to deny the existence of god and the devil, rather it is to know why god and the devil exists.

Such god and such devil come into existence through the mind of humankind. We are the fallen angels, we are the ones dispossessed, but we were not caste out of heaven, we were not forsaken by God, we fell from heaven ourselves. We are the wilfulness. We forsook God. It is I, as man and woman, denying all that is God, this is the devil arising. This is the creation of hell. It is immediate, it is *now*. Here it begins and ends.

One does not have to believe it. One can caste it aside if one so chooses, whether one believes it or not one will discover it all at the moment of death. This is how it is, exactly how it is. It is all in this moment of *now*. Still, one indulges the mind-weed by creating for oneself a heaven and a hell. Such cannot be God for such is division, such is the perpetuation of conflict. All must be God, all must be one, even the man-god's devil, for all is God-given. One has nothing of one's own, not even the air one breathes, not even the guts to process the waste. Life happens through one. One is but a player, no matter how one feels, how one hypothesizes, how one emotes. This is the reality.

Once we truly understand this then there are no problems left, for the ego is gone and all problems are the by-product of the ego-oriented life. When I, the person, totally hand over to God, then I disappear. This is the state of the spiritual mind, the state of no-mind, the *being* of *love*. This is the serene, the greatest beauty, where there is no division, no heaven or hell, no here as other than hereafter, where life and death are the one indivisible expression.

Truth presents itself here, in this space where the ego has dissolved with all of its problems and all of its related confusions. *"Thy will be done,"* as the greatest master has said, this is the handing over of all to the will of God. This is God's kingdom in this moment of *now*. This is it. It is as simple as this, so simple that the ego-mind can never, ever, grasp it. God cannot be sought for God is beyond all seeking. God is the seeker Itself.

The ego is consciousness being reflected through matter and the matter of mind creates the distortion. For example, when a stick is placed upright in water it appears to the eye to be bend at the spot where it enters and the end of the stick is not where it is perceived. Such is how consciousness is distorted through reflection. Likewise, the distortion of light from the sun as it passes through the stratosphere of the earth causes the sun to be seen in a place that is a phenomenal distance from where it actually is, according to our knowledge through science. This is not even taking the additional distortion of time and space into account where it takes eight minutes, so we are told, for the light of the sun to reach the naked eye of the perceiver. In like manner, the acquired nature of the self as the shadow of consciousness reflecting through matter is what we, mistakenly, take to be true.

The ego arises through pure consciousness being reflected through matter. It is the distortion perceived through the mind's interpretation of what is being spontaneously enjoyed through the senses and so the world as one knows it appears. Personification arises and instead of *being* the spontaneity of life one perceives oneself through the mind as being separate, thus imprisoning oneself in one's own innate limitations. This is how humankind gets deluded by seeking self-gratification through worldly delights, sexual desire being one of the strongest, and no matter how much one may seem to attain, still there is always an nauseousness arising within for all one is doing is chasing the shadow.

The shadow binds the ego and through the ego comes gross physical consciousness. Thus one is outside of oneself spilling the energy through matter into the shadowy illusion that is the acquired nature of humankind being superimposed on the absolute reality. This acquired nature is the madness one continuously swallows through one's ideologies, educational systems, societal structures, one's religious connotations, one's infatuations, loves, hates, wars, in short, one's darkness, one's own self-perpetuating ignorance.

The awakened one is the one who has flowered, the one who has opened through love, in *being* love as the spontaneity of life. This love is one's true, blissful and divine nature. But society, which is the distortion of consciousness, sells its continuity through fear. The priest exploits the fear by creating the dis-ease in the mind so he has a function in selling the cure. This is how organised religions work and this is how politics work, both aiding and abetting the spread of fear, for fearful people are in the need of leaders and it is the nature of priests and politicians to feast upon this, for they are in service only to the acquired nature of humanity. This is their vested interest.

Thus love is denied and fear stops one from flowering. The energy of the creation is thus turned to destruction. Within the confines of this commotion one's acquired nature deducts its notions of relative love. This is the limited understanding of relationship that is always dependent on some 'other'. It incessantly drives one out into the shadows of illusion, looking for a fix, looking for comfort that is always relative and always temporary. This is not love, it cannot be love. This is the claw of the feeling and emotional self, the distortion of the reality, for love is neither a feeling nor an emotion, love is the essence of *being* all that is life.

Two and a half thousand years ago Empedocles puzzled over this as he endeavoured to dissect the confusing plurality of things about him. He surmised that love is a force unifying unrelated elements thus formulating new creations and strife is the force of dissolution re-fragmenting the old. Here we can see the introduction of evolutionary theory to the analytical mind.

As a corollary to this Sigmund Freud elaborated on these two forces naming them Eros and Thanatos, the life instinct and the death instinct. But all of this is pertinent only to one's acquired nature. It is conflict re-germinating and it is the denial of love, a denial that continues in one form or another until an awakened one eventually appears to show the mind its folly. But such an awakened one must be silenced, must be crucified, when one's acquired nature is all that one is willing to serve. This is the human willpower where one chooses to live by one's ignorance.

The master is the awakened one, he or she is the flower which has bloomed and the fragrance permeates the entire garden. His or her mind has been totally destroyed. The destruction of mind is the non-recognition of it as being other than 'I' as the universality of all that is and is not. The disciple is the bud waiting to blossom. The grace flowing through the master is the divine grace of love.

But nothing happens before its time and when the moment is right the bud suddenly opens and a new blossoming occurs. Then the disciple is the master, is the enlightenment. This is one's true nature. One's acquired nature has to be destroyed, totally destroyed, for one to *be* this.

Even through destruction, dear Empedocles in whomever you are, where is this strife you speak of to be found in one's absolute reality when there is only love?

We experience evolutionary consciousness in the relative world arising through the distortion that is our acquired nature. Western philosophies are a corollary of this and we follow these distortions as the western, analytical mind that we faithfully serve in our notions that we are serving reality. But absolute reality speaks, telling us there is no such thing as evolution, there is no 'deja vous', for all past, all present and all future are within the embodiment of *now*.

In the *now* you realise truth, who or what you really are, you realise *love* and you see courtship for the play that it really is. In the *now* there is nothing to reincarnate. *Now* is looking, it is the perennial meditation, the perennial light shining through the darkness of all mental concepts, even the concept of soul. *Now* is freedom where the 'money-god' of the world has no dominion. *Now* is the unidentifiable that is the self-realisation of who or what is really in charge. *Now* is the door to the timeless.

I leave you in love.

Know thy Self

Ask your question

Q; *You refer to the goddess of love quite a lot. In Dance of the Goblins you speak of your experience where woman gave herself up to the goddess. Can you explain.*

A; I walk on the crust of this bounteous earth where every woman is the goddess of love. Show me the woman who has realised it and you show me the wonder of God.

*

Q; *I thought I would be free from this terrible blackness haunting my soul after confessing the wrong I have done to another. But it will not go away. It keeps coming back to haunt me. No matter what I do, I have been on pilgrimages to holy places, I do social work, I even took a course on counselling in my efforts to help others, still I feel as though I am rotting away inside. Is there any escape from this terrible hell?*

A; There is an narrative in a book from the ancient scriptures of the East called Srimad Bhagavatam. It is the story of Ambarisa. Allow me to recall it to you, if I may, for it answers your question much more impartially than I could ever hope to deliver.

Ambarisa was a monarch who loved God dearly. He reigned over a kingdom greater than the earth and everything he undertook he did as an act of divine worship. Once he made a vow to God where he put it upon himself to practice special disciplines for a period of one year and at the end of that time to spend three days fasting.

When the time had passed and he was just about to break his

fast he was visited by the sage Durvasa. The king offered courtesy and reverence to the wise and holy sage and invited him to partake in the feast having been prepared for the breaking of the fast. Durvasa gracefully accepted, but first he went to bath himself in the sacred river Kalindi and after bathing he entered deep meditation.

Much time passed and the king was anxiously waiting. The auspicious period for breaking his fast in accordance with his vow was about to expire. He did not wish to show dishonour to his guest by commencing to eat without he being present. However, he was also aware that if he did not break his fast within the pre-arranged period then the performance of his vow would be of no avail. Thus King Ambarisa made the decision to take some water, for he considered this would suffice for breaking his fast without showing dishonour to his guest as it did not consist of partaking in food.

However, when Durvasa returned and learned that the king had taken some water in his absence his feathers were ruffled. He felt that he had been insulted and in the heat of his anger he cursed the king. The curse took the shape of a demon that approached King Ambarisa to devour him. But the king remained calm, as God in his heart had rendered all fear impotent. The demon was baffled by this and it immediately turned on Durvasa in order to devour the one who had called it up.

Durvasa was obliged to flee for his life as he desperately tried to save himself from his own curse. But nowhere could he hide. No matter what he did, no matter where he went, there was no escape. Good works and kindness to others were to no avail. The demon kept bearing upon him. The greatest sages and saints on the face of the earth and perceivable heaven itself were powerless to help him. Even death could not free him.

Fear-stricken, he eventually found himself at the feet of the all-pervading Lord of the universe pleading for release from his own affliction. However, the Lord reminded Durvasa that he, too, was powerless to help him, as Durvasa had tried to inflict harm on a devotee of God and because of this, the curse must return with increased force upon the one who had called it up.

Durvasa was devastated by the terrible blackness engulfing his essence. There seemed to be no way of escape, not even through dying, and he now felt that the curse would haunt him for all eternity. Then the Lord in his kindness spoke to the integrity in Durvasa, telling him there is a way out of his eternal dilemma.

"The one and only avenue open to you is to go to the one whom you tried to inflict harm upon and beg his forgiveness. He is the only one with the power to release you", the Lord spoke thus.

Finding no other way open to him, Durvasa humbly approached King Ambarisa and begged his forgiveness. The king, being true to God in his heart, immediately forgave him for the wrong he had done and Durvasa was instantly freed

It is a beautiful story, is it not?

You are entangled in the web of your own self-deception. Firstly, you must stop blaming yourself. Contrary to what you feel, you are not alone, you are merely one of the masses pre-programmed towards such a reaction.

Please do realise that society has a vested interest in this. You are not isolated as you are imagining. It is all in accordance with your conditioning. This is not to blame society, for society is merely the collectivism of our acquired nature. We are the society being created and upheld by our personal masks, all being dishonest.

Take a pause right now from all the mind stuff going on in your head. Leave it down, just for this moment.

The release from your torment is in the story just told. Go to the one whom the infliction was aimed at, let it be known and ask his or her pardon.

Should time have passed and the inflicted party be already dead, then go to the ones most immediately effected by the wrong you feel you have done. It is quite obvious how you perceive that this might mean the collapse of your world, for the weight of your world is seen to be bearing itself on your question.

But have you not suffered the weight of it all for long enough? In your innocence you believed in the confessional of man, you thought this would pardon you, and now you have realised its impotence when faced with something as deeply real as your apparent dilemma.

Even your religious god has failed you in this, your greatest moment of need. You now know this religious god is nothing but another mask of pretension hiding the grim reality of how we condition ourselves.

The world you believed in does not measure up. Indeed, how can it measure up when it is totally false? Now you realise it when you feel yourself lost in your prison of personal guilt. But none of this guilt is you, it is not even a shadow of your true essence, the grace, the beauty of all that you truly are.

The terrible pain of your mental torture is real, but nothing is in vain, for much is being gained through these realisations. No more can you be fooled by the false once you come to acknowledge the truth of the situation immediate to your problem, accepting all as it is with all your integrity.

Be honest with yourself. Freedom comes first. Trust it completely and allow the consequences, whatever they may be, to unfold.

Demolish your fears by allowing the truth to be heard. The release from all your anguish is immediately before you by simply being true to the situation. You will be amazed. You will be utterly amazed.

*

Q; *You mention being caught in the web of a Spiritual Master. Can you please explain what you mean.*

A; When the disciple is ready the Master appears. This is a saying more ancient than the hills.

But how then, the mind will ask, does not everyone see the Master when he or she appears?

Let us take the Master Jesus, for example. His disciples cognised him, as did many others who were ready to see. But many did not. The soldiers who surrounded him and accompanied him on his way to be crucified could not see beyond his physical image. The high priests, who declared themselves to be the mediators of God on earth, could not see him. They were not ready, they had blinded themselves with their false philosophies, as do the priests of this day.

The Master is always present. He is never an item of past, as religions try to behold. However, are you present enough to receive Him? When you are ready, when it is right for you, then He is seen, immediately before you. The Master has myriad forms, many are not necessarily human.

Some time following the crucifixion of Jesus, two of his followers were walking on the road to Emmaus and Jesus joined them for much of the way. But they failed to re-cognise Him. Why? They had lost sight through their fears. Their Master had been tortured and crucified and they had been cascaded by their fears back into their minds. The mind always misinterprets. It was only when the Master sat down with them to eat and breaking the bread, then, their mental clouds disappeared. They recognised Him at once.

When you are ready and open to receive, then the Master appears. It is the greatest privilege on the face of this earth. I tell you now there is nothing greater. But you must be totally empty of yourself. You must be free to receive. You cannot be empty and open if there is anything whatsoever going on in your mind. Stillness is the only way. This is *being*, as in being the statelessness of no-mind which I refer to many times in the writings.

When you enter the gaze of the Master then you are gone. There is no return and this is what I mean when I say, being caught in the web of the Master.

You can only enter the gaze when you are clear, that is, when you have dropped everything, meaning, there is no mental activity, no beliefs, no comparisons, no expectations.

But nothing happens before its time and nothing happens when you are expecting it to happen. I had no idea whatsoever about any of this before I openly placed this self before a Spiritual Master. He challenged me directly and I immediately took up the challenge, not knowing who or what He was. It was only when I passed through the death of the self that all was instantly revealed. It was over, done, I had dissolved.

This does not necessarily mean that the Master coming through the person whom I encountered is the right situation for you. Whatever or whoever awakens you from the sleep of the living dead is the Master. Just be attentive, be aware. When the disciple is ready the Master appears.

*

Q; *You don't speak much in favour of philosophy or religion. Is there a particular reason for this?*

A; You could say I don't speak much in favour of anything that obstructs our knowledge of truth.

Philosophy is all mind stuff. It plays on dissection, even the holistic philosophies, there is you the personal self being perceived and there is the greater or higher self with the personal or little me trying its best to be the greater me. It may be all very well in its place, as the play on the stage of existence, but it does not allow the truth to be seen.

As far as religions go, they are all divisive, in one way or another they promote and sustain division. Division means conflict and conflict means strife. Reason alone is telling you this. I am not indicating that you should go about changing the world by preaching to the world to drop all philosophies and all religions. Even if you are moved to do so, then, that too is all right, for everything serves its purpose in the greater play of events. But do not be fooled into believing that yours is a special crusade, that humanity has been patiently waiting to receive you since the perceived beginning of time.

In truth, you are one with the whole, there is no division. I am merely telling you to *be* the dance of life, enjoy the dance, and allow it to be also enjoyed by you in others.

*

Q; *You say that one should never, enter compromise. Surely, this cannot be true. I mean, how could we settle our differences? How could we find a solution for ending conflict should compromise not be allowed?*

A; Compromise is a device of your acquired nature, or, should we say, a vice of your conditioning. It only has play in the world of the false. When you look at it honestly you have to admit that the truth cannot be compromised. It is an utter impossibility. It you think you can compromise the truth, or should you try to compromise the truth, then you are immediately serving the false.

Conflict arises through misinterpretation of the facts. The politics surrounding this always lends itself to bias, to your particular bias in accordance with your conditioning opposing the other's bias according to his or her conditioning.

Compromise comes into play where there is a no-win situation, that is, when it is nigh impossible for one party to get the edge on the other and neither are willing to be more holistic. This is appeasing the false where neither are willing to honestly transcend the conditioning causing the conflict to occur. In other words, compromise is another expression for postponement.

The conflict gives the opportunity to see deeper into yourself. However, by compromising the outcome you renege your responsibility to be true to the given situation. This is how you oblige yourself to remain as one of the masses, bowing to the yoke of falsehood. Saving face then becomes the play of events.

But, how many faces have you got to save? Look at it honestly please.

You have many faces, all acquired as part of your acquired nature, all serving this societal image you are trying to protect and you are spilling yourself into this falseness.

But where is your original face? Where are you in all of this? See it as it is and not how you think it is when you are only willing to look through your conditioning.

You see it as it is when you are fully willing to serve the truth, meaning that you have stopped serving yourself. This may call for extraordinary courage. But you must be courageous if you are to transcend your condition. You must be prepared to relinquish everything in service to truth.

Please do not interpret what I am saying through your mind. I am not telling you that you must be prepared to relinquish everything merely to maintain your own position because you think it is true. The opposing parties may also be convinced that they are abiding by truth. You need to clearly understand how your position initially has caused the conflict to occur.

The position you are taking relating to the conflict may be right or it may not be right, but the truth can only be revealed through the fact and the fact of the matter is that the conflict is occurring as a result of your position.

Should you honestly put your position aside and allow yourself to impartially look at the entire situation surrounding the conflict, as an act of service to truth alone, then truth can reveal itself. This calls for you to get out of the way.

Compromise is never a servant to truth, it only impedes it. Should you be brave enough to *be* the truth, to live the truth in every aspect of your life, then you will never be faced with compromise, nor will you be tempted to do so.

What I am saying may seem to be distant from you, like some unrealistic utopia, imaginable but not attainable. You may be feeling that should you be true in yourself then the world will take advantage. You feel that you are obliged to serve the false in order to survive. This is the compromise you make and it is exactly so how you imprison yourself.

Truth is freedom, absolute freedom. Look at the nature of the self, see what holds you back.

*

Q; *You speak of the soul being a figment of my mind. How can I accept this? After all is said and done I have to die and meet my maker. Do you expect me to abandon my soul for this nothing you speak of? And my child, what about him? Is everything for nothing?*

A; When you live in the mind, then everything perceived is mind. Let me explain. I see you are a young mother. Let us create a familiar situation.

Your child has gone swimming with friends. You are doing your work quite happily until you look at the clock and you suddenly realise it is time he was home. Then the mind flashes the message of the worst scenario. Your body tenses and your heart-beat speeds up. You know you are being silly but you cannot calm yourself down. No matter how much you try to reassure yourself, still the condition of anxiety continues and not only that, but it keeps getting worse.

Really, is the child to be blamed for this? Or his friends who are keeping him late? You phone the swimming pool. You are told, "Everything is okay, nobody has been drowned and the school group have all left the premises safely". Perhaps, he has been kidnapped, or run over by a bus, the mind kicks in again. You cannot find ease until he walks in the door. Then you are ready to kill him for the worry he has caused you by coming home late.

Now, let us look at the situation. The child has to account for being late but he does not have to account for your worries. They are your own responsibility. Your child is not wearing you down. You are doing it all to yourself.

So, what has this to do with your question? Well, it is answering your question, for your question is all about worry.

You think that you have a soul. What makes you think so? Have you ever really questioned the reality of this mental concoction? Have you ever questioned why you need to believe that you have a soul? Is permanence not the problem, this mental idea of lasting forever?

This is very close to your heart when you are a young mother. You love your child, but your love is tainted by your attachment. The fact of the matter is, your child is going to leave you. Not alone that, but your child is going to eventually die. But you would prefer to die first. Why? You could not suffer his loss. It would be too painful for you should he die now.

Death is inevitable. You know this, yet, you cannot honestly accept it. So what do you do? You convince yourself with your fairytales of there being some heaven in the sky, or somewhere beyond, and you feed this nonsense into the innocent mind of your child.

You are terrified of death and you go along with such illusions through your fears. You spend all your life running away from the truth, that is, from facing into your fear of death, so the concept of soul is nurtured. It is something to appease your fearful mind, while deep in your heart you know it cannot be the ultimate truth.

I am telling you to listen to your heart, not to your mind. First, look at your attachments, how they bind you. See it as it is. Love your child, but do not be attached to your child. Then your child has freedom to love you and he is no longer obliged to try and understand you as you come at him through your fears. The greatest gift you can give to your child is this freedom.

It takes great courage to face into your fears. The biggest fear is the fear of not being. The concept of soul is merely a result of this fear. It comes from your reactionary state. This causes your blindness.

When a flock of sheep are terrified by wolves they run in blindness, even over the edge of a cliff. Is this not how your mind reacts to the notion of death? I say, face into your fear. See what is driving you over the edge. Look at the mind. Impartially look. Stop allowing yourself to be carried away by this flooding of thoughts.

In other words, calm down, taste the stillness. Let go of the psychological props being fed into you by this mass hysteria. You are pure, blissful presence directly behind all of this mental disease. And so is your child. I say, *be* life, be as you truly are. Stop feeding your thoughts. Let the world of madness dissolve.

Then, in this state of simply *being* that you are, ask yourself the question. Enquire into the truth of your presence. Hear the truth behind the concept of soul. Hear it when you are listening to your heart, not your personal heart that is always attaching itself to something, but your true heart that is freedom itself. First you must allow your fears to dissolve. Then you will know the reality.

I am not asking you to believe me. That would be merely expecting you to replace one belief with another. Anything you believe in cannot be the truth. Believing you have a soul is not the truth. Neither is it true by not believing that you have a soul. You must drop all your beliefs and look at the fact.

The truth is in the fact. Life is now. Here and now you are. Any movement away from now is the mind. This is the fact of the matter.

All I am saying to you is to be still. Stillness is the way. When the mind is still then there is nothing needing to continue, nor to be continued, for all is now. Be easy with yourself. Rest in the stillness.

*

Q; *You say, there is only this 'I' of myself. That I can understand. Then you talk about everything being one, even everything being God. Does that not mean that I am God? Is this what you are trying to tell me?*

A; Your mind is not God, nor can it ever be God. The mind is the personal self trying to be God. This is the ego, the personal shell, or psychic entity, that you falsely take yourself to be. It is the cause of all your problems.

The intellectual mind, by its very nature, impedes cosmic consciousness. The character of your question is intellectual. It does not come from the heart. Therefore my answer cannot be helpful, for your heart is not open to receive it. See clearly where the question is coming from. Please look into that. Put nothing upon it. Expect nothing. Just see it in yourself. You do not have to be enslaved by your mind. Find the silence within you and stay with it. The answer is in the silence.

*

Q; *If I am God then why have I made such a mess? Look at all the suffering in the world, the injustice, the terrible atrocities. Are these of my making? Is this what you expect me to believe?*

A; I am not asking you to believe anything. Simply, ask yourself who is making the mess? Ask yourself what is going on immediately about you?

All suffering, all injustice, all atrocities start in the self. Find the source of the self and you will find the source of all adversity. Your world is of your own making. See it as it is and not the way you think it is.

There is an awful lot more in the greater picture of what appears as existence than can ever be captured by the limited mind. Your reasoning is labouring through the restrictions you have placed on yourself. Sooner or later your thinking must cease. Where is your world of strife when it does? See what is going on.

Believe it or not, all is perfect right now. This god, whom you are alluding to, is the creator of your mental world and as so, you see a world full of selves apparently trying to fix it, trying to make better what your mental god has failed to complete. See what is going on in the entire thinking process. Stop being ruled by the reactionary mind.

Stop imagining that you can know God, that you can understand the mind of God, when you cannot even understand your own. Let understanding yourself be your one and only quest. Rest with this. Then everything else will follow.

*

Q; *You talk about the importance of seeking the source of the self and you seem to be challenging Christianity. I was born a Christian, as a Christian I live and inevitably I am going to die.*

I believe my spirit will not die, as I am led to believe by the church, although there is nothing certain about this. But surely, all needing to be done in faith is to surrender oneself to God. Is this not enough?

A; Yes, should the surrender be complete. You know this in yourself should you be truly earnest and search deeply enough. Complete surrender is in handing all of yourself over to God. "Thy will be done" are words given to you to this effect. Embrace these words in all their fullness.

This means acknowledging everything as divine will. It also means that every act you undertake, you do it as the will of God. But be careful here, for your actions could still be your own particular notions of what you consider God's will to be. Many organised religions are a ready example of this. It is the wilful mind still at its play.

Why not be a little more direct and question yourself as to what you have got of your own to surrender.

The body you claim to be yours is certainly not yours. You do not even have command over its breath, for it breathes on its own accord. The blood flows through its veins in accord with its own intelligence. The cells of your body function independently of the you whom you think you are. Any moment your body could suddenly stop and there is not a thing in the world you can do about it.

So, in truth, what have you got to surrender? You have nothing apart from what you think you have got.

The type of surrender the mind understands is nothing more than a business arrangement between the personal self and your mind-perceived god. This is the god of the church specially designed for appeasing your acquired nature. It is utterly false, a blasphemy to your true nature that you can never see, never understand, while you continue holding onto the notion that God is apart from you.

Your Christian church, whatever its denomination, does not uphold the truth, neither by act nor creed. It serves its own purpose and dogmatically so, at that. If you feel compelled to believe in its mind-god, then by all means do so, but do it with all the love of your heart. Give yourself completely to it, but not, of course, to the fanatical point of excluding others as you are being wrongly led to do by many of its bishops

Regulations of the church instigating exclusion of any kind whatsoever are even contrary to the mind-god that the particular church itself propagates. The exclusive dogmas littering Christianity are an immediate example of this. This is the satanic nature of the theological mind. Believe it or not, all theologies are satanic for they all support their own particular mind-god.

I know this is difficult to accept, particularly when you see the millions of dedicated followers throughout the world paying homage to their visiting Pope. This is not an attack on the man, he is doing his best in the most extraordinary circumstances, but it is an attack on the office. The office needs to be challenged, but only by the love and truth of your heart. Give in love.

Give yourself through the yoke of the church if you must, but I tell you now, you are limiting yourself. You are trapping yourself through your fears and the clergy of the church play on your fears.

The clergy are serving the false. They are not doing it with open intention, of course. The intent has long been established. They are merely the custodians of mind-made rituals replaying the past. This is so deeply entrenched in your psyche that you cannot even comprehend your spiritual side being free from it. There is close to two thousand odd years of convincing going on. You cannot even imagine the weight of it all bearing upon you.

Jesus, the living Christ de-mystified the religious exclusiveness pertaining to the high priests of that particular time. This was welcomed by his immediate followers. You will even find it noted in scriptures how the curtain hanging in the temple was torn from the top to the bottom as Jesus died on the cross. The inner sanctuary cloaking the secrecies and self-given privileges of the high priests were bared and those who could hear the message of Christ in their hearts were freed from the yoke of the high priest's mind-god.

Then the founders of Christianity arrived and, taking a leaf from the past, they re-mystified the message of Christ when setting up their church as intermediary between you and their mind-perceived deity.

You are being spiritually blinded by their ritualistic magic welded to your mind through deep superstition. For example, you are conditioned to believe in the Eucharist as being the body of Christ. This is totally false in the manner it is being presented. It is nothing more than an adaptation from pre-Christ rituals that had already accomplished its spell-binding hold on the ignorant and fearful masses of yore.

Should you dare to challenge some of the top theologians of your church about this, they can hardly deny it. They will probably say, so what, as they offer you bundles of supportive evidence selectively taken from scriptures.

It takes extraordinary courage to break free from this conditioning. Even though, when you look at the history of your Christian church you have to admit it is nothing more than a seething den of corruption, yet you actively or passively continue to serve it, being programmed to do so and held fast by your personal fears. You are afraid to step away, to step out of the crowd of mass conditioning, so you go along with the deception.

I tell you now that the time is here for its dissolution. The theological mind-god has come to its end. That, which is your true nature, is saying to your church with all its bishops, cardinals and figurative heads, "Enough is enough, get behind me, Satan". Indeed, many of its priests are already saying it, all those who are seeing the light and responding through the love in their hearts.

The time is already upon us. This is a time of great turbulence, terrible desolation. Brother is rising against brother, sister against sister, daughter against mother, father against son. Such occurs at the ending of epochal time where there is terrible trepidation, an unprecedented ocean of tears, for it has to be so in time of dissolution.

You feel that surrendering to God is enough. And I am asking, who are you? What have you got of your own to surrender?

Are you not here to realise the truth, the truth of all that you are, to love and serve through *being* all you are? Now is the time to realise it.

Should you realise it, should your personal self totally dissolve, then, only then, can you truly know life. Then, only then, can you truly understand that God is not apart from you.

Stillness is the way. Experiencing the stillness of God, even for one millionth of a second, then all your fears instantly dissolve. But while you cling onto your personal self you can never realise that which is immediately beyond and you are obliged to continue being fooled by your personal notions of surrender.

"Be still and know that 'I' am God". Who is this 'I'? Look into the 'I' whom you address as yourself. Consciously look. Complete surrender is allowing the total dissolution of the self. Challenge your fears. See what is holding you back.

*

Q; *It sounds as though you are predicting the end of the world. Some crackpots are always about predicting that the end is nigh. We hear of such notions from monks who lock themselves up from the realities of life. Even the priests have been going on about this, filling us with fear. That might have been accepted in the dark ages but surely you do not expect us to accept it in this modern, scientific age. Things are now more clearly understood. I feel I must challenge you here.*

A; It is not the ending of the world, it is the ending of self. The Christians have put their own interpretation on this. They have completely miscued the words of Christ.

Christ speaks through parables, he uses symbols to give intonation of transcendental consciousness, of how one is to transcend one's state. He uses phrases like 'the kingdom of heaven is nigh'. He is speaking into the limitations of mind-consciousness in order to explode the mind.

Then the mind construes its own interpretation of the message coming from the living Christ. This is how Christianity comes into being. When you understand this through a deeper awareness then you can see how all forms of Christianity are on an erroneous footing.

You cannot expect to understand the limitations of Christianity simply by dismissing Christianity. Everything has its purpose and you can only transcend your limitations through clear understanding. This only comes about through a higher state of consciousness.

I am not disagreeing with you, I am simply saying to allow your mind to come to stillness. Rather than judging these religious connotations relating to the end of the world, pause and allow yourself to see through clear understanding.

Those who believe that the world is coming to its end in some future time are totally wrong. They interpret the words of the scriptures that some terrible end will suddenly occur. Their god will appear in the heavens and there will be a judgement of all. Many will be cast into hell for all eternity and the chosen ones, the do-gooders, will ascend into heaven for a holy rave-up that is guaranteed to last for ever. If you are in to rave-ups, if such is your foray, then go ahead, fool yourself with such rubbish!

Then the crackpots emerge, the ones who are sick of it all, as well as being sick in themselves, and they appear to you as being different, the only difference being is that they are beginning to wake up while the world is still fast asleep.

Let us look at it openly please. The mass suffering of humankind, as understood by the conditioned mind, has always been happening. It is always a source of anguish to the mind that is less that ten per cent conscious.

You have allowed yourself to believe that the end, as the Christian interpretation of the so-called last day of judgement, is something fearful to be dreaded, something too frightening to comprehend and you swallowed the bait, allowing it to sway you, until you dismissed it completely from your mind.

Instead of dismissing it, why not dissolve it? Why allow the horror of it all to remain in your subconscious awaiting the moment for some lunatic to arrive with the spark to re-ignite it again?

There has been unimaginable suffering for countless people torn apart during wars, even nuclear disasters. Such has already occurred and it is occurring right now.

Is death not the end of your world? But the mind switches off, how easily it misses through its religious beliefs, or disbeliefs, or through its false belief in its mind-god.

How can you truly know? How can you ever know while you cling onto the self with all its attachments? How can you expect to know while you choose to be less than ten per cent conscious?

Know the stillness, *be* the stillness. Stop clinging onto shadows. Allow the noisy self to dissolve, for you cannot hear through the noise of your mind.

You are right in your observations that most of the monks get it wrong. However, there are monks who live and discover much through silence. Now I am not indicating that you should live as a silent monk, or anything like that. You don't have to leave your post, whatever it is, in order to experience the silence.

It is not just experiencing silence, rather, it is *being* the silence of no-mind. This, you can be, no matter where you are, no matter what may be occurring about you, even if millions are falling with deathly disease and your body is falling as well, still, the silence remains, for the silence of no-mind always is.

But you are filled with your fears and all of these fears arise through your mind.

There is no fear in the silence. Let us examine it further. There are monks who are at one with their true nature. Again, let us be careful here, for there are many monasteries being inhabited by those who consider themselves as apart from the rest. These are merely the drop-outs more dangerous than the drop-outs boozing themselves to death on the sidewalks of life. At least the destitute alcoholics are being partly honest, for they are less opposed to the truth of their sorrowful plight.

I say, come out of your mind, come out from the tomb of the living dead. Allow the mummified wrappings of fear to dissolve. Come out. Know through the stillness. You have been unable to hear through the noise of your thoughts. Life is so full, so immediate, it is beyond all your imaginings. Be still, stop feeding yourself into the graveyard of the living dead.

There are people in certain parts who cultivate the stillness. They may be seen as monks, but they are not apart, for they have realised how to be one with the whole. Telepathy, clairvoyance, omniscience in the manner of what needs to be known is instantly known, all is available to them. How extraordinary, you might say to yourself. Yet, they are quite normal. You are the ones who are outside of yourselves, you are the ones who are abnormal.

Look through the silence. See through the silence. You can never know, you can never realise through the mind.

The end of the world is the end of the self. It is only from there that you can truly know Christ. Being Christian you can never know while you continue listening through your theologies, your dogmas, playing on your fears.

Look through the silence. Be brave. Let go of your world. Let is dissolve. Then you will know the end, for you will have passed through it yourself.

*

Q; *I feel I must interrupt. For the life of me, I don't know what all the fuss is about. I come from a secular society where we no longer consider such daftness. I mean, we are too preoccupied paying our bills, having sex, and getting along with our lives. We don't waste time with such abstractions. It appears to me that in Ireland you are still tied up with your Christian theologies and with all this daftness about the end of the world.*

A; How refreshing you really are. How free and open you are. Even through the darkest clouds the sun continues to shine. As a woman you are naturally closer to the pulse of life, which is love.

Have you noticed how most of these theologians are men? They are the saints of division who seem to have forsaken love in their lives. They dress themselves up in fancy costumes and wear funny looking hats! They bamboozle close to half the world's population with their ideologies. Not only do the multitudes believe in them but they fight among themselves as they divide their own interpretations even further! This is the calamity of the entire western world and, secular or not, you are still a part of the ongoing melee.

It may all seem to be very well, the clouds may seem to have passed, but such clouds can never really pass while we continue to accept this retarded consciousness expressing itself as the true way to love.

This type of religiosity is so embedded in the human psyche, and there is such a vested interest with the power-mongers involved, that nobody is truly free to be the fullness of life.

You feel it does not affect you. But, believe it or not, it does. Where do you go when your child dies? Where do you go when your lover dies? Indeed, where do you go when you, yourself, are facing death? In all probability you find yourself praying to some mind-perceived god.

How can you know your child? How can you ever really know your lover? How can you be one with your child, be one with your lover, living or dead, while the state of your consciousness is tarnished.

You are preoccupied keeping pace with your bills and your sexual desires. This is all very well on the surface. However, should you really wish to know love beyond the shallowness of sexual expression, then you must pass through your conditioning. You must come deeper into the depths of *me*, this *me* whom you are. Here I say unto you, let no man with his priestly frock, dare stand in your way, nor let no woman who had abdicated her essence by taking to wearing such a frock, stand between you and truth.

The end of the world is merely the ending of all this nonsense. Be life, be the love that you truly are. You are one with God.

When you make love, is it not the goddess in you fulfilling all that is life? Do you know? Are you aware of such completeness? Or, are you being scavenged by the shallowness of sex?

What if I were to directly challenge you on this? Could you

answer me openly and honestly? Feel the penetration of the question. Allow it to work. Now, answer yourself. Be true to yourself. You are the goddess incarnate. Feel her presence within you and serve it well.

The first hurdle has been transcended. No longer do you suffer the mental taboos relating to sex. But do not be complacent. These mental taboos have merely changed their appearance. Be awake, be alert. Serve life, serve love, be true to yourself.

*

Q; *You mention the unmanifested point at the centre of a circle being the door to eternity, or something to that effect. I have experienced a moment of great expansiveness, it seemed like a flash in eternity, then it was gone. From this, I sense the truth in what you are saying, but I would like to understand it more.*

A; Eternity is *now*. There is only *now*. *Now* is the point at the centre of the circle. I use the illustration of mathematics simply to give you a sense of what is being said. It is to help you to see beyond the mind, to see into the timeless. You are already aware of this, the awareness is in your question.

Now is the timeless in mind-perceived time where existence meets eternity. Let this rest in your mind. The purpose of the illustration is to offer the mind a chair.

When using the circle as a means for explaining, *now* is the point at the centre and existence is all which is circumventing the point. Existence is spiralling outwards. That which is within the point at the centre of the circle is eternity itself. The illustration is being created to allow you to travel in through the point. You will find as you go in, so also you go out. One could say, it is symmetrical

Nothingness is eternity, or, nothingness is the eternal mind exploding into existence in the *now*. There is only *now*.

For the mind of the scientist, *now* is the 'big bang'. This is the fact of the matter. The scientist measures through the mental concept of linear time. He thinks that time began at a particular moment in the far distant past. This is not true. Time begins now. Everything perceived relative to time is actually circular, not linear.

In the *now* you are exploding into that which is being sensually perceived about you as your particular existence. In other words, the eternal mind is becoming the particular, or personal, mind as you try to equate and understand through the senses. This is human consciousness.

Bear with me. I am saying it as it is seen. This is not conceptual

First and foremost, you must be prepared to let go the mind. You must allow the stillness to cultivate itself. All you have to personally do is to prepare the ground.

Take the seed, for example. The seed cannot know itself as the tree. First it must enter fertile ground. Then what happens? The seed must die to itself. Only then can it sprout as a tree. The seed holds the potential, or the potential is within the seed. The seed must give itself up, this being its universal intelligence as part of the universal mind. The seed cannot know itself as a tree, nor does it need to know. The transformation takes place through the fertile ground.

All you need do is to stop doing for yourself and allow the stillness to fertilise the ground within you. Then everything else must follow. You are the seed, you are the potential. But you, as the self, must die before you can be the nothingness, just as the seed must die before it can be the tree.

The moment of expansiveness that you experienced is merely a flash of this. It means that you are ready. Let go the mind. Stop feeding it with explanations. Let the stillness envelop you, just as the fertile ground envelops the seed. Allow it to happen and stay out of the happening yourself.

*

Q; *My life is in turmoil since I took the decision to leave my lover. You told me to be honest with myself, to stop trying to change him, to acknowledge the situation between us exactly as it is and to make my decision from there. It is painful being honest, it's like obliging myself to see what I have been refusing to look at. There was no other way, I accept. But why this pain? I am literally torn apart inside. I desperately want him, even though I know it is useless. He will not change. He will not grow up.*

A; Yes, it is painful, indeed. You opened your heart, you gave him your love and then you found you were giving your love not to a man but a boy.

You felt in yourself that things would improve, that he might change over time. You did your best by trying to change him into a man, you tried to make him see, and, at the end of it all, you frustrated yourself through trying.

The fact of the matter is, the boy cannot be the man. While the boy is there, the man is not. When the man is here, the boy is not. But nothing can happen before its time. He is not ready to be a man. There are many reasons for this. It may be due to his mother, his father, his peers, there are countless maybes and all maybes are futile. The truth of the matter is, you can only deal with yourself.

You have loved and now you feel you have loved in vain. But nothing is in vain. Everything has its purpose and everything has its consequence. The pain and torment you have brought to the fore is also serving its purpose. It is all part of shredding the dross of your personal selves. The love you display is self love and his love is also self love. By this I mean you only love what pleases you. Then, when it pleases you no more you stop loving it.

You have taken the decision to end the affair. The situation pleased you before, but it is not pleasing you now. Why? Is it not because you are wanting more? You feel you deserve more. Yet, you are getting exactly what you deserve. Life gives you exactly what you ask of it.

Life does not listen to your mind. It listens to you. Then the problem being, you fail to listen to life.

You have been serving your own pleasures, both of you taking from each other for your personal selves. It has all been an exercise of taking as you both were absorbed with the new fascination. You could call it the innocence of falling in love, if either of you had been innocent. But you know that is not the case. You both have openly and wilfully indulged in taking, you could even say, to the point of scavenging each other. Now your tanks have run dry and you are calling on the world, including me, to refill them.

But I am not here to console you, nor would it be right of me to do so. This is not the way out of the situation. The answer is in the situation itself.

See what you are doing. Acknowledge the truth. The pain is here simply to help you acknowledge, to help you to see, to understand. It is here as life's gift. Accept it, embrace it, start allowing yourself to grow through it.

Take to a course of giving. Consciously give, even if you have to force yourself to give, then force yourself to do so. Give to everyone about you. By giving I mean, give your presence, your attentiveness. Notice others, really take notice. Do this for a month, consciously do it. I guarantee that you will suddenly discover love itself embracing you, like nothing you have experienced before. Try it and see. Then ask me your question.

*

Q; *I want to wake up, to experience the stillness of no-mind that you talk about, but I can't stop thinking. Can you help me?*

A; Simply stop engaging the thoughts. I know, this is easier said than done. But the time might arrive when it may be easier done than said.

All thinking is mind. Then why not give the mind a new exercise to undertake. Instead of going along with each wave of thoughts, change your tack right now and seek the source of each thought arising. This calls for silent observing.

You are not your thoughts. Start out by seeing thoughts as separate from you and keep looking impartially at them without engaging yourself.

For example, you have seen a good movie. Then you find yourself thinking about it. There and then, stop. Let go of the thoughts. But you tell yourself they are pleasant and amusing. Really? What are you doing? You are actually entertaining your mind. You consider that it makes you relaxed, it helps you to get through your day.

This is the trick of the mind, the problem being that the mind has taken over and you are possessed by a psychic entity feeding itself off the emotional strings of your beautiful body. It does not have a body of its own, it does not need one, it can have any body it wants.

You are not your mind. But you have been spending all your life under the yoke of the mind. You try to stop thinking. Then, in the midst of your trying you get a flash of instant awareness. It is like being locked up in a windowless dungeon for twenty or thirty years and then being set free. The light is so dazzling that you feel you are stricken with blindness. In the dungeon you could see a little, just a little, and you can settle with this out of habit. You could look at your nails, at the spider on the wall, not much, but it sufficed. Now you are blinded with light. It is a disturbing experience and it makes you afraid.

Such is the initial feeling of being in the statelessness of no-mind. Allow yourself to pass through the fear. Nurture the thought-free state, it begins from here.

You have been living through the mind as a straight-jacket reactionary to your thoughts. It is the only way you have known how to live. You know how it is. The entire world is stampeding this way, everyone wanting to engage in pleasant thinking, billions of thinking minds creating such a mental racket, yet, all but a reflection of your own thinking mind.

How do you stop thinking? Firstly, cease trying to stop, for trying is thinking itself. Be still. Seek out the source of your thoughts. Start with the pleasant ones. It is easier. When you become aware of yourself thinking, there and then let the thoughts go. Do not finish the mental story. If you find that you are too engrossed to stop there and then, well, focus your awareness on your energy being drained. Be conscious of this. Thoughts drain your energy

For example, you have a hot date. For weeks, for months you have been trying to go out with this person. Then suddenly it is happening. You are pumped with excitement, the mind is going wild, you are living through all the probabilities. I can see you know what I mean. Then the moment arrives.

What happens? The setting is perfect, the date is perfect. Most of these hot dates are perfect until the chill of reality sets in! But what happens within you?

You have burned yourself out. Your energy is gone, depleted. It has happened through your mind. You have smothered the actuality before the romance even started and the grim reality is that you actually know it.

You can see in yourself the necessity to take this controlling habit away from the mind. Otherwise, you must remain a reactionary puppet where misery mostly always ensues.

You cannot know life, you cannot be the spontaneity of life, when you are engaged through the mind.

Thinking is not life, it never was and it never will. Thinking is always about something outside of now, whereas, life is within you right now. Life, as you experience through your senses, is no where else. See it as it is. Be it as it is and not as you think.

Whenever you are in your most intelligent state, you are in clarity of mind.

What is clarity of mind? Clarity of mind is freedom from mind. That means, there is nothing going on that impedes you. Then you are freedom, you are the spontaneity.

You know how it is. You ask someone a question, but they are not really listening to you, they are only listening to their thoughts. You may feel infuriated. How can anyone hear what you are saying when they are only listening through their minds? This is the cause of all the problems in the world. I say, all the problems, not some of the problems, but all the problems.

Human consciousness is a malfunction in communications between discursive minds and while technology may seem to be making things better it is also making things worse.

Look at the internet. See what is going on. It is all mind stuff. I know it is brilliant and very useful for obtaining information, even towards the betterment of humanity, or the easing of human suffering, nonetheless, most of its use is in serving the mind-weed.

Good, bad, or indifferent, all thinking is mind-weed. Pull out the weeds, let the seed of your essence sprout. Stillness is the way. Fear not the stillness.

*

Q; *I am a little bit confused about the inner space you mention in your chapter relating to Ufos. You also refer to time and the timeless, that leaves me even more confused and makes me wonder whether Ufos are real or not. Can you explain?*

A; This is a scientific question, is it not? You are seeking information for your mind. By answering you as such, I am merely adding to your load and this will not be particularly helpful.

Science, as you know it, is affirmative. It works by applying certain rules and formulas to the search, or research. Then the findings can easily be affirmed by the re-application of the same rules and formulas.

This is all very well while you are examining the known through the known. Such is the scientific world. But the formula is impotent when you apply it in your efforts to understand the unknown.

The known is relative, whereas, the unknown is relative to nothing. You must first break free from the grove of the relative. This is how new discoveries are made.

Someone discovered that the earth is round. It is shaped like a ball, just hanging on its own from nothing in space. You can easily imagine how such a suggestion was received by the minds of that time. It could not be accepted. It does not even make sense. How could the earth be possibly round? Everything would be falling away. How could you sleep at night holding onto such a ridiculous notion? No, you cannot accept it. The earth is flat. You are absolutely positive about it. You are entrenched in this belief and you are perfectly right, for this is the limited consciousness of that particular time.

Today you accept that the earth is round. You can jump on a plane and affirm it yourself. The proof of it is here in the realm of science. But Ufos are not. Science has not yet attained their speed. Yet, Ufos are as real as the idea of the earth being round is real. Merely because you have not the means to affirm it within the realm of the limited known does not mean they are not here right now.

However, human consciousness is moving this way. But all this is explained well enough in the chapter on Ufos. Seek the source of your question. Do it in stillness and soon you will realise what is meant by inner space. You can never get hold of it through your mind, the mind will always be confused. You must first realise the no-mind. This can only occur through stillness. Then you are clearing the way for the realisation of the truth behind Ufos and the meaning of the timeless to happen to you in your own experience. In other words, you will know it yourself. The answer is within you.

*

Q; *I am not very pleased at the casual way you explain the situation between Catholics and Protestants in Northern Ireland. Also your attitude towards Christianity galls me. Do you not realise that Jesus Christ is the only son of the one true God? Where have you been all your life?*

A; Right here, where I always am!

However, I do understand what you mean and how particularly important it is to you.

You are a fiery young woman from Belfast. You were born there and raised as a devout Catholic. You have no other choice in a deeply divided society. Your Catholic allegiance has been consolidated more by those opposing it rather than by the Catholic church itself. But Jesus, you feel, belongs to you and not to the Protestants! Is it not so?

You have experienced a lot of pain. Some of your close friends were senselessly murdered, all because of this division. The bitterness of it all is poisoning your heart. You feel somebody must pay.

This is exactly how the torment and hatred continues. Should you have children, then it will be passed on to them, either consciously or unconsciously.

The fact is, only you can end it. You can end it right now by letting it go. This Jesus, whom you call the only son of the one true God, is he not reported to have said, "Love your enemies"? Now this is a bit much to expect, is it not? Somewhere in your mind you are saying, "Well, that is all right somewhere else, but not right here in Northern Ireland, these enemies are beyond loving".

However, I am not asking you to love your enemies. But I am asking you to let go your enemies. Stop carrying them about in your mind. Let go of the bitterness. It is living in you. In yourself is the only place you can truly correct it. Do it right now, I tell you. Do not miss this opportunity, it may never pass your way again. It is not the others fault, no matter who, or what, they are, or whatever they may seem to have done.

Feeling bitter towards others only imprisons yourself. Release them from your mind. Give them back their freedom to be ordinary human beings. See them as human beings, as children of God. Help them to be pure, but only through consciously seeking the purity in yourself.

Let the bitterness go, let it bleed from your heart. You are deeply, deeply wounded. But you can only find healing when you let it go. The Jesus you speak of is the light of every heart, even those who seem to persecute you. They too, are imprisoned like you.

Why be a mirror of bitterness to them. Let it go, allow yourself to heal, allow the love, that you truly are, to embrace you. Be love in yourself.

I am not suggesting that you should go around expressing love to everyone. That is just another form of emotional turbulence. What I am saying is to be love in yourself. Feel it, embrace it, let it embrace you.

Allow the healing to commence. Allow your heart to be its natural purity. Allow yourself to taste your true, blissful nature. Then the others will have the opportunity to see their true nature in you. You will be a clear mirror for them.

This is the only way you can love your enemies. Jesus made the suggestion, now I am giving you the formula. Ultimately, there is neither Jesus nor I to give you anything, for all is within you, yourself. Taste it, be it, be the love that you truly are. Then all is well.

*

Q; *In your book, Dance of the Goblins, you write about the psychic realm. Can you say a little more on this. I'm asking because there's times when I feel as though I'm psychic myself. I sense when something is about to happen, or when I'm in the company of certain people there's moments when I feel as though I know what's going on in their minds. It scares me at times, especially when there's things I see that I don't wish to see. Also, I'm beginning to notice so many coincidences happening to me that I feel I'm losing it. It might help me to hear your comments.*

A; There is nothing unusual about your perceived condition. You are merely going through a shift in consciousness. This is a movement towards a deeper understanding.

You may also be noticing how the past is dissolving, those things that appeared as fundamental before are losing significance, certain beliefs, for instance, or particular behaviour patterns that you had previously adhered to as a matter of self obligation. It is somewhat like the snake shedding its skin. What is left behind is the empty shell. The snake is now free of itself, so to speak, and it is no longer restricted by the weight of its past.

The world about you is the skin you have just about shed and now you can see it more clearly. The people of your world have not changed, but you have changed. There are times when you feel that you are looking right through them. Not only are you aware of what they are thinking but you are even aware of what they are going to be thinking. It is as though they are playing a trick on you by acting naively. But they are not acting naively. They are as they are and you are looking at the discarded skin of yourself. You must move on, for life obliges you to move on.

If you must be with people then seek the company of the wise, not the worldly wise, for these cannot appear wise to you any-more. All worldly rhetoric is now nothing more than an empty shell. There is no turning back. You cannot turn back, for you cannot un-know what you know.

You are obliged by the awakening to continue moving into the unknown. You are discovering there is less turgidity to impede you as you move into the finer realms of consciousness.

You realise that everything is more instant and this is appear-ing in your life as the coincidences you mention in your question. Previously you were in the density of the forest, that is, the human consciousness at large, and you had to battle with the turgidity which is the ignorance of self manifesting about you.

This is the fire burning off the dross. You are much lighter now. Coincidences occur when you rise above the forest, like the bird on the wing hovering above the trees. There is less to impede your vision and what needs to be seen is immediately seen.

Be the spontaneity, move with it in stillness, that is, move in the freedom of no-mind. You are coming closer to your true nature. It is a joy to behold.

*

Q; *You mention in your book and I quote, 'priests and politicians are in service only to the acquired nature of humanity'. I find this difficult to accept. I mean, I am from the United States and I see our foreign policies are geared towards helping people, towards maintaining justice in the world. Look at the situation in the Middle East with Saddam Hussein, for example. If it were not for U.S. foreign policy, I mean, if the United States armed forces had not been called to intervene, then who would control him?*

Our politicians, as well as other politicians, are genuinely concerned. They are serving the good of all. And what about the Soviet threat that hung over the world for a half century or more? I accept there is a hell of a lot of corruption going on, as we have seen from the antics surrounding the impeachment trial of our president, but still I fail to understand how you can feel there is truth in such a generalised statement that the politicians are merely in service to this acquired nature of humanity that you speak of. I don't wish to appear impolite, but surely it is obvious that many of our politicians are honestly serving the good.

A; Firstly, let me complement you on your question. This is what is usually done in politics, where everyone appears polite to one another while they are secretly searching for a vulnerable spot to stick in the knife.

Such is the falsity being served when courtesy is overshadowed by politeness. The word courtesy originates from the mythical courts of the kings who led and protected their flock from their seats of divine wisdom. But this can never be more than myth in a dishonest world.

The word polite has its root in politics. See the difference and know what you are saying when you mention, "I do not wish to appear impolite". Observe how the conditioning works and look into the source of your question. Do not take this as a personal attack. I am merely responding in a manner through which you are given the opportunity to awaken.

Let us get one important fact straight. There is no such think as an honest politician. Honesty and politics are poles apart. The very nature of politics is dishonesty. You cannot *be* your true nature and also be a politician and whenever you are not being your true nature then you are being dishonest.

Let us look at it more closely. The politician is hungry for power, that is, power over people. This is his, or her, primary concern. Do not be fooled. This is first and foremost with every politician. It may start out as a cause for justice to be served and many are genuinely blinded by causes, but, at the end of the day, this hunger for power exposes itself.

Coupled to this is the lusting for power over land and resources, not necessarily lusting for personal ownership, but lusting for power, for immediate access. The system of things practiced by the West is an immediate reflection of this.

I am not differentiating the West from the East, nor from the North, nor the South. Your question comes from the West and the answer is always located in the question. So we need only to look at the western system.

You mention the Soviet threat being contained by the politicians of the United States who appear to you to be honest. This will certainly appear so when you only look through fixed binoculars, that is, when you only see and equate through your conditioned mind.

If you happen to be a Soviet citizen here now before me, then the texture of your question would, in all probability, be exactly the same, although your interpretation of events would be different. You would be defending the apparently honest Soviet politicians while seeing the politicians of the United States as being the major cause of injustice in the western world.

Firstly, you must seek for the truth in yourself. Otherwise you will continue to remain a reactionary puppet for the politicians. They will continue to lead you for as long as you continue to be as one of the masses.

Regardless of how intellectual you might seem to become, you are still nothing more than a reactionary, political puppet while you fail to truly know and understand yourself. This is the problem of mass hypnosis. You are hypnotised into believing what the masses believe. In politics this is known as public opinion.

Now public opinion wins wars and loses wars. This is what happened with your nice war in Vietnam. The cost became too great when public opinion went against its continuity. So it had to be stopped when it started becoming a public disgrace. No honour of substance could be awarded to the soldiers who returned from the battle, as the battle itself was not about valour. You do not refer to this in your question, nor to the many situations of Latin America closer to your home, but it needs to be mentioned so you might find the answer in yourself.

Politicians are dishonest. The Vietnamese people suffered because of this, as did the American soldiers and their families who were led to believe that they were the defenders of justice. You can accept this now because all of it is past.

But can you accept the present?

There is no point in I going into the details of the Middle Eastern situation. We would need to go back to the formation of Christianity, to the deeply-rooted religious nature sustaining the divide.

Religion is divisive, it is part of the human psyche continuing through time and the masses are the manifest fodder feeding its continuity. This is the fact of the matter. The ongoing division between the Christian West and the Islamic Middle East has become so ingrained in the psychic pulse of humanity that it is now accepted as normal. It is like losing your hair, a crisis at first and then you come to accept it. Particularly so, when it suits as a matter of convenience.

Was it not the western politicians who supported the long drawn-out war between Iraq and Iran when it was convenient for them to do so? Was this not a convenience for draining the resources of the Islamic fundamentalists at that particular time when they had the appearance of being a threat to the West? Is this not part of the play that has been going on for close to fifteen hundred years? Is it not a war for power over people and resources? The weapons have changed, but the intent remains more or less the same.

Is it not the story of the ongoing past regurgitating itself?

Do not take this up wrongly, I am not simply speaking about war, or the cause and effect of war, who is right and who is wrong, nor am I speaking about different faiths or creeds, I am simply speaking about human consciousness. When we follow our reactionary nature and jump into the affray we immediately lose sight of this, as we are then led to take sides according to our conditioning.

You are a western Christian simply because you happen to be born in the West. Should you have been born in Iraq, then, in all probability, you would be a Muslim and looking upon the Americans as the demons and wrongdoers of the world. This is exactly how Saddam Hussein looks upon the West. The Iraqi war with the West is between his conditioning and your conditioning. Everything else relating to the conflict comes as a result of this. See it as it is and not as you are being led by the politicians to believe.

The politicians will always allude that the source of the problem is with the opposing side, for each side rarely accepts to look at itself unless it is forced to do so. Even should the politicians be obliged to look at the conditioning causing the conflict, their vested interests will still lead them to look at the conditioning of the others, but rarely their own.

You must impartially look at your own conditioning. Only then do you have a chance to truly understand and transcend it.

The politicians are only interested in power. Their vested interest is in sustaining division, in creating enemies so they can appear to be the defenders of justice and order. When the Soviet politicians were suddenly obliged to wake up from their dreams, when they were obliged to genuinely look at the Cold War games, because of the enormous drain on their resources, then what happened as a result? Let us look at it honestly please.

The arms industry in the West had become big business. Even the Israelis were big into the production of arms and their economy had become heavily dependent on this. But an arms industry cannot be profitable should there be no enemies.

The Soviets decided not to play anymore, not to oblige by appearing as the enemy any more. The West was suddenly in crisis. What occurred? What came next?

The advertisement went out to the world, 'enemy desperately wanted, must be fierce and threatening'. Saddam Hussein obliged. I am not trying to say it is as simple as that. There are many complications and great complexities too numerous to mention, this is the nature of politics. But, behind all the apparent complexities leading to war there is the subtle play of political deception.

Politics is a power game, at the personal level, at the national level and at the international level. Power is not corrupt, it is the players in the power game who are the corruption. This is immediately visible when you impartially look at the play of events surrounding the impeachment trial of your country's president. But there is no one in particular to blame, for this corruption is the turgidity of human consciousness. It is what keeps us bound to a false reality, if there is such a thing.

You need to look more holistically. In order to do so, you must first look at yourself, at the conditioning enshrouding your mind.

You say there are many honest politicians. But should you look at it more closely you will probably find that the only honest politicians to be found are those who are being honestly dishonest.

*

Q; *I cannot get over my grief. Last year I tragically lost my wife. I try to be strong for the sake of my children. They are teenagers now and they are becoming silent towards me. I feel it's my fault their mother is not with us. She did ask me to go with her that day, but I was too busy. I ... I never saw her again. Why is life so cruel? Death ... it is so callously final.*

A; Life and death are one and the same. This may sound flippant right now, but it is the truth. One moment you are here, the next moment you are not.

When death comes suddenly and unexpectantly, it is always tragic. We are not prepared for death, and only because we do not allow ourselves to understand it. Fear keeps driving us away.

Allow me to focus on your grief, your sorrow, that terrible emptiness you are feeling within. It can never, ever be refilled, it can only be forgotten. This is the world's way of dealing with grief, by moving far enough away from it. They tell you that time will heal.

I tell you that time never heals, time only helps you to forget, until it happens again.

The fact of the matter is, everyone dies. The mind knows that, but it can never honestly accept it. In fact it is only the mind itself that dies. You do not die, you were never born to die. The body falls away, this is inevitable, but you do not fall away.

I am speaking to the stillness within you behind all your mental and bodily activities. You take yourself to be the mind and body. This is the error. You are setting yourself up for the pain and despair. See what you are doing to yourself.

Should you touch the love that you really are, should you realise your truth, then you will meet the love and truth that your wife really is behind all your mental impressions.

You both served this love together, in whatever way you served it together, even to the point of regret, of regretting you did not give more when, according to your mind, you had the opportunity to give. But this is a false assumption. You have served according to your lights, she has served according to hers, and the play of events that occurred between you, occurred accordingly.

Everything is as it is. The love that she is, where is it now?

I say it is right here within you. All you need do is to die to past impressions to realise it. You could say, this is getting on with your life. But I say, it is even more than that. Your wife is your life. The love that she is, is right here within you.

Ultimately we are all this love. But we fail to realise it when we allow ourselves to become obsessed with the false appearance of the personal. Then suddenly the personal is gone, and we feel that our love has gone, because we fail to see beyond it.

Your wife is love. Give to love, instead of giving to your grief. You do this through what appeared to you as her personal appearance by letting it go. Free her from your mind. Allow her to be in your heart.

People foolishly say, 'my heart is broken'. In truth, the heart can never be broken, the heart does not grieve, for the heart is love. All grief comes from the mind. Your wife is no longer here with you through her mind. But the impression of her mind-presence still lingers in yours. It is this that is causing your grief. You are grieving over an impression. Look at it closely. I can see you are smiling. Your heart is smiling. It is meeting her now.

*

Q; *Everything seems to be very rosy from where you're sitting. What can you know about the torments of the world? What can you know about strife? What can you really know about loss? Real loss, the pain of losing your child, for instance? It's not all sweet and lovely as you seem to feel. There's pain, there's suffering, the world is full of suffering. It's as though you've closed your eyes. You don't seem to care about this.*

A; The world is as I am. You choose a world of pain and suffering and then you complain about that which you get. Show me this pain you speak of, right now, apart from the pain of listening to me!

Where is this world of pain? Right here, this very moment? Where is it, here and now?

Let me remind you exactly where it is. Is it not all in your mind? You may very well add, what about the millions who are starving and homeless? Surely they are not in my mind, this you might say.

But where are they right now? Where is it happening right now? Is it not in your mind? Is it not here, right here, that your world of misery commences?

The mind will go on talking about the starving millions, it will feed itself on their wretchedness, but does it cause you to move an inch towards relieving the suffering world, towards feeding those who are starving? Be honest with yourself. See what you are doing. See how you are using the wretchedness of others to feed your misery.

When you allow yourself to be swamped by the sufferings of your particular world, then you are obliging yourself to live with the pain. Everything becomes a misery and all you can relate to is the misery appearing about you. You walk out your door into the sunshine of life. A bird is joyously singing. You pass it by without even seeing it. Then you meet up with some other like-minded person who is feeding the misery of the world and you block up the footpath as you pour out your miseries to each other. Neither of you are really listening, of course, for you are only listening to yourselves, to your own particular stories.

You choose to be miserable. You allow yourself to be imprisoned by it and then you try to imprison everybody else about you.

Go on, be miserable if you must. You have been doing it for so long, it has now become a habit and the only way you know how to relate.

But truly, is it not the love you feel you are missing in your life that is causing you to complain so much?

Look at yourself whenever you are moved to speak by complaining. See that there is no end to the complaints of your world, see how it goes on forever. See what you are doing. See what you are really doing. I am asking you to stop and to look at yourself. Ask yourself, does it really have to be so?

Must you continue inflicting yourself with your world full of anguish? Must you continue denying yourself the love that you really are?

You can give it up right at this very moment. You can break free from your self-inflicting prison. Why go on choosing it so? Why not choose freedom?

Try it for a day, just one solitary day. Consciously choose to spend one day without complaining and then see how you feel about life.

Yes, indeed, you are correct in what you observe, how everything seems rosy from where I am seated in existence, for everything is rosy. There is neither torment nor strife, but far from how you see it, it is not isolating. Should you chop off these limbs, the physical pain will be felt, but I am not going to worry, or feel miserable about it. Neither am I going to whine on somebody's shoulder. I say, be as you are. Choose what you must. But why not choose to be the spontaneous joy of life, so your presence can feed joy to your world? There is an abundance of joy in your true nature.

But, are you free to receive it?

*

Q; *When I look at you I see your sincerity. But I think you are a flirt. I have experienced this before. It could be dangerous.*

A; You are quite right in your observations. I am, indeed, an outrageous flirt. It is like a compulsion, part of the package, so to speak. I am being continuously moved to flirt with anything crossing my path. I flirt with cats, with dogs, with birds, even with ladies!

Just a little while ago I was compelled to flirt with an unfriendly bull. It was his field and he was rather possessive about it, for he was not too happy to share it. He showed it through his rather aggressive behaviour! He snorted, pawed at the ground, made threatening gestures when I tried to befriend him. Then I did exactly the same. I snorted, pawed at the ground.

But he could not see the funny side! It was as if he did not have a sense of humour! He seemed to become a sort of confused. He started eyeing me as though I was some freak of nature!

What happened next? Well, he turned his backside on me and went back to his grazing in a casual air of indifference. This is, indeed, unsporting. Indifference is like being served a flat pint of Guinness!

Once in Australia, when I was walking barefoot through the sand dunes, a beautiful queensland-brown snake gracefully crossed my path and entered the bush directly before me, probably to find itself something to eat.

It stopped there in stillness, silently watching some little lizard, or something it liked, waiting, it seemed, for the right moment to pounce.

But its tail was sticking out of the bush, just a little bit sticking out, exposed to my compulsively flirtatious nature.

What did I do? I grabbed it, of course!

In an instant the tail disappeared from my hand and what amazed me even more, my body reflexes caused me to jump at least ten feet backwards. I must say, I was stunningly amazed. I had never experienced such a long jump before. It was close to an Olympic gold and backwards at that!

The body reflexes are amazing. The body, it seems, has an intelligence all of its own. It a sort of takes care of itself and this is a good thing, perhaps.

Indeed, how little of us would survive if we had to depend on our minds to respond.

Then, the body stood there, crouched, waiting for just that split second for the focus to return through the senses. You know how it is, a movement occurs, then a split second later the mind is upon it. The silly old mind is forever trailing behind, always a split second away from the initial 'big bang'.

Is it a wonder why the scientists are being so exasperated? And they still think they can discover it all with their minds! How silly we are to believe they can.

Then the focus returned. And right there in the exact same spot where its tail had been when I was first moved to grab it, right there in that exact same spot, I now saw its head. It was staring at me with one of its eyes and with this long, funny-looking thing sticking out of its mouth!

It seemed as though it was trying to figure me out as to what was this crazy-looking thing daring to pull on its tail!

It was an amazing experience, both of us holding our positions, motionless, just flirting with each other!

Eventually the snake got bored. Or, perhaps, it may have considered the lizard more tasty! It gracefully retired back into the shade and we continued on our separate ways, enriched by the brief encounter.

Yes, your observations are good. I am, indeed, a compulsive flirt. But it gives me a tale to tell, does it not? Or a tail to pull, should it need pulling!

***

INDEX

Absolute; A/aloneness 58, <u>147</u>, 171/2. A/freedom 48. A/knowledge 203/4, A/reality 24, 95, 127, <u>152</u>, 211, 224, 263-265. A/stillness 53, 144, <u>169</u>, 216, <u>222</u>, <u>249</u>.

Allah; Allah/'I' 200.

Aloneness; Aloneness dissolved by the light of your heart <u>184</u>. A/death <u>56-58</u>. A/eternal <u>146/7</u>. A/freedom171/2. A/humankind's bewilderment <u>218</u>. A/immortality <u>251</u>. A/separation from God 51. A/sexual 153. A/strife in relationships 34. A/fear of the unknown 58.

Ananda; (Sanskrit term for bliss) 235, 240-242

Anaxagores; (Circa 500-428BC) Greek pluralist philosopher who surmised that the universe is organised by the force of Nous, ie. the mind 246.

Aristotle; (384-322BC) A student of Plato and founder of the Lyceum 246

Avidya; (Sanskrit term for the veil of ignorance covering one's true nature) 119.

Awareness; A/awakening consciousness 18. A/body 249, 250. A/consciousness <u>113/4</u>, 135, <u>171</u>, 200, 216, 226. A/consumerism 189, 193. A/experience 48/9. A/inner 29, 120, 122, 130, 144, <u>146/7</u>. A/love 66. A/meditation 162. A/reincarnation 133. A/pure 49, 113/4, 137, 207. A/static beliefs of society 105/6, 115/6, 124. A/unperceived limitations 111.

Being; Be/becoming 120. Being/consciousness/bliss 235, 241/2. B/God 156/7, <u>200</u>. B/life <u>20-24</u>, 29, 65, 144, 148, 163, 170, 215/6, 222/3, 255. B/love 33, 48/9, 51, 78-80, 83, 157, 263. B/meditation 162/3. B/no-mind 130, 163, 243. B/now 229. B/radiant presence 143. B/timeless 54, 104, 135. B/truth 7.

Big Bang; 27, 217.

Freedom from the known 20. F/love 48, 54, <u>193</u>. F/master consciousness 188, 258. F/meditation 159, 171-173. F/mind 119-121, 145, <u>147</u>, 256. F/money-god 196. F/no-mind 130,136. F/now 255, 265. F/reason 257/8. F/secret closets 255. F/silence of the timeless 136. F/silent understanding 169. F/transcendental consciousness 256, 257/8. Woman's sword of freedom 80.

Freud, Sigmund; (1856-1939) Viennese scientist acclaimed for his works in psychoanalysis, theory 264.

Galileo Galilei; (1564-1642) Philosopher/scientist 8.

God; The god of man's acquired nature 35, 177. God consciousness 259. Children of God 88. God/Christ of Christianity 120. God/devil <u>261</u>. God directly speaking through the circumstances of your life 82. God/Eastern philosophies 95. False gods of organised religions 7, 56, 89, 91/2, 186. Finding God 94. God/illusion 133. God/love 33, 63, <u>157</u>, 238. God/master/teacher 259. Man's idea of God 8. Man's demi-gods 77. Mind god 96, 260. Mind-weed god 59. Money-god 12, 65, 82, 109, 185-202, 209, 265. God/no-mind 54. God/now <u>262</u>. Philosopher's god 244, 259. God realisation 238, 260, <u>261</u>, 262. Religion as a business arrangement with God 123, 201. Scientific god 34. God/soul to be saved 166/7. Woman is man's most immediate God 80, 81, 237.

Goddess; The Goddess/*She* 80. G/woman's innermost nature 78, 79, 183.

Heaven; The collective lie 35. H/death 109, 166. H/escapism 17. H/false belief 255/6. H/false psychological pillar 166. H/hell 261. H/illusion 133. H/mind-weed 261. H/no-mind 261. H/personal self 148, 150. H/reincarnation 85, 129, 133. H/selfish love 47, 80.

Hell; H/acquired nature 65/6, 83/4, 260. H/altars to hell 178. H/awareness 29, 30. H/bliss 200, 201. H/Christian priests 91. H/custodians 177. H/electro-magnetic net 194. Facing hell 191. H/false psychological belief 166. H/freedom 193, 255. H/here

V/beliefs 120. V/immortal state 241. V/western mind 240. V/western self 119.

Vedas; (Ancient Hindu scriptures) 120. V/objective mind 122/3.

Virtue; V/vice, the one karmic recurrence of the masses 134. V/vice, stillness and the absolute reality 169.

Void; V/first realisation 41. V/'I' 207. V/matter 228. V/nothingness 207. V/point and now 230. V/point and relative consciousness 214. V/timelessness 229, 230.

Vortex; V/being 214. V/'I' and the mind 23. V/'I', the eye of the vortex 211. V/infinitesimal point of the void 214. V/humanoid world 218/9. V/now 223. V/relative consciousness 206. V/time and humankind 214. V/time and the mind's objective creation 215/6.

***